Walter Savage Landor, Stephen Wheeler

Letters of Walter Savage Landor

Private and Public

Walter Savage Landor, Stephen Wheeler

Letters of Walter Savage Landor
Private and Public

ISBN/EAN: 9783744688581

Printed in Europe, USA, Canada, Australia, Japan

Cover: Foto ©Thomas Meinert / pixelio.de

More available books at **www.hansebooks.com**

Miss Rose Paynter.

LETTERS

OF

WALTER SAVAGE LANDOR

PRIVATE AND PUBLIC

Edited by

STEPHEN WHEELER

DESORMAIS

With Portraits

LONDON

DUCKWORTH & CO.

3 HENRIETTA STREET COVENT GARDEN

1899

CONTENTS

PART I
PRIVATE LETTERS

CHAPTER I
1838—1839

PAGE

CHAPTER II
1840—1841

CHAPTER III
1842—1843

CHAPTER IV

1844—1847

CHAPTER V

1848—1857

CHAPTER VI

1858—1863

PART II

PUBLIC LETTERS

CHAPTER I

1838—1840

PORTRAITS

Introduction

AUTHORS, Landor said, should never be seen by authors, and little by other people. Yet it may be that authors and other people besides will see much of him in the following pages. The rule he lays down need not be followed exactly, or without a saving clause. In one's first judgment of a book, doubtless it is better to avoid too intimate a knowledge of the man who wrote it. The personal bias works unfairly, sometimes in the direction of undue adulation, sometimes of unreasoning dislike. But before the final appreciation, we should surely seek to know a great deal about an author and his surroundings. As Sainte Beuve said, there are questions to be asked. And to the particular questions which the great French critic held to be essential, the answers, in regard to Walter Savage Landor, are given more or less distinctly in his private letters.

Such briefly are the considerations which led me to ask, indeed I may say to importune, Lady Graves-Sawle for permission to transcribe the greater part of the letters she received from her old friend during a period extending over a quarter of a century. But the letter that follows will speak for itself :—

PENRICE, CORNWALL.

DEAR MR WHEELER,

In acceding to your earnest request that some of my letters from my dear old friend, Walter Savage Landor, should see the light, I have consented to entrust them to you for selection, because we have agreed that they illustrate the genial and affectionate side of a nature which some have thought rugged, and this in a way not to be discerned in the published memoirs of his life. They cover nearly a quarter of a century. I could wish for the sake of those who read them that these letters to my family had been less extravagantly eulogistic; but if they had been too closely pruned, they would have lost something of their originality.

In our happy family circle at Bath, Mr Landor found a rest for his impatient spirit; and the welcome always accorded to him there soothed and cheered his solitary life, and was repaid by the out-pouring of his enthusiastic and poetic nature.

My mother's near relationship to the Rose Aylmer of his boyish romance was the first link in the chain of this long friendship, for he remembered her as a little girl running by her sister, Rose Alymer's side. They never met after that until 1835 at Florence, and the intimacy continued which ceased only with their lives. It must have been to the charm of that inherited name that I am indebted for the many lovely verses—then so carelessly appreciated and now so deeply valued—with which he honoured a young and ignorant girl.

The pen-and-ink sketch, by W. Fisher, was given me as an intended caricature: it is, however, a faithful portrait of him when in one of his irascible moods. He was as full of fun as a boy; but if sometimes his boisterous spirits outran his discretion, a re-proving look would instantly restore his balance.

These letters may not add one laurel to his brow, but their tenderness and grace will cling round his memory like the perfume of the graceful cyclamen, the flower he loved so well. To your sympathetic care and judgment I consign these records of the past. I may scarcely hope to see them in print.

Yours sincerely,

Rose C. Graves-Sawle.

Feb. 1898.

In a previous volume [1] I have related the story of Landor's friendship with the Hon. Rose Aylmer, Lord Aylmer's daughter, and how he afterwards came to know her niece, Miss Rose Paynter, now Lady Graves-Sawle, to whom most of the letters here printed were addressed. If in dealing with them I have erred on the side of too profuse selection, the fault is entirely mine. But it seemed a pity to leave out anything that would throw light on his surroundings, and, I may add, on the influences that have so often helped to inspire his compositions. This also was my reason and excuse for begging that other portraits might appear with this volume. They are a commentary not only on the letters but on much of Landor's published writings. To one of them might almost be given names borrowed from the Conversations.

In the portrait sketch of Landor himself there is indeed a touch of caricature, and it bears quaint

---

[1] "Letters and Unpublished Writings of Walter Savage Landor." London : Richard Bentley & Son. 1897.

traces—which we preferred not to obliterate—of a sudden, perhaps a surreptitious hand. Yet in spite, or perhaps because of that, it is a more natural, a more convincing likeness than the oil-painting by the same artist in the National Portrait Gallery. It is unmistakably Landor in his less serene moments ; whether irate at the shocking rascality of kings or in wrath at the imagined larceny of his spectacles, one cannot tell. It is Landor, if we may say it, down to his boots. Recollect, however, that Mr Landor, pacified and benignant, and more elegantly arrayed for a ball at the Assembly Rooms, or a dinner party in Great Bedford Street, was a very different figure.

On the revelations of character in these private letters there is no need to enlarge. Readers may judge for themselves, and note how the voice raised so loudly in public, on behalf of the weak and oppressed, the victims of despotism, cruelty, or neglect, was subdued to a wistful tenderness when it spoke of friendship, love, and family affection. Landor's natural kindliness, his consideration for others, the passionate delight he took in the society of his children, were qualities not less conspicuous than his detestation of whatever he thought wrong and false, in life, literature, or politics. The public letters printed in the second portion of this volume are the proper complement of his private correspondence. They are now collected for the first time, from a periodical no longer in existence. It might be easy to show that Landor was not infrequently mistaken in his facts, and sometimes misled in his deductions; but for all that, his opinions on the questions of his day are of interest both for the language in which they are set forth, and also, in many cases, because they touch on problems which once again await solution.

While this volume was in the press, one of the friends mentioned by Landor in his private letters passed away. Mrs Lynn Linton, whom he first knew as Miss Eliza Lynn, held his memory in affectionate regard, and I had hoped that she would read what is written here. From other and older friends of his, still living, I have to ask forgiveness if, unhappily, there is anything here that recalls to mind things best forgotten.

Before coming to the correspondence, it may be as well to offer a few words of more formal introduction. When living at Fiesole, in the thirties, Landor met Mrs Paynter, whom he knew when she was a little girl. With her he could talk of his boyish devotion to her sister, the beautiful Rose Aylmer, who had died in India in 1800. Mrs Paynter gave him a lock of Miss Aylmer's hair, which I found carefully preserved in his writing desk. The name and features of one of Mrs Paynter's daughters also reminded him of the romance of his youth. The letters in the first part of this volume include a few addressed to Mrs Paynter, but the majority were written to her daughter, Miss Rose Paynter, now Lady Graves-Sawle, after Landor's return to England in 1835, during his residence in Bath, and during the last years of his long life which were spent in Florence.

———

PART I

PRIVATE LETTERS

CHAPTER I

1838—1839

A

CHAPTER I

1838—1839

ON January 30, 1838, Walter Savage Landor entered upon his sixty-fourth year. Three years earlier, he had hastily left his wife and children and his pleasant villa at Fiesole, to find "a solitary and a late repose" in England. After paying visits to various friends, he took a lodging for himself in St James's Square, Bath. We read in his correspondence of frequent excursions to London, Warwick, Llanbedr, and elsewhere; and the earliest letter here printed was written from Gore House, Kensington, the residence of his old friend, the Countess of Blessington. Long afterwards, Mr Augustus Hare relates, Landor would talk of his visits to Gore House, of Count D'Orsay and Lady Blessington, "with Disraeli sitting silently watching their conversation as if it were a display of fireworks."

But his headquarters were fixed at Bath for twenty years to come. His daily life there is described in a letter to his sister (1845):—"I walk out in all weathers six miles a day at least; and I generally, unless I am engaged in the evening, read from seven till twelve or one. I sleep twenty minutes after dinner, and nearly four hours at night, or rather in the morning. I rise at nine, breakfast at ten, and

3

dine at five. All the winter I have had some beautiful sweet daphnes and hyacinths in my window." Toward the end of 1838 he was writing historical plays. "Andrea of Hungary and Giovanna of Naples" were published in one volume early in the following year. The "Book of Beauty for 1839" (published about October 1838) contained two dramatic scenes. In September 1838 he wrote and published a long letter to Daniel O'Connell, in which he advocated a reconstruction of the Irish Church and the planting of Irish colonies in Canada and Australia. In 1839 he was writing letters to the *Examiner*, in which he criticised the published opinions of Lord Brougham. About the same time he made the acquaintance of Charles Dickens. " Tell him," he wrote to Mr Forster, "that he has drawn from me more tears and more smiles than are remaining to me for all the rest of the world, real or ideal." It was at Landor's rooms in St James's Square that Dickens first conceived the character of Little Nell. Landor wished afterwards that for his own part he could have bought the house and burnt it to the ground, in order that no mean association might degrade a spot so sacred. In the letters now to be given, there are frequent allusions to Dickens, whom Landor's friends, Mrs Paynter and her daughters, had met both in Bath and London.

Of the verses with which the letters are interspersed, some few have never appeared in print, while the rest, to be found in one or other of his published writings, or in the periodicals to which he contributed, are inserted either because they were in the nature of epistles in rhyme, or because they illustrate the prose letters in some way. The first little poem was dated the day before Miss Rose Paynter's birthday, or eleven days before Landor's own.

<hr>

Two Birthdays.[1]

January 18, 1838.

Ten days, ten only, intervene
    Within your natal day
And mine, O Rose !—but wide between
    What *years* there spread away.

<hr>

To Mrs Paynter,[2] at Bath.

LONDON, *May* 19, 1838 [postmarked].

My DEAR MRS PAYNTER,—

. . . Yesterday I breakfasted with Milnes.[3]   He invited a good number of his cleverest friends to meet me.   I did him wrong in fancying I had lost

---

[1] Not published.   The manuscript of these lines is in Lady Graves-Sawle's Album.

[2] Miss Rose Paynter's mother, half-sister to the Hon. Rose Aylmer.

[3] Richard Monckton Milnes, afterwards Lord Houghton, had met Landor first at Fiesole in 1833.   His verses to Landor's son, Walter, aged nine, were printed in " Memorials of a Residence on the Continent." London, 1838, p. 92.   The quotation from Landor is on page 22.

The day after this letter was written Landor breakfasted with Crabb Robinson, who writes in his " Diary " :—" A great deal of rattling on the part of Landor.   He maintained Blake to be the greatest of poets ; that Milnes [also present] is the greatest poet now living in England."   A year later the *Quarterly Review* was recommending " the honourable member for Pontefract " to intermit the homage he rendered "at the fantastic shrines of such baby idols as Mr John Keats and Mr Alfred Tennyson."

a portion of his kind feelings.   He gave me another volume, in which is the whole poem to Walter and a quotation from me ; and he expressed the most earnest wish that I should remain in London and meet again his charming sister, Lady Galway.[1]   She used to sing to me with as much good nature as Rose does ; and I hope Rose will find as handsome a husband as she has done.   He has not all his wife's talents ; they are extraordinary ; beside that, her voice is thought one of the finest in the world.   Lady Blessington has persuaded me to remain a few days longer, that I and D'Orsay may be accompaniments to her in a picture. So flattering a wish is not to be denied.

Something, I know not what, has been said for me to a man in office.   His reply was—" If Mr Landor wishes anything for himself, the earliest and greatest attention shall be paid to it." . . . Adieu.

———

To a Lady.

June 5, 1838.[2]

Why, why repine, my pensive friend,
    At pleasures slipt away ?

[1] Miss Harriette Monckton Milnes was married to her cousin, Viscount Galway, in April 1838. Carlyle said of her—"She sings, plays, reads German, Italian, etc., to great lengths, looks really beautiful, but somewhat *mooney*, with her large blue eyes, and, indeed, I do believe has more in her than we yet see. Her husband, the Viscount Galway, is a furious, everlasting hunter of foxes ; I mean furious on the foxes, *good* to all other things and men."

[2] Mr Forster wrongly included these lines among the poems ad-

Some the stern Fates will never lend,
        And all refuse to stay.

I see the rainbow in the sky,
        The dew upon the grass,
I see them, and I ask not why
        They glimmer or they pass.

With folded arms I linger not
        To call them back ; 'twere vain ;
In this, or in some other spot,
        I know they'll shine again.

An Alabaster Hand.[1]

Presented to Miss Paynter by Lord Elgin.

He who, rais'd high o'er wars turmoils,
Rescued from Time his richest spoils,
    Had laid them at thy feet, O Rose!

dressed to Ianthe. The original manuscript, dated as above, is in Lady Graves-Sawle's Album. A copy was sent a month or so later to Lady Blessington. The piece is printed in Landor's Works, 1846, ii. 644.

    [1] These verses were afterwards printed in "Dry Sticks." Lady Graves-Sawle writes:—"Among the many distinguished English families who had taken up their residence in Paris, partly from motives of economy, partly for the sake of the society, was Lord Elgin, of Elgin Marbles reputation, and to him I showed with pride Mr Landor's letters. Lady Elgin's salon was the rendezvous of all the celebrities to be met in Paris. She conversed in French with remarkable fluency, and a marked Scotch accent, on every subject of interest on or off the *tapis*. Mesmerism had a great charm for her, and I well remember her and some of her guests sitting in a row, all waiting to receive the mesmeric influence of Dr Gilbert. Hahnemann, the Homœopathist, was also to be

But Britain cried, To me belong
Trophies beneath whose shadows sung
   The choir of Pallas where Ilissus flows.

Of purest alabaster, well
   Expressing what our speech would tell,
   Beauteous, but somewhat less divine
Than Pheidias, taught by Pallas, plan'd,
Elgin presents the only hand
   That throbs not at the slightest touch of thine.

               BATH, *Nov.* 27, 1838.

To Miss Rose Paynter in Paris.

            [BATH], *December* 16 [1838].

DEAR ROSE,
         You ought to be very happy, for you
have taken all our happiness with you, and you know
how much there was of it. What kindness it is in
you to write to me so early after your arrival at Paris.
When on one side of you is sorrow at leaving the
most affectionate of mothers and sisters ; on the other,
all the pleasures and all the hopes inviting and
soliciting you. Consider what a precious thing it is
to be so beloved by everybody. It will never make
you proud—may it always make you happy.
    You had hardly left Bath before the weather

seen there. On my leaving Paris Lord Elgin sent me a marble hand,
restraining a bird, accompanied by a note couched in terms of such
affectionate interest that I have preserved them among my treasures of
the past."

seemed to change expressly for your journey.   Every
cloud left the sky—a few were remaining to cover a
brow or two.   Put another red letter to the calendar
in your pocket-book, for you have performed a miracle.
You were rather late.   The coachman said he could
not stay another minute; I begged for three, only
three, and ran like a lamp-lighter up to Gay Street.
This has perfectly cured my sprain.[1]   Happily I had
just reached York House when your carriage made its
appearance.   How I dreaded a delay which might
have made the Admiral[2] receive you with somewhat
less of pleasure in his countenance.   On another
occasion there would not be so very much in this:
but there are few of us who do not know how a little
grief swells a greater.   Have you never seen two
drops of rain upon a window, where the larger has
been quiescent until the lesser was drawn into it—
then it dropped.[3]   Knowing the Admiral's exaction
of regularity and precision, you will acknowledge I
had some reason for my apprehensions.   But you
know also his very great regard and affection for you
—and you may not know that men sometimes look
displeased when they are only pained.

[1] " I forgot to tell you that I fell in Milsom Street and sprained my
ankle."—Landor to Lady Blessington.

[2] Admiral the Hon. Frederick, afterwards Lord Aylmer, was Miss
Paynter's uncle. "The Admiral" is frequently referred to in this
correspondence, as well as in the verses in " Heroic Idyls," page 227.

[3] " As one drop of water hath an attraction for another, so do felicities
run into felicities."—Landor, Works, 1876, iv. 11.

Collins has this instant sent me the new almanack. It is hardly worth while to look into it. I know already what it will not tell me, that the coming year will be without its spring. Did Mama ever let you into the secret that she sometimes writes Italian poetry? She wrote these about midnight on *the* Friday.

I PENSIERI DI MAMA.[1]

Si, reposa la mia Rosa !
La mattina pallidina
Segnera per infelice ;
Chi sà, chi sà, quanti amici !
Sosterranno dire addio
Tutti quelli—ma non io.

I never prided myself on my talents for translation, so that I have attempted to give the following as much the air of an original as possible.

Calmly fall the night's repose
On your eyelids, blessed Rose !
When pale morning shines again,
It will shine on bitter pain.
Friends who see you go away
(Ah how many friends !) will say,
" Blessed Rose ! adieu ! adieu ! "
I may bear to say it too . . .
But alas ! when far from you.

---

[1] These Italian verses, with a slight alteration, were printed in the "Book of Beauty," 1847, and were Landor's own, notwithstanding the fact that on another ooccasin he attributed them to a mythical Italian poet.

Now for all this you will surely execute the little commission I gave you, beginning "Conquer—and then."[1] The other less important one I request you to defer and alter. I have been wearying my brain to devise how I could present to you some trifle on your birthday. To those who have any regard for us, all things are of equal value. Wear for my sake on the nineteenth of January[2] the small white flower which you tell me has been admired in Paris. To-morrow I will procure for my dear Julia[3] what she wants much more, and you will render her the gainer by the exchange.

I have brought your rose-tree into the house this morning. It lost its last leaf the day you went. It has now put forth a small bud. It ought not to have done so until I had received your letter—but perhaps it was conscious that I had in fact received several; and this before me is only a continuation of the delight they gave me. . . . You have much to do, much to see, much to enjoy : I will not allow you to sacrifice too many half hours in writing to me : for I

---

[1] The following stanza, in Landor's handwriting, is in Lady Graves-Sawle's Album :—

> "Conquer (and then give conquest o'er)
> The fickle realms of Charlemagne ;
> But bring us to your native shore
> A Brito worth his golden chain."

[2] Miss Rose Paynter's birthday.
[3] Landor's only daughter.

know that I always shall possess a quiet little nook in your memory, and that you will always believe me, Dear Rose.

Yours very affectionately,

W. LANDOR.

To Miss Rose Paynter.

BATH, *Jan.* 1839.

DEAR ROSE,

What I have said again and again, is very true.   Never did Madame de Sévigné write so admirably to a daughter as you have written to a mother and a sister.   And how worthy are both of them of such an affection !

. . . We are now almost as happy on our side of the Channel as you are on yours.   Observe, I do not answer for all the young men, I only answer for those who are gainers in happiness by every conquest you make, by every delight you receive or inspire. No doubt you have heard already that the Priors [1] have left Bath.   I spent the, their last, evening with them.   Two or three days before they went, I met Mr Call at their house.   He had just left Paris, and I was disappointed at hearing from him nothing in the world about you.   Kenyon

---

[1] The Priors, often mentioned in these letters, were a well-known family in Bath. Mrs Prior was a sister of Lady Aylmer. Her first husband, General MacKinnon, was killed at Cuidad Roderigos. She afterwards married Andrew Prior, Esq., F.R.S.

and Southey and Robinson [1] have also been there lately. . . .

In the commencement of Napoleon's career I remember Madame Tallien, Madame Recamier and Pauline. I remember one more, certainly not less beautiful than the most distinguished of these, but contented to hide an illustrious name, with many talents and every virtue in deep obscurity. These are the only French ladies I ever saw worth looking at. Perhaps I ought not to say this exactly. The Duchesse de Grammont [2] was handsome, rather past her perfection, but retaining a part of her bloom and all her graces. If you meet her you will be pleased with her. . . .

Let me return to those who will interest you more.

---

[1] Mr John Kenyon, "lover of frolic and fancy," was an intimate friend of Landor's, and a kinsman, as everyone knows, of Mrs Browning. His volume of "Poems for the Most Part Occasional," was published in 1838. A portrait of Landor, by Fisher, in his possession, was given by his executors to Crabb Robinson, the Robinson of the text, who bequeathed it to the National Portrait Gallery.

[2] "The Duc and Duchesse de Grammont were our neighbours in the Avenue de Paris, Versailles. The Duchesse was a sister of Count d'Orsay. She had then the remains of great beauty, and fair hair of wonderful length. She told me that her brother had made a wager that he could produce a hair from a lady's head measuring two yards. The bet was taken, and he wrote to his sister to send him one hair in a letter. She sent him two or three, which exceeded the exact two yards, and the bet was won."—R. G.-S.

Antoine, Duc de Grammont, died in 1855 ; the Duchesse, who survived him, died in 1882. Their son, often referred to in these letters as the Duc de Guiche, now became Duc de Grammont. He was Foreign Secretary, under the Emperor, on the outbreak of the Franco-German war.

On Christmas Day I dined in Gt. Bedford Street.[1]
Was it requisite to tell me to drink your health?
Unless indeed you knew it would be a pleasure the
more for making it an act of obedience. Fred[2] has
come sometimes to visit me in the evening. You
will be delighted, on your return, to find him so
improved. He is extremely amiable as well as
clever, and is only in want of occupation. I am
convinced he will be distinguished, and particularly
if his profession should be the army. The Admiral
is looking well. When he mentions you it is always
with delight. Why cannot he be perfectly contented
(I asked him the question) in the society of which you
form a part, without a view of what is equally inconsistent with his habits and his age. He is playing the
very worst and most hazardous game of *ecarté*, but I
hope and believe he will rise from the table before he
has lost anything more.

However we old people, it seems, have not half
your prudence and judgment. Yet Paris, I am afraid,
will now rob the Isle of Wight of the glory it acquired
last summer, and steal away a few of the roses you
gathered on that coast. I heard the Duchess of
Devonshire say that nothing was so good as an hour's
repose (*nap*, I think, was the true word) before dressing

[1] Where Miss Paynter's mother was living.

[2] Miss Paynter's brother, afterwards an officer in the Indian army.
He was present with his regiment, the 31st Bengal Infantry, at the
battle of Maharajpur.

for dinner. I doubt whether even she went to three parties in an evening. This is an improvement on the customs that prevailed in the former state of my existence. May it never satiate you, or take away the freshness of enjoyment! Try to steal this important hour, and it may serve as an *egis* to defend you from the *ennui*, and what is better, be a powerful ally in your career of victory. I have visions of glory for you, and sometimes walk in my sleep by the side of your triumphal car. You must not disappoint us all, but bring back with you "The Briton worth his golden chain." There cannot be more than one such in existence. . . .

I find that I have been nearly two hours about this letter, and am now in the Sunday morning. We (you see how I dare to identify myself with your family) have been half baked in a dull and stupid party at Lady D——'s. Even the brilliancy of Miss Caldwell [1] could not render it supportable. She played a few tricks of cards, such as I venture to say that you with all your cleverness will never learn. In another week, or ten days, a gentleman is going from Bath to Florence, and has offered to carry anything for me. Will you take the trouble to write a note to Fisher, requesting him to send you the trifles he was about to convey to my villa in the

[1] "My earliest Bath friend, sister to dear, good Lady Belmore."— Landor to Forster. Feb. 6, 1854.

spring, and give these, together with the few you have so kindly taken charge of, to Mr M—— when he calls for them.

It was my intention to exert my powers of calculation to their full extent, and to contrive that a letter of mine should reach you on your birthday. But on second thoughts it occurred to me that it was the very day on which a letter would come the most inopportunely. And now, Mr Hume[1] is leaving Bath on Wednesday, and passes through Paris : he will bring you this, with more good wishes for returns of happy years than all the paper in all the Bath paper-mills could contain. . . .—Dear Rose,

Your sincere, affectionate friend,

W. S. L.

To Miss Rose Paynter.

[BATH, *March* 1839.]

DEAR ROSE,

At last I am able to send you a little book.[2] . . . If you attempt to read it before you set out again, I shall begin to think you guilty of curiosity—the only bad thing I can ever be induced to think of your sex. O! that cruel chapter in

---

[1] Mr William Wentworth Fitzwilliam Hume, who was afterwards M.P. for Wicklow.

[2] This was the volume containing Landor's historical dramas, "Andrea of Hungary and Giovanna of Naples," which was published in 1839. The author's profits, if any, were to go to Grace Darling.

Genesis which will not allow us, as good Christians, to disbelieve or doubt it! But let us hope that it is wearing out in the world, for I have heard nothing about it lately. . . . I have exempted her [Giovanna] from the levities of her court and of her age, that due honour might be done to her ; while I thought it requisite for that court and that age, that nearly all the other personages should partake in them. I merge my own gravity in the well of truth. . . .

Believe me (indeed you will easily), it is a horrible thing to have many literary friends. They are apt to fancy that, however your time may be occupied, you must at all events have enough to read what they send you. Alas! alas! There are few who have time enough to read even all the very good books that have been written, old and new; and who çan neglect the good for the bad without compunction and remorse? . . . In regard to small authors, restless for celebrity, and wriggling on their level walks like worms exposed to the sunshine, I have scarcely ever seen one of these poor creatures who did not at one time excite my smiles, and at another my pity. .. . . When years have stored your mind with observation, you will continue to prefer Goldsmith to Bulwer, Miss Edgeworth to Lady Morgan,[1] Madame

---

[1] A passage in Landor's "Imaginary Conversation" between the Cavaliere Puntomichino and Mr Denis Eusebius Talcranagh, as printed in the first edition (1824, ii. 139) gives one the impression that he had small esteem for the clever, fascinating and kind-hearted author of " The

de Sévigné to Chateaubriand: in other words, the
very best to the very worst.

So I find that you have been made acquainted
with Lady Bulwer's[1] declaration of hostilit:es against
me.   I disdain all defence.   He who wants any
deserves none.   The two notes will serve perfectly—

DEAR LADY BULWER,
By this morning's post I have received a letter
which obliges me to entreat your patience.   It appears to be known
among my friends and relations that you intend me the honour of
dedicating your novel to me.   The report was first spread, I believe,
by the person or persons whom Fraser engaged to read it over.
Now I have been *implored* by those whose happiness and contentment I feel myself most especially bound to consult, "never to
allow my name to be implicated in matters of such delicacy."
I have been implored not to give intolerable pain to a sister,

---

Wild Irish Girl." He seems never to have rhet her, but Lady Graves-
Sawle writes :—"Lady Morgan was our next door neighbour in William
Street, in the fifties.   She took a fancy to me, and liked to drive with me.
She was a very small woman and *contrefaite*, with fine expressive dark
eyes, and abundance of Irish wit and dash.   She used to send her
invitation cards to dinner with '*Côtelette Musicale*' in the corner.
Ministers, ambassadors, poets and painters met under her diminutive
roof, and who so happy as their hostess !   She was very fond of her
nephews and nieces, and used to say that nepotism was maternal instinct
gone astray."
[1] Lady Bulwer (Rosina, Lady Lytton) had intended to dedicate her
novel, "Cheveley," to Landor, whom she knew in Italy, and later in
Bath.   Her reminiscences of Landor were published in *Tinsley's
Magazine*, June 1883.   "Cheveley ; or, the Man of Honour," came out,
in the end, with a dedication, dated Bath, March 27, 1839, "to No One
Nobody, Esq., of No Hall, Nowhere."   The husband of the authoress
was not the only real person satirised in the book ; Landor's friends,
Lady Blessington and Mr Forster, both coming in for their share of
detraction.

grievously afflicted by a hopeless malady of many years, when I had destroyed, with my own hands, the most elaborate of my works,[1] lest it might disquiet the peace of my mother, then in perfect health. Do not imagine, dear Lady Bulwer, that I consider the expression of your friendship as a light and valueless distinction : I trust I shall be worthy of retaining it, and not the less for the sacrifice of my pride to the sacredness of my affections.—I remain,

Dear Lady Bulwer,
Your ever obliged,
W. S. LANDOR.
ANSWER.

DEAR MR LANDOR,

You need not fear. The Dedication shall be with pleasure withdrawn, as I dislike Dedications at all times, and should be sorry to compromise you, even in the moral and virtuous atmosphere of Gore House. I remain (privately)

Your sincere friend,
R. LYTTON-BULWER.

Rude as the close is, yet it was impossible I could doubt that the Dedication was withdrawn if not "with pleasure" at least with complacency. A virtuous and right mind would at once have approved of my motive; and it seems impossible to me that any language could be more proper than my letter. I have submitted it to the judgment of four friends.

[1] This seems to refer to a projected history of his own times. "I attempted to trace and to expose the faults and fallacies of every administration, from the beginning of the year 1775. I was born at the opening of that year ; and many have been my opportunities of conversing, at home and abroad, with those who partook in the events that followed it. On looking over the large quantity of materials I had collected, and of the papers I had composed on them, I found, among the latest, no mild reprehension of some living statesmen. . . . I threw these papers into the fire, no record of them is existing."—Landor's "Letters of a Conservative," 1836.

Only one has thought it light. I could not think of giving "intolerable pain" to a sister so afflicted with asthma that she cannot speak without difficulty, nor take an airing in the most easy carriage. If she has not shown the same kindness to my family as she always did to me in our early days, that is only a reason the more with me for showing my compliance with her wishes. And indeed I now find that if she had invited Julia to her house it would have been painful to them both. A vainer man might have exulted in the celebrity to be expected from Lady Bulwer's Dedication. To me it could afford neither pride nor pleasure. With the exception of Louis the Fourteenth, no man ever was so frequently mentioned by contemporary writers. The best poem, and almost the best novel, of our days, were dedicated to me— " Kehama " by Southey and " Attila " by James[1]; and I hear that my name is to be found in twenty places of the first authors. I wish to keep myself as free as possible from the small fry ; and, if they either praise or abuse me, that they will favour me in preference with their abuse. I have not shaken off the "mortal coil" of Lady Bulwer, but I am grateful that she has removed it.

For the remainder of my life I will keep aloof from the concerns of others. The little good I can do

---

[1] In later years Robert Browning dedicated "Luria" and Mr Swin-burne dedicated "Atalanta in Calydon" to Landor.

without effort and without inconvenience I will do—
nothing more. All active exertions, all deep interests
are over with me. There is a time of repose before
we go quite to sleep, and this repose makes the sleep
more placid and easy.

. . . I must not fatigue your eyes any longer. I
find I have been writing for some hours . . . None
of your many friends think of you oftener or more
affectionately than that tiresome old scribbler,

W. S. LANDOR.

[*Postscript.*]

He will not yet believe that you are to remain in
France six months longer. To how many now in
health are six months the greater part of their remaining lifetime! To how many who are forming plans
for the future and speculating on the enjoyments of
far distant years! Your letter which came this
morning has occasioned these reflections . . . This
morning I accompanied your sister to Carpenter's
garden. I ordered him to make me a bed of Haut-
bois strawberries. . . . They are worthy of your
notice; but you shall not have one, nor half one,
unless you come back before the end of July. Since
we must go to war somewhere and have not yet fixed
where it shall be, my vote is for one against the
French, if they detain you. . . . I hope the terrors
of the influenza have passed over you. Two years
ago everybody at Clifton was affected by it except

myself. It attacked me early in March, for leaving
my windows open while I slept after dinner, and
has hardly yet left me. . . .

To Rose.[1]

My verse was for thine eyes alone,
    Alone by them was it repaid ;
And stil thine ear records the tone
    Of thy grey minstrel, thoughtful maid!

Amid the pomps of regal state,
    Where thou, O Rose ! art call'd to move,
Thee only Virtue can elate,
    She only guide thy steps to Love.

Sometimes, when dark is each saloon,
    Dark every lamp that crown'd the Seine,
Memory hangs low Amalfi's moon
    And lights thee o'er Salerno's plain.

And onward, where Giovanna bore
    Keen anguish from envenom'd tongues :
Her fame my pages shall restore,
    Thy pity shall requite her wrongs.

[1] These verses were prefixed as a prologue to "Andrea of Hungary
and Giovanna of Naples."

To Miss Rose Paynter.

[BATH, *May* 1839.]

DEAR ROSE,

Mr Mogg has just sent to tell me that he leaves Bath on Wednesday morning, and, after a few days in London, will proceed to Paris. I might run up to Great Bedford Street (*ecco il giovanotto!* run up!) to remind Mrs Paynter and your sister that if they have anything to send, they must prepare. You will have heard from them all the news. Have you as good to send in return? I mean to them, not to me? But take care I do not hear all about it, for I am very sly—worse than you suppose, which is bad enough. . . . This letter of mine is not very likely to reach you before the end of a fortnight. I shall request Mr Mogg to leave it at M. Charles Lafitte's, Place Vendôme, and perhaps it may be best if you send to the same address the little parcel for Italy.

Believe me, dear Rose,

Yours very sincerely,

W. S. LANDOR.

[*Postscript.*]

Southey [1] has written—he tells me of his intended marriage—that he has known the lady for twenty

---

[1] " Reduced in numbers as my family has been within the last few years, my spirits would hardly have recovered their habitual and health-ful cheerfulness if I had not prevailed upon Miss Bowles to share my lot for the remainder of our lives. There is just such a disparity of age as

years—that there is a just proportion between their ages, and that, having but one daughter single, and being obliged to leave her frequently, she wants a friend and guide at home. Nothing is more reasonable, nothing more considerate and kind. Love has often made other wise men less wise, and sometimes other good men less good; but never Southey, the most perfect of mortals, at least of men mortals.

Now I have opened my letter I will send you the last verses[1] you may expect from me before the beginning of next century. I here suppose you at Chantilly:

> Everything tells me you are near;
>   The hail-stones bound along and melt,
> In white array the clouds appear,
>   The Spring and you our fields have felt.

> Paris, I know, is hard to quit;
>   But you have left it; and 'twere silly
> To throw away more smiles and wit
>   Among the forests of Chantilly.

---

is fitting; we have been well acquainted with each other more than twenty years, and a more perfect conformity of disposition could not exist; so that, in resolving upon what must be either the weakest or the wisest act of a sexagenarian's life, I am well assured that, according to human foresight, I have judged well and acted wisely, both for myself and my remaining daughter. God bless you! ROBERT SOUTHEY" (Southey to Landor, March 31, 1839). Southey married Miss Caroline Bowles on June 5, 1839.

[1] Of the verses that follow only a portion is printed in Landor's Works, 1876, viii. 60.

Leave the grey carp [1] and greyer duke,
  Or by my faith ! I'll tell Molandé,[2]
On whom those dim eyes dared to look,
  For whom he dared to play the dandy.

And is that all you have to say ?
  Methinks you ask me—Very near :
Two others once upon a day
  Were cherisht, and should stil be dear.

Her little cell your rose adorns,
  To tempt you—and your cyclamen
Throws back her tiny twisted horns
  As if she heard your voice again.

To Mrs Paynter.

WARWICK, 12th June [postmarked 1839].

DEAR MRS PAYNTER,

Since I have come to Warwick I have been a most fortunate man—for within two days I received a letter from you and another from Rose. What a delight will it be to you all to meet at Passy ! Let us indulge the hope that no alteration for the worse in the Admiral's health will interrupt it. I wish he had brought you to Leamington instead of Malvern. But Malvern is the most healthy spot in the world, Leamington the most unhealthy. The Priors, whom I went to see the day after my arrival, are discontented with it. . . . In fact the place is a sink. Had

[1] Landor's " old friends " the carp at Chantilly. See his preface to " A Conference of Master Edmund Spenser with the Earl of Essex," 1834.
[2] The Countess de Molandé, the Ianthe of Landor's verse.

you come to Warwick, I could have shown you the wood-pigeons building and nightingales (or rather a nightingale) singing in my sister's garden, in spite of the eternal mowing and weeding. Yesterday the third Miss Prior[1] was married. I was invited to the wedding, but could not go, as some cousins were coming to visit me, whom I had never seen for about thirty years.

In London I sat next to Lord Canterbury[2] at dinner. By this time he has returned to Paris. I waited in vain for him to mention Rose, for it gratifies me to hear her admired, whether by young or old. The portrait[3] will be returned next month; but at present the engraving has made so little progress that I was not permitted to see it. Fisher begged me to sit again to him for a picture which he intends to keep. D'Orsay and everybody else thought the others too old looking, and D'Orsay gave him the reason—which is, my sitting in a chair raises my shoulders which are low, and shortens my neck which is long. I stood up and he has made the only picture of me which is worth a fig, excepting

[1] "June 11, 1839.—At Leamington, F. H. Stephens, Esq., Captain, 14th Dragoons, to Louisa Sophia, daughter of A. R. Prior, Esq., granddaughter of the late Sir John Call, Bart."—*Gentleman's Magazine.*

[2] Formerly Mr Charles Manners Sutton, Speaker of the House of Commons in 1817 and again in 1833. Lord Canterbury died in 1845.

[3] A portrait of Miss Paynter by William Fisher. The engraving was published in the "Book of Beauty," 1840. The portrait of Landor, also referred to, is now in the National Portrait Gallery.

one miniature, which an acquaintance of yours first
stole and then stamped upon, and then pocketted
the setting. Lady B[lessington] did not think my
verses[1] on Rose's birthday at all applicable to her
picture, and asked me for some on it. Here they
are — the event commemorated in the third line
happened earlier.

> The basket upon which thy fingers bend,
>   Thou mayest remember in my Tuscan hall,
> When the glad children, gazing on a friend,
>   From heedless arm let high-piled peaches fall
>   On the white marble, splashing to the wall.
>
> Oh, were they present at this later hour !
>   Could they behold the form whole realms admire,
> Lean with such grace o'er cane and leaf and flower,
>   Happy once more would they salute their sire,
>   Nor wonder that her name still rests upon his lyre.

I think my verses to Sophy[2] are better — for I
never can write (or do) anything I am bid.

> Sophy ! whose hand is now about to part
>   No moderate stores of pleasure and of pain,
> To one the honeyed hours, to more the smart,
>   When will return that graceful form again ?
>
> Glad as I was, or thought I was, that thou
>   Didst give thy faith where love and virtue bade,
> The light of gladness is o'ershadowed now,
>   When thou art leaving us, O pure soul'd maid !

---

[1] Printed in the " Book of Beauty," 1840, and in Landor's Works, 1876,
viii. 60.

[2] Miss Sophy Paynter, afterwards Lady Caldwell. The verses, somewhat altered, are given in " Dry Sticks."

Fairest in form and highest in estate,
  Of all our wide-spread western lands contain,
  I see thee lovely and scarce hope thee great,
  And almost wish thy talents shone in vain.

I have sent these to Rose but not the others.
You will have left Bath before my return on the
first of next month.   Remember me to James[1] when
you write to him, and tell him I shall very soon have
another copy of my book for him.—Believe me,
          Dear Mrs Paynter,
                Yours very sincerely,
                      W. S. LANDOR.

To Miss Rose Paynter, at Passy.

WARWICK, 12th June [1839].

DEAR ROSE,
          I have been spending a fortnight in London
and a week at Warwick, to which place your letter was
sent after me.   Yesterday the third sister of the Prior's
was married at Leamington.   Mrs Prior did me the
honour to invite me, but my cousin Mrs Shuckburgh had promised to come over in the morning,
and in a day or two I return with her to Birlingham.[2]
The Priors do not very much like their residence.
Leamington once belonged to my mother's great-

[1] Colonel James Paynter, C.B., 24th Regiment, was Miss Paynter's
brother.   He was severely wounded at the battle of Chilianwalla, and
died on Nov. 14, 1851.
[2] Landor's brother, the Rev. Robert Eyres Landor, was rector of Haf-
ford with Birlingham.   He died Jan. 26, 1869.

uncle, a Mr Price (?), with a part of the neighbouring parishes. He left it to his nephew in preference to his nieces. I had visited the place only once in thirty-five years. I believe it is unhealthy—it certainly is low. And now about another marriage. Indeed you do me but justice in thinking me much interested in it. Never was there upon earth a person more amiable than your sister.[1] She is become much attached to Mr Caldwell, and he deeply in love with her. How could it be otherwise if he loved her at all? You have seen him. . . . James who was at school with him says he is about seven or eight and thirty. I wish the seven or eight could be removed; but in the early part of life they are not very incommodious. It never has occurred to him that he must inevitably grow old before the object of his affections. This event when it occurs at last will only call forth fresh virtues and higher graces from your affectionate and gentle sister. . . .

A few days ago I happened to sit by Lord Canterbury at dinner. Among the many pleasant things he told me I waited in vain for his mention of you.

You know I am a Conservative, and wish things to continue as they are. I shall never like you so well if you prove me to be in the wrong in thinking that any alteration can be to your advantage. I would not

[1] Miss Sophy Paynter was married in the following year to Mr, afterwards Sir H. Caldwell.

even have you sing what you call better if it must be
differently. In fact you are beginning to get out of
favour with me already. So, come home and make
your peace directly, for I cannot wait three entire
months. I am glad, however, that Mrs Paynter and
your sister are about to see you again so soon. What
a delight it will be to all of you! How often, how
perpetually did they talk about you, and with what
fondness! Your are quite worthy one of the other.
Can all the wits in Paris say a better thing to you? I
am sure you would rather have it than the roses and
strawberries I thought of presenting to your *contemplazione* [1]—as the Italians say on similar occasions.
At the thought of your approaching happiness I too
am happier than I have been for years. You are very
right in Believing me ever,

Dear Rose,

Your affectionate old friend,

W. S. LANDOR.

[On the back page.]

You ask me whether I have ever been at Chantilly.
Yes, and I very much preferred it to everything in
France. I will give you one more trifle for your
album—only one, and I have hardly the heart even
for this.

---

[1] " Such is their idea of contemplation, and of the subjects on which it
should be fixed, that, if a dinner is given to a person of rank, the gazettes
announce that it was presented *alla contemplazione della sua excellenza.*"
—Landor's Works, 1876, iii. 78.

[Here follow the verses
        "Sophy ! whose hand is now about to part,"
printed above, page 27].

I forgot to say that I heard Garcia,[1] and think her voice, expression and acting better than Grisi's. I never liked any singer so well except Pasta. Remember I never saw Malibran.

To Mrs Paynter at Lord Aylmer's, Passy.

[BATH, postmarked *July* 27, 1839.]

DEAR MRS PAYNTER,

It is now raining as hard as it can rain, but before half an hour is over, I will run up to your house and send you all the intelligence I can collect. Do not be uneasy or let Sophy be. *The* letter is written tho' she has not received it. And now for a funny story to amuse you, and quite *à propos*. First, however, let me premise that the Goddess of Memory is sometimes led by Love to stand atiptoe on one point, to look straight forward at one object, and neither to see nor think about the world below her. And now for my story, which perhaps may be as applicable to two as to one. A certain friend of mine, whose practice it was never to begin or end a letter as other people do, nor to sign his name unless to one on business, wrote an epistle to a fair personage, every

[1] Mlle. Pauline Garcia, Malibran's sister, made her first appearance at Her Majesty's Theatre on May 9, 1839, in the part of Desdemona.

line of which was a *lucifer*, and forgot in his hurry
every particle of the address.   The letter-sorter had
the civility to bring it to my friend, who, with admirable presence of mind, said—" I have no particular
intimacy with the writer tho' you may once or twice
have seen us together."   " Lord ! sir ! " said he, " is it
not yours ? "   " Do I look like a young lady ? " said
my friend smiling.   " No, sir, but as you left your
purse one day, I thought perhaps you might have
forgotten."   " How lucky ! " cried my friend.   " Do
me the favour to accept this trifle—I am certain you
will never compromise so worthy a gentleman as—"
here my friend named a sour, morose, quarrelsome
fellow—" send it back to him under cover with no
charge for postage—indeed, it would be best to leave
it, not by the postman, but by a private hand, while
he is dining at the public table and with only the
words—returned unopened."

Now even to myself it has happened more than once
that I have found my letter without its direction at
the moment of despatching it.   Milnes is here with his
sister and Lord Galway.   I have promised to spend
the morning with them, but cannot.   They set out
for Clifton at three.   None of the party had seen
Bath before yesterday except Milnes for one hour.
Any stranger who carries a rod and line with him
would open my window and expect to catch a trout—
such a torrent is bursting over the stones.   Miss

Caldwell desired me to tell you that she would answer your letter when she is at Clifton. She spoke most kindly and affectionately of the whole family, so did dear old Lady Belmore. Poor Miss Hotham, I am afraid, is in a hopeless state of health. It grieves me, although I have seen but little of her these last thirty years. She is the only visible link in a chain to me more than golden.

I took your letter to Mr Cogan, who promised to send me an answer for you. Mr C—— has lost his son in the most deplorable manner. He had been deranged, and every sharp instrument was removed from his reach. But several months before, he had secreted a pistol, and with that he terminated his existence. The father had been studying late, and had just got into bed, when he heard a noise above him in his son's room. Fancying he wanted something which he could not find, he ran upstairs. At the very instant he opened the chamber door, a pistol exploded, and his son fell into his arms, covering him with blood. Philosophy has no defence against such blows as these; and those to whom the world is least, are the most vulnerable on the side of their children.

Early next month I think I shall go for a few weeks into Devonshire. But I am not fond of new faces, nor of many people. I took lodgings for a week at Clifton, but stayed only two days. The place is utterly ruined by that detestable bridge, and

they have cut a deep hollow-way to it and thrown
the soil over the grassy slope with its pinnacles
of porphyry-looking rock surmounting it—now no
longer.   There have been disturbances at Birmingham,[1] and about the whole neighbourhood.   Ipsley
Court[2] is but sixteen miles off; and I fancy I have
yet some cottages at Redditch in the manor where
there are the worst rogues in the kingdom, needle-
makers, fishhook-makers, etc.   These worthies, no
doubt, will find it very hard to pay me a shilling a
year for a cottage and garden, particularly as they
get by their labour only about five shillings a day.   I
do not care one straw about it if their honours will
only be pleased to stop there.

I have just been into Gt. Bedford Street.   " Sir !
duty, if you please to Missis—I sent Miss Paynter's
letter yesterday week.   I have *five* for Missis which
I must keep for the Admiral to see."   I have seen
nothing of Mr Hume.   Lady B (? Bulwer), I hear, is
in London. . . . Believe me, dear Mrs Paynter, with
best love (which is best French—*à la fiancée* or *aux
fiancées ?*)

Yours very sincerely,

W. S. LANDOR.

[1] Chartist Riots at Birmingham, July 4 and July 15, 1839.

[2] Ipsley Court in Warwickshire.   The estate was bequeathed to
Landor's mother by her great-uncles, wealthy London merchants, who
had inherited it from the Savage family.   Writing to his sister in 1830
Landor said :—" Never was any habitation more thoroughly odious—
red soil, mince-pie woods, and black and greasy needle-makers."

To Mrs Paynter, chez Lord Aylmer, Passy.

[BATH, *September 19th* 1839.]

DEAR MRS PAYNTER,

Just before dinner I met the eldest of the Miss Freemans, who asked me if I had heard lately from you. On my replying in the negative, she said, " Then probably you cannot tell me how Miss Paynter does." I was, you may well believe, a little alarmed at this." She continued, " Then perhaps you do not know that she lately has had a pleurisy ? " Is this so ? If so, is she well again ? I feel all her pain, and all your and Rose's anxiety—which will not quit me until I hear from you. Poor suffering *Sposina.* I know what that horrible pain is. It attacked me at about her age, and I could not even turn in my bed to ring the bell. I had to endure three or four hours of this exquisite pain before I was bled. . . . None of my friends are at Bath, and the weather has prevented me from going into Devonshire. I have twice walked up to the monument in Lansdowne Park—that has been my longest walk—eight or nine miles in all. I feel no effect whatever from my sprain in the ankle, thank God !

I have been reading Lady Chatterton's " Travels in Ireland," [1] an admirable work both in style and feeling.

[1] "Rambles in the South of Ireland, during the year 1838," by Lady Chatterton, London, 1839.

She has quoted some beautiful lines of our friend
Kenyon.   I remember her fifteen years ago, at
Florence, then very beautiful, still handsome and
highly interesting.   I met her again in town, last
May.   We have nothing but rain.   Our out-of-door
peaches are mere turnips.   I send away a plate of
them untouched, after one vile sample, devourer as I
am of fruit. . . .

        Believe me, Dear Mrs Paynter,
               Very sincerely yours,
                    W. S. LANDOR.

THE MOUNTAIN ASH.[1]

The mountain ash before my pane,
Rattling red berries once again,
Said, "Where, O where! can Rose remain?"

Hearing him call, I rais'd the sash
And answered him, "Sir mountain-ash!
At Passy." "Why?" "To cut a dash."

He shook his head, and in reply,
Said only, "Well then, you and I
May both go on to droop and die."

"Thanks! thanks! my fellow sufferer!
I, by your leave, should much prefer
To look out here and wait for her."

[1] These verses, printed in "Dry Sticks," p. 67, were obviously written
at this time.

To Mrs Paynter, at Lord Aylmer's, Passy.

[BATH, *September* 1839.]

DEAR MRS PAYNTER,

Beyond a doubt and beyond a comparison, you will think me the most troublesome man in the world to call your attention day after day to my illegibilities. To-day I was at your house to see the garden put in order. The cook requested me to go down below and just look at the walls. It grieves me to tell you that they are just as damp as ever. . . . I may be imprudent in doing it myself; but when I think how grievously you have suffered from the rheumatism, and how lately poor Sophy has been tortured with a malady which dampness usually produces and always aggravates, I could not defer the intelligence, however unpleasant. . . . I was afraid you might think me presumptuous and intermeddling, otherwise I would instantly have set a couple of masons to work. . . . Do me the favour to give me your directions, and for once in my life I will be a man of business. Happy as I shall be to see you all back again, I must confess I would rather there were any delay than that you should have the almost inevitable evils of a damp house. . . .

I have been buying a fine Rubens—a lion.[1] Un-

---

[1] Some friends of Landor's, to whom he showed this doubtful masterpiece, could only restrain their hilarity while they were with him. Then, as they walked back to their hotel, at midnight, the usually quiet streets of Bath rang with their inextinguishable laughter, with which were

fortunately the proprietor knew the master.   They
have just set up in the Park a prodigiously fine head
of Jupiter,[1] in Bath stone, executed by an obscure
artist of this city, who died lately, miserably poor.
In my opinion nothing of Michel Angelo is nobler—
nothing of Thorwaldsen purer.   It is colossal.   The
rain and frost will ruin it.   I offered my five or ten
sovereigns, if they would contribute to build a dome
over it.   This morning I bought an engraving of it,
and paid the money to the artist's son, who promised
to leave it at my lodgings.   If he had, I would have
sent it you with this.

I remain, dear Mrs Paynter,

Very sincerely,

W. S. Landor.

To Miss Rose Paynter, Passy, near Paris.

[Bath, *September* 23, 1839.]

Dear Rose,

It is true enough that you have not
heard from me for a long time ; and the reason is not
that I am idle, which I am, but because I hoped, from
the long absence of all letters from Passy, that you
surely were on your way to Bath.   Otherwise not

mingled "Roars for the lion !"   One of these jovial art-critics was
Charles Dickens.   Lady Graves-Sawle told me this story.

[1] The bust of Jupiter stands on the hill in the Victoria Park.   It is
six feet in height, and is carved out of a single block of Bath Stone.
Osborne, the Sculptor, died in poverty.

only should I have written, but have been, long ere
this time, in Devonshire. Tell Mama that I might
safely have been entrusted with the *tapis*, or, even
with everything *sur le tapis*. There is no commission
of hers which I would not have executed, at least
carefully. I am indeed quite as idle as usual.

> " I never sprain,
>   Dear Rose ! my brain ;
>   And if I did,
>   The Lord forbid
> That you should set it strait again :
>
>   For I have seen,
>   O haughty Queen !
>   The tears and sighs
>   That fall and rise
> Where your ungentle hand hath been."

No wonder you ask me whether you are not most
barbarous : I will answer for it you are. I scarcely
know any man but myself who is out of your martyro-
logy. I am like one of the Saints (no doubt of that—
you will say) I mean I am like one of those who
look quietly on and take delight in seeing the most
beautiful of the Creation execute the Creator's will.
But I do not approve of your making more people
mad and desperate.

By the by, I met Sir Dudley Hill[1] in town. He

---

[1] Afterwards General Sir Dudley St Leger Hill, K.C.B. He had
lately returned from the Lieutenant-Governorship of St Lucia. He had
served with distinction in the Peninsula, and in 1848 he was appointed to
a command in India where he died, 1851.

told me the wonderful news that a relation of his (the name too great to be communicated to me) was an admirer of yours. Never say, after this, that we acquire but little information in the great world. Speaking of Bath, you say—"for the short time we shall remain there." This disquiets me. Is it not too much to lose *one* of your family? But there is good cause shown ; and when the same good cause is shown again, we must submit—more than submit— give up one half of the heart to gladness, while the other half is devoured by grief.

If your family is really to continue but a little while in Bath pray let me know it. I have not been very importunate in my entreaties to hear often from you ; for the pleasures of those I love have always been and always will be the highest of my gratifications; and I do not ask you now to shorten a ride or a walk or a conversation, but, at any moment, when you really have nothing else to do or to think about, tell me if my delightful evenings in Gt. Bedford Street are soon to close. I sadly fear your wishes in regard to the picture are expressed too late. But I will write by this very post and signify them. The " Book of Beauty" is always sent to America by the first of October. To-morrow I will set out for Torquay, and return by the middle of the next month.

If Mrs Paynter thinks I can do anything in the decoration of her house, better than the servant, I will return sooner and try my hand at it. Your account of Sophy has removed from me a heavy load of anxiety. That horrible pleurisy frightened me. I can bear pain passably well myself: it is only when it rebounds from my friends that I have not the courage to face it. You would have laught at me the other day when a lady was my protectress. I was over at Marston [1] to see the Boyles when (tell the Admiral if he is with you) I delivered his message to Sir Courtney.[2] In the courtyard was a magnificent black Newfoundland dog. No sooner had I entered the gate than, before I could deliver my credentials, or make the sign of dog-freemasonry, he seized my leg. A swinging box on the ear was opposed to this manœuvre. My Newfoundlander had what the boxers (not very elegantly) call *pluck*.[3] He renewed the attack, despite some severe appellations and admirable parasol-thrusts of Miss Boyle.[4] However she conquered him—for neither my box on the ear nor a kick at the second round, which sent him upon his back, made him give in. We were pretty good friends at last, although I told him I should trouble him, at his leisure, just to look over a certain article in my

---

[1] Marston, in Somersetshire. See "Last Fruit," p. 484.

[2] Admiral Sir Courtenay Boyle, brother-in-law of the 8th Earl of Cork and Orrery.

[3] This was a word which Landor greatly disliked. "The Romans were content with *cor* and *pectus;* we with their contents." *Works*, 1876, v. 129.

[4] Miss Mary Boyle.

tailor's bill, which might as well be transferred to his account. Fred[1] will think this rare fun—for several minutes it was rather serious. I would have declined the combat and have left my enemy alone with his glory had there been any escape.

Believe me, dear Rose,

Yours very affectionately,

W. S. LANDOR.

To Miss Rose Paynter at Passy.

BATH, *Sept.* 26, 1839.

DEAR ROSE,

It is only in trance that "*on fait l'impossible.*" I pretend but to have done the possible and all the possible. You see by Lady B's[2] letter the extent of my ill-success. I was packing up my finery for Torquay when in came Marcus Hare. My place in the coach was taken and paid for, but they very civilly allowed me to defer it until Monday. Now it happened to be a gloomy day on Monday, so I ordered a good fire, instead of a fly coach-ward, and here I am yet until Saturday again. The reason why I deferred it so long is, that Thalberg plays to-day at the Rooms. I have just returned from hearing this wonderful *sonatore.* There was also Ivanhoff, Balfe, and Miss Birch. Balfe sang "The Light of Other Days"; Ivanhoff the 'Barcarola' in "Marino

---

[1] Miss Paynter's brother.
[2] Lady Bulwer or Lady Blessington.

Faliero," '*Or che in cielo.*' All three sang parts in the *quartetto* in the 'Puritani'—*a te cara amor talora.* I am happy to say that the room was very full. On Monday, finding I must remain a few days longer, I wrote to Kenyon asking him to join me here for a jaunt into Devonshire. Either he is from home or he is coming, he might have written word. Now if your family had been in Bath he would never have lost a day, I will answer for him, but would have appeared this very evening in all his radiance. On Monday I met the Admiral much to my surprise. He had been in Bath only a couple of days, and was going into Wales for some shooting.

To Mrs Paynter at Passy.

BATH, *Oct.* 9 [1839].

DEAR MRS PAYNTER,

My visit to Torquay is put off until the spring; for Hare,[1] who proposed to be there with his brother Marcus, is gone to Italy, and Marcus is come to his aunt in the Crescent. Kenyon was to have joined me either here or in Devonshire. He too, I believe, is gone to the continent. Mrs Bloomfield is now with Lady Belmore, which enlivens us a little. Rose in her last letter told me that your stay here after your return was likely to be short. I am really grieved at this—I could not quite believe it; and begged her if

---

[1] Mr Francis Hare, a great friend of Landor's.

by any chance she had a vacant half hour to tell me whether it really is likely to be the case. But her half hours neither are nor ought to be so ill-spent as in solving a question which perhaps is not yet ready for solution. I shall be sadly grieved to lose you all again, and so soon after so long an absence. Your commission has been executed. The maid told me that the "carpets are come quite beautiful," and she has put them into the bedrooms. I do believe she was inclined to lead me into these sanctuaries in order to prove her exactness in the commendations she had lavished. But probably on a second look at me she thought that I, like Richard the Third, was never made to amble in a lady's chamber.[1]

By-the-by, and this is really *à propos-issimo*, Mr —— is going to marry. The lady is handsome, rich, a young widow. The first husband was a Pole—her present, I fear, will be a stick—and a poor one. I do not know why the projected wedding should remind me of the Admiral. He was looking remarkably well, and going into Wales for some shooting. I think him perfectly in the right to choose Diana for his goddess. She does not inspire quite so much fanaticism as another

"Daughter of Jove, relentless Power."[2]

And seven or eight hours shooting with a brace

---

[1] "He capers nimbly in a lady's chamber." Shakespeare *Ric. iii*. I. i. 12.

[2] Thomas Gray's "Ode to Adversity."

of hares in pouch are *conservatives* against wild vagaries . . .

Yours very sincerely,

W. S. LANDOR.

To Mrs Paynter at Lord Aylmer's, Passy.

[BATH, *Oct.* 22, 1839.]

MY DEAR MRS PAYNTER,

When I wrote to you by Mrs Willoughby I am afraid my letter may have alarmed you about the condition of your house. I have just this instant left the workmen who laboured actually in the dark. The mason wanted me to believe it would be an affair of many days. "Give me a spade and pick-axe," said I, "and before night I finish it with my own hands or forfeit twenty pounds." I would have done it. When he saw I was serious, he promised to bring a couple of others with him. They would have gone on wrong, indeed they did when my back was turned, for I am happy to tell you the work was accomplished according to my plan. I will answer for it no water enters unless from the ground springs, as they are called.

I am not in time for the postman, but Charles will run with this. . . . It delights me to know how happily you have spent your time at Passy. . . . There are periods of life when our early days come

back again in rich clusters of joyous brilliancy like
constellations which for a while have been out of
sight. They disappear, they do not perish.

Ever yours sincerely,

W. S. LANDOR.

To Mr Frederick Paynter.[1]

DEAR FRED,

You do not seem to place a proper and fair value
on your letters; for the devil himself with all his
ingenuity and knowledge of languages could not read
the specimen with which you have favored me.
However, I am heartily glad to get it, because it
shows that you have not forgotten an old friend, and
because it is also a proof that your ideas run on with
such rapidity, no pen can follow them up with any
hope of catching them. I will deliver your message
to the Miss. . . . Do not wonder nor fight me
if taking advantage of your absence I have cut you
out. I shall be glad to see you in Bath again.
Meanwhile,

Believe me,

Very sincerely yours,

W. S. LANDOR.

---

[1] On the same paper.

CHAPTER II

1840-1841

CHAPTER II

1840-1841

In 1840 Landor was greatly disappointed at the postponement of a visit from his sons, Arnold and Walter. Another grief was the death of his accomplished friend, Francis Hare. In the autumn he wrote a third historical play, "Fra Rupert," a sequel to "Andrea of Hungary and Giovanna of Naples." I find no mention in these letters of an excursion to Devonshire in the autumn of 1840; but there are lines on Torquay in the "Keepsake for 1841" (published about October 1840); and there are verses in Lady Graves-Sawle's album, dated Exmouth, September 1840. As usual, Landor spent the winter at Bath. Writing to Mr John Forster in December he said :—"In this weather nobody can be quite well. I myself, an oddly mixt metal with a pretty large proportion of iron in it, am sensible to the curse of climate. The chief reason is I cannot walk through the snow and slop. My body, and my mind more especially, requires strong exercise. Nothing can tire either, excepting dull people, and they weary both at once. . . . Lately, from the want of sun and all things cheerful, my saddened and wearied mind has often roosted on the acacias and cypresses I planted."

He was in better spirits next year when he went to

Paris to meet his son Walter, who returned with him
to Bath. At the French capital he was astonished to
find himself something of a lion. " Imagine my surprise," he wrote, "that any among the literary men
knew even of my existence. Nothing can exceed
their civility."

To Miss Rose Paynter.

[BATH ? *March* 1840.]

DEAR ROSE,

You appear to be quite as regardless of what you
lose as of what you make the *giovanotti* lose, otherwise you could not absolutely have forgotten that you
dropt a bracelet in the Crescent. It was brought
back to me. Here ends the mystery. The snake
I find is not a snake in the grass—and although there
appears to be some little fire in his eyes, it is lambent
and quiescent. You are very kind in expressing a
wish that I had given it to my Julia. Do not imagine
I have forgotten, or ever shall forget, that you once
told me you were sure you should love her. This
alone was quite enough to drive away all sadness
from me—for Julia[1] is my darling and delight. . . .
Yesterday I received a long letter from her.

She tells me she has been lately at several parties,
beside the splendid ones at the Minister's and at
Palazzo-Pitti, and that she is about to be brides-

---

[1] Landor's daughter.

maid to Frederica de Courcy[1] who marries Baron
de Hoggier. I have ordered my agent to supply
her with money sufficient for a whole nest of snakes,
so do not wonder that I forebore to steal yours when
it fell in my way. She is good enough to make me
a present of her bust, which I may expect to find
in Bath on my return from Germany. At present I
have not heard a syllable of Arnold's and Walter's[2]
expedition. . . .

Your very affectionately,

W. S. LANDOR.

To Miss Rose Paynter.

[BATH, *April* 6, 1840.]

DEAR ROSE,

If I am writing to you a few hours after your
departure it is not to obtain a single line a single
hour earlier than I should otherwise. It is only to
tell you that I spent a quarter of an hour with your
mama, and left her in good spirits. This is better
worth writing about than anything else you can ever
hear from me. We often are comforted by hearing
the very things we know as perfectly as the com-
forter. All I said was, "consider how many amuse-

[1] According to Burke, Miss Frederica de Courcy, sister of John Fitz-
roy de Courcy, afterwards Lord Kinsale, married Baron Paul de Hoggier on April 4, 1840.

[2] Landor's sons, whom he was to meet in Germany. But the projected meeting did not come off.

ments she will find in London, how many friends and relatives, and, above all, what a consolation her society will be to Sophy." . . . But my dinner is before me, my appetite so good that you will call me a monster without feeling—without heart. . . . As for heart I have only room for one more inmate. He who has the merit to win yours shall be my friend for life. . .

Affectionately yours,

W. S. L.

To Miss Rose Paynter.

BATH, *May 15*, 1840.

DEAR ROSE,

The continuance of fine weather is the more delightful to me when I think how essential it is to your pleasures and amusements in London. Mrs Paynter read me your letters and Sophy's, and I was highly gratified at your day at the Dickens's.[1] For one moment I was on the point of joining your party.

---

[1] Extracts from Lady Graves-Sawle's diary :—

June 1838.—" We found Charles Dickens in the little enclosure at the back of his house, Tavistock House, Tavistock Square. Lying flat on the grass he gazed up for inspiration to the only tree in the little garden. He was then writing the 'Curiosity Shop,' and told us he had received letters from all parts of the world, imploring him not to kill Nell. We dined with him, and afterwards played *charades en action*, a favourite amusement of his."

April 28, 1840.—"Charles Dickens took us to see the Bolivar at the Polytechnic Hall, and we went down into the diving-bell with him."

However I was at last contented with a walk, backward and forward, in the fields behind Miss Whitehead's, listening to a cuckoo and a couple of woodpigeons. . . .

We have lately had some marriages and givings in marriage at Bath. Among the rest, Sir William Davy to Miss Fountaine Wilson.[1] The bridegroom, I hear, is past seventy. It is reported that the infidelity of this swain has thrown a melancholy over the susceptible bosom of Mrs M . . . Mrs Leslie Jones and Mrs Cotton (Lord Combermere's sister) are here. I see them every morning. They both are very clever, well-bred girls, and good humoured. In the evening I hear music at the Digby's or the Wright's. Field[2] usually plays and sings. The rose you gave me I am grieved to tell you is quite decayed. I brought a gardener to examine it, and promised him a sovereign if he would bring it about. . . . He turned out the soil and found nothing but what was perished. I washed the root and all its fibres in lavender-water, and I preserve them carefully. I had formed many projects for this gifted rose. I had been looking out for some little garden to constitute her principality. Lilies of the valley were to be the ladies in waiting;

[1] At Bath, April 20, 1840, Major-General Sir W. Davy, C.B. and K.C.H. to Sophia, eldest daughter of Richard Fountaine Wilson.— *Annual Register.*

[2] Mr Henry Field, a music master at Bath, a great friend of Mr Landor's.

cyclamens the pages.   These and the plebeian strawberries were to be all the court, and all the subjects of
my young queen.   Is it a pleasure or is it not, to think
that what is perished was once very different?   There
are many things to which we are inclined to revert,
and which too surely are not pleasant.

These are not very dark reflections : but none whatever ought to be cast on the first of May, the month
of promises, and before those feet which even the
prosaic have said, and perhaps are saying at this
moment, make the flowers spring where they tread.

It may be so : for my part I will not believe it
until I see it, either on the High Common or on
Primrose Hill.

> *Amico mio !* non lo vedrai
> Dunque se non hai vista
> Assai lunga, e chi penetra
> Le case dirimpetto alla tua.

Last night was the Master of the Ceremonies' Ball [1]
—very well attended.   I left some good music for
it. . . .

Yours affectionately,

W. S. L.

[1] The annual ball for the benefit of the Master of the Ceremonies at
Bath, Colonel Jervis, was always an important event. Colonel Jervis
was the friend both of Mr and Mrs Landor. Years after Mrs Landor
had left Bath, first for Llanthony and afterwards for Italy, Colonel Jervis
welcomed with open arms a young officer on furlough from India who, he
found, was the brother of the five charming sisters. This was General
Sir Henry Landor Thuillier who told me the story.

To Miss Rose Paynter.

DEAR ROSE,   [WARWICK, *June* 1840.]

It appears to me as if I never am to write to you but about some loss or other. James [1] is leaving you, perhaps at the moment I am writing the words. . . . No, indeed, Rose, you may not "truly say that this separation has been your first real unhappiness." All unhappiness is real, although the cause of it may be as yours has been, unworthy of producing it. The kindness of Providence has so ordered it, that we should be moved in some degree by small events, to prevent us from being shaken by greater. A few dark days precede the chillier and stormier. May the first of these be over with you, and may the last never come.

. . . My sons [2] were to have written to me on their departure from the Villa, which was to be in the first week of June. I am very anxious about them, and I might have received the letter to-day had it been written on the first. As it is, I do not expect them at Warwick before the twenty-fifth. On the first of July I am engaged to my friend Ablett [3] in Denbighshire, where we spend all the month, so that I have scarcely

[1] Miss Paynter's brother, Colonel James Paynter.
[2] Arnold and Walter Landor, then at Fiesole.
[3] Mr Joseph Ablett, of Llanbedr Hall, Denbighshire, the friend of Wordsworth, Southey, Leigh Hunt, Reginald Heber, and Landor. In 1837 he printed, privately, a volume of "Literary Hours : by Various

a fortnight for them to stay with my sister, and another fortnight to divide among my other relatives who have invited them.   Arnold says he cannot stay beyond two months in England, since it grieves him to leave his mother for a longer time.   I cannot blame him nor argue with him on that point.   It shows an affectionate heart which I am pleased at finding, although I may grieve in secret that it does not lean a little more toward me.   I shall ask him only one favour; which is that he will allow me to show him

Friends," to which Landor was the chief contributor.   To Ablett was addressed Landor's " Ode to a Friend" :—

> Lord of the lonely plain
> Where Celtic Clwyd runs to greet the main,
>> How happy were the hours that held
> My friend (long absent from his native home),
> Amid those scenes with thee ! how far afield
>> From all past cares, and all to come !
>
> .   .   .   .   .
>
>> Ablett ! of all the days
> My sixty summers ever knew,
> Pleasant as there have been no few,
>> Memory not one surveys
> Like those we spent together : wisely spent
> Are they alone that leave the heart content.
>
> .   .   .   .   .
>
>> I never courted fame,
> She pouted at me long ; at last she came,
> And threw her arms around my neck and said,
>> ' Take what hath been for years delayed !
>> And fear not that the leaves will fall
> One hour the earlier from thy coronal,' &c.

These verses were first printed in *Leigh Hunt's London Journal*, Dec. 3, 1834.   A *rifacimento* of the poem was published in the same periodical on April 15, 1835.

Bath. . . . I think I am destined to spend there all the remainder of my days, living on recollections—which, however, are more likely to wear out life than to nourish and support it. You will provide for me one expedition to break the even tenor of my existence. I shall value the copy of the Claude[1] greatly above the original, which, of all the pictures I ever saw, I have lookt at the longest and with the most delight. For these reasons it is the one I most wished to be yours. . . . You tell me nothing of Fred. Perhaps I may devise some eligible plan of life for him in Canada—an inexhaustible field for speculation and enterprise. . . .

Ever most affectionately yours,

W. S. LANDOR.

To Miss Rose Paynter at Bath.

WARWICK, [*June 5th* 1840.]

DEAR ROSE,

I am writing this in the evening of a day which must have been very sad to you.[2] . . . However, what a variety of studies and occupations are within your reach! But if you turn your mind to poetry, let me for once have influence enough with you to persuade you not to indulge in any kind of it which

---

[1] A landscape, *d'après* Claude Lorraine, still in Lady Graves-Sawle's possession.

[2] Colonel James Paynter had left Bath for India.

verges on sadness.   I am now repeating in prose what
I said before to you in verse.   Take my word for
it, if we fondle and pamper our griefs, they grow
up to an unwieldy size and become unmanageable..
Melancholy, which at first was only the ornament of
a verse, becomes at last a habit and a necessity.
Much of our subsequent life depends on the turn
we ourselves give to the expression of our early
feelings.   But why am I saying all this to you?
to you whose philosophy is so much sounder and
surer than mine?   It is because we all require to be
told as often of what we know as of what we do not
know.

The day before yesterday I had a letter from
Arnold and Walter.   They set out in the first week
of the present month, and will remain, Arnold tells
me, only two in England.   I expect them here about
the twentieth.   My sister is confined to her room, her
niece is very kind and attentive to her.   She admits
me occasionally, and desires I will use her carriage,
&c., as often as I like.   At present I feel but little
inclined to go beyond the garden.   Perhaps next week
I may go to Leamington and see the Priors.   Before
breakfast I gathered the yellow rose which I intend to
place in this scarcely legible letter. . . Perhaps I may
go up the Rhine with my sons.   They shall have
their own way.   Indeed one of them in this respect
seems resolved to leave me no alternative.   Well, if

he pleases himself, I am satisfied. With kind regards
to all my friends in Great Bedford Street,

Believe me, dear Rose,

Ever affectionately yours,

W. LANDOR.

To Miss Rose Paynter.

WARWICK, *June* 25 [1840].

DEAR ROSE,

Your letter finds me writing three or four, in
answer to invitations from relatives and friends—
declining them, one and all. Why so ? Because my
sons do not come to England. They had reached
Bologna, when poor Walter felt suddenly ill after his
late meazles. Arnold either felt the same, or pretended it. Walter, in spite of his severe fever would
have proceeded, but Arnold was resolved to return,
and, after much difficulty prevailed on the good and
affectionate Walter to abandon his determination of
going onward. He, I mean Walter, expresses the
deepest regret at it, and trusts he shall be more
fortunate another time. Arnold on the contrary
tells me at the close of his letter that he never
comes to England at all unless with his mother and
the whole family. He has not the humanity to express
the slightest regret at my disappointment nor to defer
to another moment the resolution he announces. If
you live long in the world you will find perhaps many

such instances of hardness and ingratitude, but I hope it may be in persons not quite so near to you as this is to me. . . . You will see me even more stupid than usual; as much delighted to hear you sing if not as formerly, yet more than by anything else. Delighted is not the word—for nothing can delight me. So be it—but neither can the worst calamity crush my mind. I will see none of my friends while there is any weight of sadness on me. I will walk it and reason it away. There is only one thing on earth worth an effort from me, and that is to grasp back again the senses that seemed for an instant resolute to leave me.

I remain, dear Rose,
Yours affectionately,
W. S. LANDOR.

To Miss Rose Paynter.

BATH, *July?* [1840].

. . . This evening I had the honor of walking beyond Mrs Whitehead's with Miss Rackham and Miss Carter. Miss R. asked me to write in her album, premising that she had always been afraid of making such a request, but that you assured her she might. My reply was—"It is impossible Miss Paynter can have heard of my resolution and promise never to write but in one." I ought to have said, "never to write in any for the future." But it would have been less graciously expressed. On Thursday I

dined with . . . The dinner was splendid. Strawberries, &c., in profusion. There were only Col.
Acklom, Sir Henry Baynton [1] and myself to pay our
homage to our fair hostess, to the somewhat less
fair Mrs L. . . . and Mrs M. . . A Piedmontese
lady came in the evening and sang admirably. So
did Miss . . . I went to Digby's at ten. Field was
just leaving. The Miss Wrights were there.

I would lay a wager you have never yet opened
Digby's book. [2] Do not wonder if you hear of me
becoming a Catholic, and cultivating my little garden
behind some convent in the Abruzzi or Calabria. I
am by no means tired of the world, and never am
likely to be sentimental, but I have sometimes hours
of deep seriousness, as far removed from sadness as
possible. I do not write poetry on these occasions,
but I sometimes translate from the Spanish. These
are from Don Diaz Labrusca, [3] who appears to have
been in love with a French lady. I have seen a
curious fragment of his autobiography.

> I value not the proud and stern
> Who ruled of old o'er bleak Auvergne,
> Whose images you fear'd to pass
> Recumbent under arching brass,

---

[1] Admiral Sir Henry Baynton, K.C.B.

[2] Doubtless the first volume of "Mores Catholici, or Ages of Faith,"
by Kenelm Henry Digby : London, 1831, &c. For some verses on his
book see Landor's *Works*, 1876, viii. 281.

[3] These verses are printed in Landor's *Works*, viii. 207, but with regard
to Don Diaz Labrusca such books of reference as I have consulted are
silent. Either he was an imaginary personage or not a celebrated one.

Nor thought how fondly they had smiled,
Could they have seen their future child.
And yet, Antinöe, I would pray
Saint after saint to see the day
When undejected you once more
Might pass along that chapel floor ;
When, standing at its altar crown'd
With wild flowers from the ruin round,
Your village priest might hear and bless
A love that never shall be less.

Labrusca, you see, was a very cold poet and (no doubt) as cold a lover. *I* was always of the same kind, while I appeared in either capacity. These were translated in the year 1801—and written in the same year. I wonder that I could recollect them—you will think them scarcely worth writing out, much less reading—you are at this moment drinking your coffee happy and making happy. . . .

Saturday, 5 o'clock.

To Miss Rose Paynter.

RUTHIN,[1] *Oct.* 1, 1840.

DEAR ROSE,

If I thought my letters worth a single straw I would not write to you within a week or fortnight. . . . But really the fine weather you have had in Devonshire is more than a sufficient apology for you, and your pleasant walks a full indemnity to me. Here in

[1] Landor was staying with Joseph Ablett at Llanbedr Hall, near Ruthin. Denbighshire.

Denbighshire we have scarcely had a day without rain
since my arrival, and the weather was just the same
for a very long time before, that is while I was taking
my long solitary walks over the cliffs or along the
shore at Exmouth. I am never tired of solitude
where there is sunshine, but sometimes this gloom is
rather more than external with me.

Remember your promise to sing your favourite
song[1] as often as I wish to hear it. These are your
words. I will not press too hard upon them—but
often as I may ask I shall wish fifty times oftener. I
am glad that you are pleased with Sidmouth. Formerly I enjoyed some delightful rides in the country
round it, and remained there several weeks. Within
these few days I have heard of most extraordinary
effects produced by brandy, and as much salt as it
will hold in solution; and I have heard them from
two persons who tried this remedy. I am anxious to
state this in the hope and confidence that it may be of
service to Mrs Paynter. The same medicine taken in-
ternally, with an equal quantity of hot water, removed

---

[1] This may have been either Gabuzzi's "*Mi vien da Ridere*," set to
music by Cimarosa ; or the old ballad, " Early one morning, before the
sun was dawning." To the first Landor wrote a reply, both in Italian and
English (see Appendix). The second suggested the lines—

Does your voice never fail you in singing a song
So false and so spiteful on us who are young?
When, lady, as surely as you are alive
We are seldom inconstant till seventy-five.

Works, 1876, viii. 124.

from me the most violent spasms, which had continued for several months, and from another a rheumatic gout. I know your good sense and goodness of every kind so well that I am not afraid of your thinking this uninteresting. On the contrary, if it should be of any service to Mrs Paynter, you will consider it more interesting than anything I have written or could write to you. So shall I.

On the fourteenth of October I leave this place for Cheltenham, where perhaps I may remain a few days. Three or four at most. Then for Bath, I have innumerable invitations. Some (probably) cordial. But I have acquired all the habits of an old bachelor, even regularity, and I like my own room, my own chair, and—what is never tiresome to one person in the world, my own company.

You tell me you have been walking seven miles without being *much* tired. I think it too far: I should have the courage to tell you so even if I had the honor to be of your party. However, I will hope it was not this which caused you two sleepless nights; and I am certain it was not the alleged court mourning: *what* it was I am not likely to know at present, if at all. There are things in the world fairly worth even two sleepless nights. I think I myself have paid almost as high a price heretofore. At present I do not carry any such coin about me. You are perfectly right in reckoning on my economy as regards the Princess.[1] I would not be the only one in the house wearing black. Added to which it would puzzle me to find the money, now that you have given me to understand that you have not ten odd pounds to spare me. . . . *Coraggio!* next week I shall be as rich as Crœsus. Shall I be happier than I am? Certainly not. I shall only be just as happy, even though I should receive another letter with *Rose* upon the seal. . . .

To Mrs Paynter.

GORE HOUSE, *Friday Morning* [*May* 7th, 1841]

DEAR MRS PAYNTER,

Doubtful how much time I may find amidst the hurry of London to give any account of myself, I take advantage of the early morning. I did not leave my cab at Gore House gate until a quarter past six. My kind hostess and D'Orsay were walking in the garden[2] and never was more cordial reception. After dinner we went to the English opera,[3] *The Siege of Rochelle* and a *Day at Turin*, by Mrs Maberley. Nothing could be worse than the first except the

---

[1] Princess Augusta, George III.'s daughter, who died Sept. 22, 1840.

[2] At one period Count D'Orsay's walks were confined to the garden of Gore House, except on Sundays : the only day on which he could defy the bailiffs.

[3] "May 5, 1841. At the Royal English Opera House, for the benefit of Madame Balfe, Balfe's popular opera of the 'Siege of Rochelle :' to conclude with a new operetta, by Mrs Maberley, 'A Day near Turin.'" —*Adv.*

E

second. The Hanoverian Minister, very attentive to Miss Power,[1] a Carlist viscount, and Lord Pembroke[2] were the only persons who stayed any time in the box. I had not seen Lord P—— for twelve years. He is grown old, and almost plain. Yesterday he dined with us : otherwise we were alone. Immediately after breakfast I went to introduce myself personally to Colonel Stopford.[3] We had been long acquainted by correspondence; and if there is not too much pride in me to say it, with mutual esteem. A more gentlemanly or more noble-minded man I never conversed with. His wife was overjoyed at our meeting, talked to me of Llanthony, and of the walk I took her over the hills, and of the grouse we started. Presently came in the Minister of Caraccas and General Millar, who took the command of the armies of Columbia on the retirement of Bolivar. Stopford was the Adjutant-General. They are great friends. He seems very intelligent, is extremely handsome for a person no longer youthful, but suffers from several wounds, one of which penetrated the liver. Neither of these men think highly of Bolivar as a soldier; both of them like all his family, and

---

[1] Lady Blessington's niece.

[2] Robert, 12th Earl of Pembroke (1791-1862).

[3] Colonel Stopford, formerly in the Guards, had married a Miss Thuillier, Mrs Landor's sister. He went to America to become Adjutant-General in the army of Columbia, under Bolivar. Landor dedicated the first volume of the " Imaginary Conversations " to him.

were pleased with the gracefulness of his manners. And now appeared my niece Teresita.[1] She struck me as being very like my dear Julia, rather less beautiful, but more intellectual. I am afraid her health has suffered by too close an application to study. Lord Pembroke, Montgomery, and all the other public men I have conversed with seem to think that the Ministry[2] must resign immediately. It is not true that the Queen persists in retaining them against the wishes of the people. She, like her predecessors, is quite passive on this occasion. Prince Albert is thought to have suffered in his health by the unwholesome situation of the new palace. Other reasons are given which are much less probable.

To Mrs Paynter.

[GORE HOUSE] *Saturday Morning* [*May* 8, 1841].

. . . We went this evening to the German Opera.[3] Never was music so excellent. The pieces were " A Night in Grenada " and " Fidelio." Madame Schodel sings divinely, and her acting is only inferior to Pasta's. Grisi never quite satisfied me excepting in

[1] Miss Teresa Stopford, who afterwards married Lord Charles Beauclerk.

[2] "All the world thinks and talks of nothing but the Division next week, and its consequences. The Whigs are clamorous for a dissolution."—"Greville Memoirs," May 7, 1841. Lord Melbourne resigned in the following September.

[3] May 7 1841. German opera : Theatre Royal, Drury Lane, "A Night in Grenada" by Conradin Kreutzer, to conclude with Beethoven's grand opera of " Fidelio."

Norma. There nobody can surpass her. I have seen enough of viragos in real life—they no longer can interest or even amuse me. Both D'Orsay and Lord Pembroke were enchanted with Madame Schodel, and Lady B[lessington] and Miss Power, both good judges, and the latter a fine composer, were breathless. To-night we go to the Italian Opera. At dinner nobody but Lord Pembroke. Yesterday I missed seeing Mademoiselle Rachel, who had just left Mrs Stopford, but I found there Miss Strickland, authoress of the "Queens of England"—and went to find my old acquaintance, Miss Porter, and my new one, Miss Poulter. Afterwards I went to Kenyon's. He and Bezzi[1] were out, but Bezzi saw me in Regent's Park and overtook me. I hope to see them this morning, but I find I am too late for my passport, which I cannot have before Monday. As the steamer sails on Sunday I shall go without one.

I left behind me only one thing, but the most important of all, the little key of my carpet bag in which my dress coat, &c., were packed up. I was forced to cut it open, and how to manage with it or without it is a puzzle. Lady B[lessington] and my other friends here wish me to stay until after Monday, when Mlle. Rachel[2]

---

[1] Signor Bezzi was an accomplished Italian gentleman, a great friend of Mr John Kenyon's. It was he who discovered the portrait of Dante on the whitewashed tower of the Bargello in Florence.

[2] "I went to see Mdlle. Rachel make her *début* last night, which she did in *Hermione*."—"Greville Memoirs," May 11, 1841.

acts. I had heard that she is plain. Miss Stopford tells me she is quite the reverse, and that her manner is charming. This morning I shall know if the Ministers resign. If they do, I shall call on Lord Normanby.[1] I will never pay a visit to a man in office. Some of my friends have left their cards on me—but I really have never been at home, and on the opera nights nobody is received here. Walter has written to me from Leghorn, where all my family have been for the benefit of sea bathing, and will remain the whole of May. . . .

Believe me, Dear Mrs Paynter,
Sincerely and affectionately yours,
W. S. LANDOR.

[Here may be inserted some amusing lines, not by Landor, in which his approaching journey to Paris is discussed. They were composed at the time by Miss Rose Paynter, and perhaps nothing could give a truer impression of the impulsive energy and serene indifference to mundane details with which Landor would fling himself into some new enterprise. The author of the verses, written so long ago, now protests that they are mere doggerel, but they happily preserve a marked trait in his character, as well as the extravagance of Landorian speech.

---

[1] Secretary of State for the Colonies in Lord Melbourne's administration.

CONVERSATION (NOT IMAGINARY)

BETWEEN MR S. L. AND MRS P.

Mrs P.

Pray, Mr Landor, may I know
How you intend to France to go?

Mr S. L.

Indeed, I really cannot say,
My friends must *putt*[1] me in the way.

Mrs P.

The Diligence, or the *Malle-Poste*,
Men generally prefer the most.

Mr S. L.

I never of such things take note ;
Rather than do so—I'd be shot!

Mrs P.

Well, but the *coupé's* snug enough,
One must sometimes learn how to rough.

Mr S. L.

Rather than with French scoundrels go,
Strike off my head, at one good blow !
'Twould drive me raving mad.   Why, Zounds !
I'd rather pay ten million pounds.

Mrs P.

How *would* you go then—would you walk ?
(How wildly the poor man does talk !)

Mr S. L.

Oh, I shall take a coach and four ;
Or with a courier ride before.

---

[1] By Mr Landor, *put* was always pronounced as if the word rhymed with *hut*.

Mrs P.

Indeed, I think 'twould try your strength,
To take a ride of such a length.

Mr S. L.

I'm never tired—never know
What in my life 'tis to feel so.
I once walk'd fifty miles in rain,
And when 'twas fine walk'd back again.

Mrs P. to Rose.

My dear, he really is too bad.

Rose.

Oh ! but mama, you know he's mad.
At all events, one thing is flat,
The walk has not improv'd his hat.

A LETTER IN RHYME.[1]

PARIS, Hôtel Vittoria, Rue Chateau Lagarde,
Half-past Twelve, May 1841.

.   .   .   .

Well, on Sunday I parted,
Not very light-hearted.
At midnight we stand
Upon Gallic land.
I rise very soon,
For on Monday, at noon,
Light or heavy my heart,
Perforce I must start.
A little more cost
Attends the *malle-poste;*
But then, as to comfort,
We surely get some for't.

---

[1] Landor's letters were not infrequently versified, but a single specimen
must suffice.

With a nymph by my side,
As blythe as a bride,
All the day thro'
And all the night too.
As we talk'd the whole day,
We had nothing to say,
Or little to think,
Ere in slumber we sink.
But this morn I'm as tired
As could be desired.
I, who boasted that naught
Can tire me, am caught.
No excuses to offer
Against you, fair scoffer!
'Will you permit me a little digression?'
Says Rose, 'We have brought the old fox to confession!'
Pooh! nonsense! all stuff!
Tho' I did not look gruff,
There was for confession little enough.
At Paris the quietest lady would laugh,
And the quietest man say 'too little by half!'

I did not half praise the *malle-poste* as I should.
In England no public conveyance so good;
There is plenty of room for the feet and the knees,
And the arms on each side may extend as they please.
Whereas, in this matter, a thousand reproaches
May justly be cast on our cramping mail coaches.

And now to continue.   Pursuing our way
From the Madeleine into the Rue St Honoré,
What should I see,
Fixt upon me,
But those two bright eyes
Which confounded the wise,
And fix'd that FitzGerald, whom fifty beside
To fix or to soften

Often and often
Vainly have tried.
'Is it *you*?' 'Is it *you*?' we cry both of us. 'It's
An incredible time since I saw you and Fitz.'
'Come and dine with us.'—'No, not to-day?'—'Will you fix
On to-morrow? Be sure you're no later than six.
Well! I find you as lively and youthful as when
I was brightest of maids, and *you* boldest of men!'
'Alas! my sweet lady! no very great praise!
You hardly were born in the best of my days,
When eyes bright as yours, and voices as sweet,
With *my* voice and *my* eyes were happy to meet.'

'Of my praise or my thoughts how unworthy are you!
I was born in those days, and remember them too.'

With a little less pleasure Jane looks in her glass,
But Fitz is as hearty as ever he was.
A wrinkle the more, or a wrinkle the less
May creep on us men, and cause trifling distress,
But thirty years hence you may witness how sad is
A suspicion or shadow of one upon ladies.

And now a few words on my Florentine guest,
Who is gone, as I wish'd, rather early to rest.
I find my poor Walter as thin as a lath,
And wish he were quietly with me at Bath,
At morning and evening taking his fill
Of health and fresh air upon your Primrose-hill.
He would find, I suspect, even health and fresh air
The sweeter for one certain nymph being there.

Tho' here is brave Walter, methinks I would rather
My Julia, dear Julia, were now by her father,
With her fair open forehead, eyes modest and mild
And a voice, I do think, like my own, when a child:
I fancy her (what will not fathers suppose?)
As beauteous, and nearly as graceful as Rose.

Now waltzes are over, and arms disengage,
Rose, write to me twice, if not thrice, in an age,
And I who have almost as little to do,
Will write, if you let me, as often to you.

To Miss Rose Paynter.

PARIS, *May 26,* 1841.

. . . Last night I was at Miss Clarke's. She lives
in the same house with Chateaubriand. Having a
touch of the *grippe*, he did not make his appearance.
I was not sorry for it. He is a notable charlatan. As
nobody can leave Paris without making one *bon mot*,
or an attempt at it, when my opinion was asked
about him, and his popularity had been extolled, I
replied that he appeared to me a small bottle of sugar
and water, fit only to catch flies. Miss Clarke was
the first person who received Lady Bulwer. Of
course she was also the first to be ridiculed by her.
For Lady B. knew that all things in France take their
turn in due order. I do not like to repeat what you
will hear too surely from others—that Mrs ——[1] left
Paris in disgrace. It is reported that she pretended
that her daughter was about to be married, and ordered

---

[1] The name, that of a once celebrated lady novelist, had better be suppressed. George IV. said of one of her books that it was "the best and most amusing novel published in his remembrance." The escapade referred to in the text made no little sensation at the time. The lady is said to have given out that her daughter was engaged to an English duke. The only foundation for the fiction was the fact that the ladies had been invited to a ball at Devonshire House.

a superb trousseau, which she sold immediately and decamped.

Your favourite old oak in the Bois de Boulogne has been uprooted. The fortifications in this quarter are much advanced. Surely it would have been more considerate to finish the other parts first that we might enjoy the pleasantest ride near Paris. My favourite walk was always the Jardin des Plantes. Formerly I used to walk there as soon as it was opened, and again in the evening. In seven months I went but three times to the theatre and four or five to the opera—nowhere else. "What a stupid man! no better in his youth than in his age!" The same on—

> " I once walkt fifty miles in rain
> And when 'twas dry walkt back again."

Rose, one day *walking* with her beau,
Not *flirting*—for she walks not so—
As we—who often see her know,

Cried, " See that vain old man! Last May
I do declare I heard him say
That he can march three miles a day.

He now is going into France :
How they will quiz him if perchance
He hazards such extravagance.

Ah ! his poor head has got a twist ;
He fancies he can use his fist
As you would, if he should be hist.

See how he totters in his gait !
Neither his walk nor sight is strait :
We soon shall earth him, sure as fate."

On

"The walk has not improved his hat."

Being somewhat *hot-headed*, is not an old hat likely to fit me better than a new one? I wish you had seen it in all its glory. What think you of my talking with a king and queen and displaying it before them? Such in the most legitimate sense are the Prince and Princess Czartoryski—he having been proclaimed King of Poland by the deputies of the nobility and people. Knowing my devotion to royalty, but probably more attracted by my hat than by me, he conversed with me the greater part of the evening. . . .

The Louvre is now occupied by the exhibition of modern painting—a sad disappointment. I hoped to pass every morning there. We have been at some private concerts. On Sunday there will be fine music at St Eustache. If civility and kindness are sufficient to make a place agreeable, I ought to be quite contented at Paris. Never have I received so much attention anywhere. . . .

To-day, Wednesday, Dr Virchy called on me, and the first question he asked was, whether I had seen or heard lately of Miss Paynter. I told him I had had the pleasure of seeing her fifteen days ago, and that she had picked up as much bloom in three, as she had lost in a month by sitting up late, etc., etc. He appears to be a man of the first order. I very much doubt whether there exists in France another such intellect. He says Lord Granville [1] can never quite recover.

Probably you have seen in the papers all about the elopement.[2] The lady is frightful, and the gentleman a fool. That of course, in running off with an ugly woman—but equally in all things beside. He tried his fortune with Mlle. Rachel, who replied that her profession was her *parti*, and that she desired no other. This is wise; but it is a species of wisdom more likely to diminish than increase. She will change her mind when she grows old, and when nobody, not even a Frenchman, can love her. How few are aware of the right moment, men or women ! Generally the choice is made too soon, and then the repentance is necessarily the longer, and usually the more poignant.

Out of reverence for the talents of Mlle. Rachel let us hope that she may never, soon or late, be destined to act a part in a domestic tragedy. I forgot to say that I visited Versailles again. A few of the old portraits are interesting. It is wonderful how resemblances are transmitted through several genera-

[1] Ambassador at Paris.

[2] "It was reported in Paris that the eldest daughter of the Infant Don Francisco de Paula had eloped on Tuesday morning with a Polish gentleman. The fugitives were believed to have proceeded in the direction of Brussels."—*Examiner*, May 16, 1841. Writing on June 10, the Paris correspondent of the *Court Journal* said :—"The elopement and subsequent marriage of the Spanish princess, Isabella, with Count Geropski is still the subject of general conversation here."

tions.   Here is a portrait of a Dauphine of Auvergne.
I remember to have seen a descendant of hers sur-
prisingly like it, after two centuries and more.   The
most beautiful face among the portraits is the Queen
of Prussia's, by Gosse.[1]   Never was wounded pride
so delicately exprest.   She is in the act of being
received by Napoleon.   She suppresses the swelling
heart and rises with majestic beauty above the man
who conquered only her kingdom.   You yourself
would not have been greater in her place ; and only
a few of your enthusiastic admirers would find greater
beauty in the expression of your countenance.   You
see I have not learnt to flatter by my recent inter-
course with the French. . . .

Sincerely and affectionately yours,

W. S. LANDOR.

To Miss Paynter at Versailles.

BATH, *July* 24*th* [1841.]

DEAR ROSE,

It delights me to find that I have not entirely
slipt out of your memory. . . . I have little news
for you.   A few weeks ago I went over to Clifton to
visit Lady Belmore. . . . A good many people were
assembled that morning, and before I went away

---

[1] "Napoleon receiving the Queen of Prussia at Tilsit," by Nicholas
Gosse, who died in 1878, aged ninety-one.

there came our handsome friend James FitzGerald.[1]
He said he had a manuscript book of yours, which he
had quite forgotten to return before you left Bath, and
he asked me how it might be conveyed to you.   My
reply was, " By your own hand—nothing less can obtain
or deserve forgiveness for such negligence." . . . Mr
C—— is residing with his family, having left the army.
His mother told me he had nothing to do now but look
out for a wife, adding, "with a few thousand pounds,
beauty, some accomplishments—music in particular—
a companion to him in his studies."   Moderate man !
I suspect, however, that he has something more to do
than to *look out*.   We may look out for the stars at
midday, but there is something to be carried with us
if we hope to find them.   Whether he has that about
him which may bring his star nearer, you are a better
judge than I. . . . Mrs Napier[2] has been extremely

[1] Mr James FitzGerald, one of the FitzGeralds of Coolanowle, Queen's
Co., afterwards went to the Colonies and became Auditor General and
Comptroller, New Zealand.   He died in 1896.

[2] The wife of Colonel, afterwards General Sir William Napier, historian of the Peninsular War.   She was a niece of Charles James Fox.
Her daughter, Elizabeth Marianne, was married in 1838 to Philip, 4th
Earl of Arran.   Another daughter, Miss Nora Napier, married Sir Henry
Austin Bruce, afterwards Lord Aberdare, and died April 27th 1897.   Miss
Pamela Napier married Mr Miles, M.P. for Bristol.   The Napiers at
this time lived at Freshford, some seven miles from Bath.   Landor often
visited Freshford ; and although he and Napier disagreed about the
character of Fox, they were excellent friends.   " You don't draw your ale
mild," Napier once wrote to him, "any more than I do ; but if Pam or
Johnny (Lord J. Russell) call you out, I will be your second."   Colonel
Napier's daughters acted as his private secretaries, writing out his
History as he dictated it ; but they found time to attend the balls at the
Bath assembly rooms, often walking the seven miles through muddy

unwell, and is still far from recovered.   Miss Napier returned with her.   She possesses the same admirable understanding as the others, with somewhat less beauty.   But this, we are told, and no doubt you believe it, matters little.   It grieved me to hear that Lady Arran has been suffering under the influenza. The air of Ireland, I fear, is ill adapted to her constitution.   Besides, thoughtful as she is, and abounding in resources of her own, she enjoys and requires society.   Lord A. avoids and hates it. . . . I shall remain in Bath only a few days longer, then to my sister's at Warwick, afterwards for a week into Staffordshire.   I have declined my friend Ablett's invitation into Denbighshire.   Bath is the place of rest for me—always was—always will be.   Solitude—retirement, rather, has the same charms for me as ever, and in these days of political excitement I have reason to be gratified that all factions are as civil and courteous to me as before.   Neutrality has not usually any advantage.   I seldom go anywhere but to Digby's, not Digby the Catholic but to Simon.   Last week there was a small party in his beautiful garden—in which the fruit and cream appeared to be as attractive as the flowers.

roads for a dance. In a biography of Napier it is stated that he was "extremely democratic in his views."   In confirmation of this, Lady Graves-Sawle relates that when she was walking with the Colonel and one of his daughters a rustic labourer stood aside to let them pass, whereupon Miss Napier was somewhat roughly reprimanded for getting in the poor man's way.

If you happen to make an excursion to the *Petit
Trianon* you will find one rock, and only one,
smoothened in part and made commodious for a seat.
It is just above the pond. Perhaps it may exercise
your ingenuity to discover whether this was done
purposely, when all the rest were made rough as
possible. I was vext at seeing the windows of
that apartment, which was once occupied by Marie
Antoinette, taken out, and four panes substituted for
one. Forty years ago there was not a very large
panel in all Europe ; these upper windows had the
largest. I at that time occupied the apartment for
several months. Happy days they were from first to
last—the happiest and most tranquil in the whole of
my existence. I wish you exactly such in the near
neighbourhood. Can a letter end better than with
a wish so cordial? Mine has already been so long
that *any* end of it must be welcome. Among my
follies is this, that I am apt to think I am conversing
when I am writing. . . .

Ever sincerely and affectionately yours,

W. S. LANDOR.

To Miss Rose Paynter.

WARWICK, *Sept.* 25 [1841].

DEAR ROSE,

. . . Your commands, that my letter shall be a
prosy one, are likely enough to be executed. This is

F

a proof to me that you like novelty. . . . Do you fancy that no time can sober me? The fact is, I am never less poetical or less romantic than when I think of you. . . . It is flattering to me to be remembered by the Duchesse de Grammont. Pray tell her so, and that I was delighted by the letter which Count D'Orsay read to me from her son on the high college honours he had attained. I have frequently heard that they are all such as a wise and anxious mother could wish them.

You know that my hatred of politics is unfeigned— you also know that the dearest of my friends are Conservatives. Neither party can ever be of the slightest use or advantage to me; and I was not very highly pleased when I was desired and invited to ask for something. If the change of Ministers[1] is beneficial to any of your connections I shall by no means regret it, for I am confident that the present men will bring about what the others failed to accomplish. The Duke of Wellington is the only man of either party in whom I can discern the semblance of greatness. The rest are clever scene-shifters and expert prompters, nothing more. Did you ever meet the Percies in Italy? They have lately returned to Guy's Cliff, and I spent yesterday with them. Mr Percy[2] is the

---

[1] Sir Robert Peel's Ministry came into power in Sept. 1841.

[2] Afterwards Lord Charles Percy, his brother becoming 5th Duke of Northumberland. There were two Mr Bertie Greatheads (or Greatheed) of Guy's Cliffe, father and son, and nephew and grand-nephew of the 5th and last Duke of Ancaster, who died in 1809. The elder Bertie Greathead (1759-1826) was one of the group of literary triflers who about the

brother of Lord Beverley, and Mrs P. is the daughter of an old friend of mine, Bertie Greathead, nephew of the last Duke of Ancaster. They have an only daughter *chi farà furore.* Mr Crampton gave me his dog Oscar, whom I ordered to become her vassal, and he kissed hands on the occasion. It is sad to think that I shall not see your sister or you for several months yet. However, I am resolved to cut short my visit in Staffordshire, that I may at least have the pleasure of meeting Mrs Paynter in Bath. I had proposed to be there on the twenty-fifth. I will if alive be at St James's Square on the tenth. Walter leaves me on the ninth. It will grieve me most bitterly to lose him. God only knows whether I may ever see him again, or any of the rest. Adieu, dear Rose,

I am,

Ever affectionately yours,

W. S. LANDOR.

year 1784 founded the Society of Otiosi at Florence, and were afterwards laughed at in England as Della Cruscans. He also wrote some plays, one of which, "The Regent," was brought out at Drury Lane in 1788 ("Dictionary of National Biography"). His son, Landor's friend and Mrs Percy's father, died in Italy in 1804 aged twenty-three. Lord Charles Percy's only daughter died seven years ago. Mr Guy Duke, Landor's grand-nephew, informs me that Mr Greathead of Guy's Cliffe was thought by some of Landor's family to have been the author of "Guy's Porridge Pot," a satirical poem in dispraise of Dr Parr, which has sometimes but wrongly been attributed to Landor himself. Bertie Greathead, the younger, could not have been the author, as the first and second editions were published in 1808 and 1809, after his death. But the elder Bertie Greathead, who lived till 1826, may have written it. Miss Berry, Horace Walpole's friend, was a frequent visitor to the Greatheads of Guy's Cliffe.

To Miss Isabella Percy.[1]

If that old hermit laid to rest
  Beneath your chapel-floor,
Could leave the regions of the blest
  And visit earth once more:
If human sympathies could warm
  His tranquil breast again,
Your innocence that breast could charm,
  Perhaps your beauty pain.

To Miss Rose Paynter.

[BATH, *Oct.* 14, 1841.]

DEAR ROSE,

Ought I not to be a little vexed and almost angry with you, telling me as you do, that you are going to ask me a favour? And what at last is this favour? That I will send you the "Book of Beauty"![1] Supposing it not to be your right by the title it bears, yet it has grown yours by custom. One volume contained something, I forget what, unworthy of you and unreadable; this I withdrew for a time. And when I offered it to you again, you rejected what had been disfigured by a cross. In future I will always try to do better, and so long

[1] The lady to whom Landor addressed these verses died a few years ago unmarried. They were probably written about the same time as the preceding letter, and were printed in Landor's Works, 1846, ii. 670.

[2] The "Book of Beauty" for 1842, published about October 1841, contained some verses of Landor's addressed "to Zoe, June 1808," written just before his departure for Spain.

as I receive the "Book of Beauty," I beg permission to consider it as only held in trust for you. This is the fourteenth of October, yet the fair editress has not yet sent me my copy. When it comes I will pack it up, together with William Spencer's[1] poems. These are edited by Miss Poulter, a cousin of my kind-hearted old friend, Lord Guildford. She is come to reside for six months in Bath, and has taken the lodgings over me, leaving her fine London house in Green Street. She is extremely pleasant in conversation, and her poetry is thought to be of the highest order. You will not entertain the same opinion of her criticisms when you read a passage on my writings in the Biographical memoir prefixed to the volume. I had not the honor of her acquaintance when she wrote it, and I wish I could send you the work without it, or at least without your knowing or

---

[1] The Hon. William Robert Spencer, grandson of the second Duke of Marlborough, was an accomplished writer of *vers de société*. Jeffrey, in the *Edinburgh*, spoke of his "flashy, fashionable, artificial style," and the authors of "Rejected Addresses" made fun of him—which he took good-naturedly enough ; but his verses to Lady Anne Hamilton—

> "Too late I stay'd ! forgive the crime,
> Unheeded flew the hours "—

deserve a place in any anthology of minor poetry. After leaving Harrow, Mr Spencer read for a time with Landor's old friend, Dr Parr, who seems to have treated him more as a man of the world than as a pupil. "Billy !" the Doctor would say, "there is no occasion for you to trouble your head with all we talked of last night : indeed, I do not remember what I said." Mr Spencer died in France in 1834, and is buried at Harrow.

Miss Poulter published in 1841 "Imagination, with other poems."

finding out that it is there. Poor William Spencer, the delight of all society, lived unhappily with his wife, died far away from her and from his children, and received the last solaces of his existence from the assiduous and unwearied affection of Miss Poulter. You will be sorry to hear that Dickens[1] has been extremely unwell. Barnaby Rudge is drawing to a close, but something of equal ability is certain to succeed it.

I hope you sometimes by way of variety meet and converse with men of genius. Possibly they may not be the most desirable companions for a constancy; but the intellect has its sympathies as well as the heart, and no one ever regretted the indulgence of them. I wish you may happen to meet with Madame Colmache.[2] She is an excellent person, free from all affectation, a good wife, a good mother, courteous, friendly, sincere, instructed, and intellectual. But your earliest days in Paris will require no addition to their brightness. Whether you would let me or not, there is no happiness of yours in which I do

---

[1] "He was still in his sick-room (Oct. 22, 1841), when he wrote : 'I hope I shan't leave off any more, now, until I have finished Barnaby.' On Nov. 2, the printers received the close of Barnaby Rudge." Forster's "Life of Dickens." The next book was "Martin Chuzzlewit."

[2] This lady, who is still living, was the wife of Talleyrand's private secretary. She gave Landor a pair of spectacles which had belonged to Talleyrand, and he gave them to Sir Henry Bulwer, who would value them, he said, even though, being a diplomatist, he could see through a brick wall.

not to a certain degree partake. I rejoice in your meeting Mrs Caldwell, give her my kindest remembrances, if you have any time to think about them. It may be that we shall all meet in February; it may also be that we shall not. I dare never look far forward; I dare not take up hopes to play with, lest they cling to me too closely. Last evening I was at Lady Belmore's. She continues quite as well as she was when you left Bath. . . . If you meet Rio[1] again make my compliments. He is a man of great abilities, courage and integrity. He was about the publication of an interesting work which I have long expected. Walter has left me grieved and solitary, but by permitting his return I have a better chance of seeing the rest. Poor dear Julia thought that Walter might succeed in bringing me back to Italy with him. I soon found out that, anxious as he was to come to me, he

---

[1] I am indebted to Mr Walter Slater, whose collection of Landor's rarer writings is probably unsurpassed, for a reference to "La Petite Chouannerie, ou histoire d'un collége Breton Sous l'Empire," par A. F. Rio: Londres, Moxon, 1842. On pp. 294-299 are some verses of Landor's, dated March 19, 1840, which I have not met with elsewhere. M. Rio describes them as "une touchante élégie de Landor sur les écoliers tués au combat de Muzillac." They begin

"Cities but rarely are the haunts of men."

The volume also contains verses signed R. M. Milnes. Regarding Landor, M. Rio wrote, not untruly :—"La stoïque indifférence de l'auteur pour la gloire littéraire a été cause que ses ouvrages n'ont pris que lentement la place qui leur appartient parmi les productions contemporaines." M. Rio is better known as "the graceful and pious historian of Christian Art." See "Life of Lord Houghton," by T. Wemyss Reid.

came in the character of her ambassador. There is
only one thing in the world in which my sweet Julia
could not prevail with me. To stand firm on some
occasions requires more power and more energy than
any active effort, and wrenches both the mind and
body more. I think my strength and spirits are rather
the worse for this resistance, and long walks are in-
effectual in bringing me back sleep and appetite. I
shall soon, however, be more reconciled to the absence
of my sweet-tempered boy, who is much improved by
his residence in England, and the last shades of gloom
will have disappeared before your return. I have been
to visit your flowers—they are doing well, and the roses
I planted seemed glad to see me. Present me very
respectfully to Lord and Lady Aylmer, and

Believe me ever, dear Rose,

Your affectionate

W. S. LANDOR.

To Miss Rose Paynter.

BATH, *Novr.* 21, 1841.

DEAR ROSE,

The Admiral was here a few days ago, and looking
as well as usual. The moment I heard of his arrival
I called on him. He told me he was about to write
to Paris. In case he should not have done so, I am
saying all this to remove your apprehensions. . . . .
To-day I dined with Napier with only a family party.

He introduced me to the papa of your distinguished admirer, Mr C. Beauclerc. I had met the ladies of the family before. One of them married the brother of Mrs Hare. Mrs Napier and two of her daughters are gone into Berkshire for a few weeks. To-morrow I shall meet the others in the Pump-Room, where we have excellent music, but the space of the seats is contracted, there being none under the orchestra.

Discontent is gaining ground in England, and there is malevolence where there is not discontent. Bishop Baynes[1] has had another cornstack burnt down. Two days afterwards I met him at Lady Arundel's and we talked much about it after dinner. I expressed a wish that it might not have been the work of an incendiary. He replied that he "could only wish the same thing." I had not time to read a single article in the " Book of Beauty " or the " Keepsake." The moment they arrived I sent them off to you. The only tolerable things in either, I suspect, are Miss Garrow's.[2] She

[1] Bishop Baynes, Principal of the Roman Catholic College at Prior Park. " By far the most interesting spot in the neighbourhood of Bath," Miss Mary Russell Mitford wrote, " is Prior Park, built by Allen, the book-seller, the friend of Pope and the original of Fielding's Allworthy ; afterwards the residence of Warburton, and now the site of a Roman Catholic College." " Recollections of a Literary Life." Bishop Baines, Miss Mitford adds, was the son of a Yorkshire farmer, and " had risen to the rank of Vicar Apostolic, titular Bishop of some Eastern See, and to the highest influence among his English co-religionists."

[2] There are some lines by Miss Garrow, " on the portrait of Her Majesty " in the " Book of Beauty " for 1842. " I have been much puzzled by the impression which Miss Garrow's poetry has made upon certain very competent and usually very fastidious critics, Mr Kenyon,

had written out for me long before her beautiful verses on the Queen. December in Bath will be the longest and dullest month of the year. In Paris I hope you will find it the pleasantest and shortest.

Believe me ever, dear Rose,

Affectionately yours,

W. S. LANDOR.

Walter Savage Landor, &c. You will find a long poem of hers in the recent ' Keepsake.' " " Recollections of a Literary Life," by Mary Russell Mitford, Dec. 5, 1841.

CHAPTER III

1842-1843

CHAPTER III

1842—1843

IN 1842 Landor received a visit from his eldest son Arnold; but not much is said about it in his letters. He seems to have gone twice to London. His account of a visit to the Royal Academy in the spring or early summer may perhaps be held to refute the justice of Edward FitzGerald's observation that Landor "appeared to judge of pictures as he does of books and men, with a most uncompromising perversity which the phrenologists must explain to us after his death." His artistic sense was not always perverse, though he often went strangely astray through a want of technical knowledge.

In the autumn of 1842, Landor was again in London, this time to attend the marriage of his niece, Miss Stopford. Next year he was visited by his son Walter, and his much-loved daughter, Julia, of whom he writes with the fondest affection. Of his literary pursuits at this period, and of the unabated vigour of his mind, there is proof in the critical studies of Catullus, Theocritus and Petrarca, written for the *Foreign Quarterly Review*, some imaginary conversations printed in the " Book of Beauty " and *Blackwood's Magazine*, and numerous letters to the *Examiner*. Robert Southey died in March, 1843, and Landor, the poet's oldest surviving friend, was active in advocating a public recognition of his merits as a distinguished man of letters. He also wrote an inscription for his tomb at Bristol, but this was not accepted.

To Miss Rose Paynter.

SUNDAY MORNING [*May* 15, 1842].

DEAR ROSE,

Down to the present hour I have received no letter from Arnold. I wrote to him on the twelfth of April, and desired he would set out from Italy on the first of May at latest, and give me notice a few days previous. The blowing up of the train at the Versailles railroad[1] has filled me with terror and dismay. I cannot help thinking it possible that he may have been upon it. Rarely as I have any painful or unpleasant dream, I dreamt on the morning of the sixth of May that he was dead. It is said that every man has some superstition. I have none—absolutely none. But I have always felt beforehand a fainter or stronger intimation of coming evils—in such a manner as to leave me no power of obviating them. I remain in the house all day. I stand on my feet at every knock,

[1] May 8, 1842.—"Horrible occurrence on the railway between Paris and Versailles. . . . The list of killed was officially set down at fifty, but it was generally thought that many more perished in the flames." —"Annals of our Time."

open my sitting-room door and turn back desperate. Old fathers, you see, and young lovers have some points of resemblance.

I cannot quit the house even for a long walk until I hear from Arnold, or see him.   From the thirteenth to the sixteenth I have every moment been expecting him, or shall expect him—and cannot tell where we shall meet, whether in Bath or London.   For this reason I have declined the invitations of my friends in town. . . .

The good Napier girls have sent me a pic-nic letter as they promised.   To relieve the heaviness of mine and to let you know what they forgot to tell you about the General,[1] I now enclose it.   I do really think one or two of them would even give up a flirtation for five minutes to write to me or converse with me.   This is a great deal to say, and perhaps too much! but I say it only of one or two, and only when they have had a pretty long flirtation first. . . .

I hope the waters of Wisbaden will be of service to Mrs Paynter.   There is always a great deal of gay society, which I hope will to some degree indemnify you for what you must lose by your absence from Dorsetshire. . . . Bath is still gay.   I have three or four cards for dinner but don't go.   To-morrow evening is the only one I shall pass out of my own house.   It

---

[1] In the beginning of April, General William Napier had gone to Guernsey, as Lieutenant Governor.   He resigned this post in 1847.

sometimes rains at Wisbaden—and rainy days are writing days—you may make them the pleasantest of all days to

W. LANDOR.

To Miss Rose Paynter.

[*May* 17, 1842.]

. . . A letter from Arnold came to me this morning at the same moment as yours. On such an occasion I opened his first. Never in future will it happen to any other letter in the world. His was dated on the sixth. He proposed to leave Florence on the seventh, Leghorn on the eighth, and to be with me at Bath in thirteen or fourteen days from setting sail. If he suffered by the sea, he would stop at Genoa and go to Lyons by land all the way thence. I may expect him to-morrow night or Thursday or Friday. I wish he came through London that I might meet him there. . . .

Do not moralise so gloomily on the bitter thought, "how transient is friendship." The loss of friends, by some cause or other, is the commonest accident of life. Weak minds bear it better than strong ones, and presently lose the sense of it in loquacity and complaint. . . .

COMPOSED IN A WALK TO WESTON.

Che cosa mai, che cosa
Davanti agli acchi vedo!
  Per ubbedire a Rosa
  Io breve tempo chiedo.

Leva una sua parola
Tutta mia dappocaggine
E crea versi sola
Sua invocata immagine.

A rimedar buon senso
Da lei mi viene imposto.
Mi scrivera in compenso?
  No, riderà piutosto.

Ma basta quel' riso
Bel fiore di bel viso.

La Prima Dama dicĕ.

Poeta chi lavora
Per te, bella Signora!
Bella, ma troppo altiera!
Dimmi, che cosa spera?

La Seconda Dama risponde.

Spera da me, Signora?
Ed avrà lui ognora
Silenzio e pressa mano.
Dimmi, se scrive in vano?

G

To Miss Rose Paynter.

[BATH, 1842.]

DEAR ROSE,

. . . I cannot tell which are the verses you think the best : it appears to me that some of the others are quite equal to those which I find in the envelope.

There is no time of life or stage of friendship, whether in the flow or in the ebb, when it is safe to speak to a lady any *whole* truth about her. I do not believe you will quite pardon me while I am telling you that I find one or two conventional expressions. For instance no *sigh* ever *echoed*, and no Muse ever was inspired. The Muses are the inspirers : it is Rose who is the inspired.

All delicate points in criticism are liable to be called *cavils.* But Boileau wisely says—*Rien n'est beau que le vrai*—and he says it of poetry. You shall, however, have your revenge. Although I thought a single stanza sufficient answer to Bettina,[1] I found it easy to supply her lover with more. My Italian friends have marvelled that anything fresh could be added on such a subject, and in a language in which there is scarcely any other. Miss Garrow and Bezzi are vociferous about it. . . .

[1] See Landor's Italian verses in "Dry Sticks," p. 200.

To Miss Rose Paynter.

[GORE HOUSE], *Saturday Night* [*June* 1842].

DEAR ROSE,

We have not been to the opera this evening, as Lord Pembroke and the Duc de Guiche came to dinner. He is on a visit to Lord Tankerville,[1] but has the good taste to prefer the society he finds here, particularly D'Orsay's. D'Orsay was never in higher spirits or finer plumage. Yesterday we went at two o'clock to hear Rossini's *Stabat Mater.*[2] Certainly the air sung by Staudigl, *Pro Peccatis*, is very sublime. It would be presumption in me to say anything about the composition. I think it less simple, and feel it to be less affecting than some I have heard in Italy. Many great masters, I believe, have tried their hands at it, and several of these are thought to have succeeded.

After the *Stabat Mater* we went to look out for

---

[1] Lady Tankerville (*née de Grammont*) was the aunt of the Duc de Guiche. She was sent to England, when a young girl during the Reign of Terror, became the intimate friend of Lady Palmerston, and died in 1865.

[2] There was a performance of Rossini's *Stabat Mater* at the Prince's Theatre on June 29, 1842, when, says the *Athenæum*, "the beautiful singing of Mdlle. Lutzer, Mdlle. Pacini, Signor Mario, Herr Staudigl, and a very steady chorus, was set off by an orchestra at once powerful and delicate, well conducted by Signor Gabussi." Mention is also made of "the bass air, *Pro peccatis*, in itself among the finest modern songs of its class—how much more so when sung by a Staudigl."—*Athenæum*, July 2, 1842.

some proper setting for the miniature, unsuccessfully at present.

Instead of going to Chiswick for the horticultural display, with my friends the Stopfords, I took advantage of the absence of people from the Exhibition.[1] Three pictures struck me particularly. A scene in Hamlet, the play scene, by Maclise. The Queen is most admirable; but Hamlet is vulgar and too old. In reality he could not be twenty. All the accessories are admirable. There is another piece containing only Ophelia. She is sitting under a withered tree; her feet naked, and hanging over the water in which she was so soon to die. The flowers are going down the stream. She has thrown in almost the last of them. Her countenance is mild and melancholy, and very beautiful. Even in the position of her feet there is pathos.

Landseer has several pictures all worthy of his skill and genius. One of them is equal in execution and invention to any work of the English school. He calls it the Sanctuary. A hart has been pursued, and has taken to the water of a wide lake in Scotland. He has just reached a desert island, just within his utmost power of swimming from the main-

[1] At the Royal Academy in 1842 were exhibited, "The Play Scene in Hamlet" (No. 62), by Daniel Maclise, R.A.; "Ophelia" (No. 71), by R. Redgrave, R.A.; and "The Sanctuary" (No. 431), by E. Landseer, R.A. The first picture is now in the National Gallery, the second in the Tate Gallery, and the third at Windsor Castle.

land : he is weary and stiff: a long line of light and ripples shows you his track : the moon is half above the hills he has left behind him : and he has this very instant frightened from the shallows a flock of wild ducks: they fly away and leave him to his weariness and his solitude.   He seems to be as conscious of the one as of the other.   Such is the power of Landseer, who knows the hearts of all the brute creation.[1]   I only wished that you could see these pictures, though I am not among the privileged who attend you on such occasions.   At this distance I cannot mar your pleasure by my remarks.

A German boy named Rubenstein [2] (I think) has been playing to us on the pianoforte.   Never did I hear anything so wonderful and of so pure a taste at the same time.   Wonder, where it exists at all, generally predominates over every other feeling— not so in him.   He appears to be about eleven or twelve years old.

[1] " Do we never see the past and the future in the pictures of Edwin Landseer? who exercises over all the beasts of the field and fowls of the air an undivided and unlimited kingdom, καὶ νόον ἔγνω." Landor's Works, 1876, viii. 365.

[2] " We have little faith in prodigies, less patience to see the best years and hopes of a child's life expended and prematurely destroyed in the mechanics of musical education.   But it is absurd to be beyond the will or power of making exceptions ; and we must needs do so in the case of this young pianist (M. Rubenstein).   As to age, a year more or less is of little consequence ; and whether he be accepted as eleven, or rated as fifteen, he is remarkable as a player."—*Athenæum*, May 21, 1842.

Sunday Night.

This morning I saw Lord and Lady Aylmer at church. The place and the party I was with would but permit me to make my bow. I could not give them the satisfaction of telling them that I had seen you and Mrs Paynter well and happy two days before. On Saturday I leave this place. I have written to Arnold—for where there is no dishonour there ought to be no dissention. That, and that alone, opens an impassable gulf between parent and son. . . .

Ever affectionately yours,

W. L.

WARWICK, *July* 20 [1842].

DEAR ROSE,

Old people, and especially old friends, are very apt to be troublesome and unreasonable. I doubt whether by turning into a gossip I have any better chance of making my way at present. A few days after my arrival in town, the Duc de Grammont dined at Gore House. He is on a visit to Lord Tankerville. Be sure he did not forget to make enquiries about you, some of which I could answer and some not. He told me that his younger son, a fat little boy when I saw him last, is only changed into a fat great boy, and just gone into the army.

D'Orsay has just finished an exquisite painting of the Duchesse. . . .

Among the extraordinary men I met this last time in London was Bab-boo Tagore.[1] He came early and there was nobody to receive him but myself. When he left the dining-room for the opera, he came round to me and said a thousand Oriental things. Expect to see me in a turban when we meet, with diamonds and rubies in it. He makes everybody grand presents. I can receive none I shall think of any value since the vegetable ruby of Wellow,[2] bearing a name more precious than itself.

I went twice to the British Museum, and found our friend FitzGerald in excellent health and spirits, full of Lycia and colonization. . . .

Believe me,
Ever affectionately yours,
W. S. LANDOR.

[1] Babu Dwarkanath Tagore, a wealthy and distinguished Hindu, head of a well-known family in Bengal. He first visited England in 1842, was graciously received by the Queen, and played whist with the Duchess of Kent. The Court of Directors of the East India Company gave him a dinner, and the Lord Mayor at a city banquet proposed his health. In returning thanks, Babu Dwarkanath Tagore said that England had "protected his countrymen from the tyranny and villainy of the Mahomedans, and the no less frightful oppression of the Russians." The worthy Babu again came to England in 1845, and never returned to India, dying in London on August 1, 1846. There is a "Memoir" of him by Kissory Chand Mitha, Calcutta, 1870.

[2] A place about six miles from Bath, a favourite spot for picnics; but the allusion must pass unexplained.

To Miss R. Paynter in Devon.

[BRISTOL, *Aug.* 1842.]

DEAR ROSE,

I daresay you will be curious to know how the most negligent of escorts fared in regard to his luggage.[1]

It came at about two. I dined here at Bristol a quarter of an hour after, and am proceeding to Cheltenham, where I sleep to-night. . . . I remain at Colton Rectory, near Rugely, a whole week. "Mr Landor! I never take hints!" Well, do not then, but enjoy your health, your society, and everything enjoyable in life. My letter had a narrow escape from my soda water. Adieu.

Ever yours,

W. S. LANDOR.

TO LADY CHARLES BEAUCLERK [2]

ON HER MARRIAGE.

No, Teresita! never say
That Uncle Landor's worthless lay
    Shall find its place among your treasures :
Although his heart is not grown old,
His rhymes are, like himself, too cold .
    For bridal bowers and festal measures.

[1] Landor not infrequently arrived at his destination without the key of his portmanteau ; or would felicitate himself on having brought the key and then find that the portmanteau had been left behind.

[2] Published in the "Book of Beauty" for 1844, but written in 1842

He knows you lovely, thinks you wise,
And still will think so, while your eyes
Seek not in noisier paths to roam,
But rest upon your forest-green,
And find that life runs best between
A tender love and tranquil home.

To Miss Rose Paynter.

[GORE HOUSE], *Wednesday, Sept.* 7 [1842].

DEAR ROSE,

It is my intention to write you not a note but a letter, such as was occasionally the custom in this country and some others, even at so late a period as 1839 or '40—in short, within the memory of man. To be circumstantial—which I seldom am—I arrived at Gore House early on Monday. In the morning, beside Lord Allan, and some other people, there called Lord Auckland,[1] whose administration as Governor-General of India has been lately so much condemned. At dinner the Duc de Guiche, Sir Francis Burdett,[2] and Sir Willoughby Cotton.[3] I had

When reprinted in Landor's Works, 1846, ii. 668, a few alterations were made in these verses.

[1] "The Opposition continually taunt the present Government with having approved of Auckland's policy, when it appeared likely to be successful, and now finding fault with it when unexpected failure and disaster have occurred." "Greville Memoirs," Sept. 3, 1842.

[2] Sir Francis Burdett had been the friend and disciple of Horne Tooke. He was for thirty years Member of Parliament for Westminster; but from 1838 to his death in 1844 he sat for North Wiltshire.

[3] General Sir Willoughby Cotton commanded the Bengal column in the Afghan expedition of 1839. He afterwards held the chief command

not seen Burdett for many years, and never liked him much, he being always querulous—yet once upon a time we were in the habit of dining together daily. Those were bright hours, even my presence could not interrupt their brilliancy. We fell into politics, that is, he dragged me in. We do not differ in them quite as much as you imagine, only that he likes them and I detest them.   Sir W. Cotton is a very intelligent man and a good officer.   On his march in India, he told me, he saw the temple that Alexander built in honour of his horse Bucephalus.   He says it is in the finest style of Greek architecture, and still entire. . . .

I pity C— B—, he is certain to find out these things. The laws of nature have usually been called regular. They may be, but here they are more capricious than even those of fashion, and a thousand times more cruel. What poignancy there is in the effervescence of *dissimilars*! and what sadness even when it subsides! There are calms worse than tempests, and more to be deprecated in the voyage of life. All these reflections are but sand and shingle—we now come to

in Afghanistan till his departure in November 1840. I cannot identify the ruins referred to by Sir W. Cotton, but Cunningham in his "Ancient Geography of India," regards Jalalpur, on the banks of the Jhelum, as the site of the once famous city of Bucephala, founded by Alexander, in honour of his charger, killed in the battle against Porus.   Sir Willoughby Cotton has not always been fairly treated by historians of the first Afghan war.   Sir William Fraser, in his Memoirs, described him as "one of the finest types of soldiers that I have known ; combining determination, courtesy and sagacity."

the solid beach, and I promise you that the remainder of this paper shall be worth half a column of the *Morning Post.* The marriage[1] which brought me to London was celebrated this morning. Six brides-maids are now become necessary on these grand occasions, as six horses were formerly. They were all such pretty girls, but Teresa too is very lovely, far beyond *them.* Lord Charles is an accomplished man, of fine manners, and extremely handsome. His morals and temper are equally unexceptionable. There were sixteen persons at the wedding and seventy at the breakfast. This was given at Mivart's hotel in grand style. At church there were the Duke and Duchess of St Albans, Lord and Lady Essex and their families, Sir Robert Stopford[2] and his daughters, and a very pretty girl who knelt by me, but whose name I have forgotten. Have you heard that the Duc de Luxembourg is about to marry a girl of 18— a Miss Cochrane, with some fortune (£15,000) and much beauty. The Duc de Guiche left us this morn-ing to shoot with his cousin, Lord Ossulton.[3] We

[1] On Sept. 7, 1842, Landor's niece, Miss Teresa Stopford, was married to Lord Charles Beauclerk, son of the 8th Duke of St Albans. She died in 1858, and the present Viscount Milton is her grandson. Landor's verses to Lady Charles Beauclerk were published, with a portrait, after a painting by J. Hayter, in the " Book of Beauty " for 1844. In " Hellenics," 1859, p. 259, are verses on her death. Lord Charles Beauclerk died in 1861.

[2] Rear-Admiral Sir Robert Stopford, G.C.B., a distinguished naval officer, was at this time and until his death, in 1847, Governor of Green-wich Hospital.

[3] Lord Tankerville's son.

miss the liveliness of his conversation—he talked
Memoirs.   Can you read this?   My lamp is not
clear.   W. S. L.

To My Daughter.[1]

By that dejected city, Arno runs,
Where Ugolino claspt his famisht sons.
There wert thou born, my Julia! there thine eyes
Return'd as bright a blue to vernal skies.
And thence, my little wanderer! when the Spring
Advanced, thee, too, the Hours on silent wing
Brought, while anemonies were quivering round,
And pointed tulips pierced the purple ground,
Where stood fair Florence : there thy voice first blest
My ear, and sank like balm into my breast :
For many griefs had wounded it, and more
Thy little hands could lighten were in store.
But why revert to griefs?   Thy sculptur'd brow
Dispels from mine its darkest cloud even now.
What then the bliss to see again thy face,
And all that Rumour has announced of grace !
I urge, with fevered breast, the four-month day.
O! could I sleep to wake again in May.

---

[1] Landor was expecting a visit from his son, Walter, and his daughter
Julia, and these verses appeared in *Blackwood's Magazine*, March 1843.
Reprinted, with slight alterations, in Works, 1846 and 1876.

To Miss Rose Paynter.

[BATH, *May* 27, 1843.]

DEAR ROSE,

My letter I hope for your sake will be a short one, but when we begin our letters, as when we begin our lives, we have no notion how long they may run on, or what they may contain, or where they may end. . . . Yesterday I dined with the Longs—your friend FitzGerald and the Baroness Browne-Mill[1] were all the party. I sat by the Baroness, with whose manners and conversation I was charmed. I expected to find nothing but severity, taciturnity, and coldness. Quite the contrary. She admired Mazzini and more than tolerated Byron. You yourself, if you ever favoured me with so long a conversation, could hardly have sustained it better.

My sister has written to me again, desiring me and Julia and old Walter to come up to her, at latest by the first of June. I have begged a reprieve until the third, by which time I shall hope to hear in Great Bedford Street about what you have done at Greenwich. Julia, whom I gave her aunt's letter, said, " we shall not see Rose then all next month! " You perceive you have already given her the confidence of familiarity, and it is the only time I have heard her say anything in a tone of regret. The old man Walter

---

[1] Baroness Browne-Mill was the recognised head of the Low Church party in Bath.

rode yesterday with the Miss Tyler. He and Julia
are gone, I believe, to Great Bedford Street. It will
not be until after your Greenwich expedition that you
intend to see Dickens, I suppose. Lady Aylmer, I
hope, will be pleased with him ; indeed, I am sure she
would be if she knew the high opinion he entertains of
her niece.

You are under a great obligation to my friend
General Napier. He has written me a long letter
which requires an immediate answer. So now you see
land. . . . Dear Rose,

Ever affectionately yours,

W. S. Landor.

Saturday morning.

To Miss Rose Paynter.

[Llanbedr Hall, *July* 1843.]

Dear Rose,

. . . Had I been at all aware but a week
ago that you were going to Brighton I would have
requested Mrs Paynter to have taken lodgings for me
there, and I should have entered them about the tenth
of August. Most unfortunately I have now promised
to spend a fortnight with my brothers, at Colton and
Birlingham, and then a few days at Cheltenham with
a friend,[1] who is not only blind but also bereft of the

[1] Mr Rosenhagen was a pensioned Treasury official, and had been
private Secretary to Mr Perceval. Mrs Rosenhagen was the sister of

best and dearest wife any man ever possessed. What would you think of me if I could disappoint him? The others I should not have cared about.

The weather has been so rainy ever since we came into Denbighshire that Julia has been tempted but once to mount a pony under the guidance of Walter. I suspect that if she were at Brighton, her equestrian skill would have been insufficient for her to accompany you. Julia and I must have lagged behind—not perhaps quite unpardonably. I confess I am not very fond of riding a hack myself, and I should be in perpetual fear about poor Julia. Even much better horsewomen have sometimes made me tremble for them, with little cause perhaps. I remember an instance of it in the Park at Bath which occasioned me the longest fit of fear I ever experienced in the course of my life.

I hope you will be happier at Brighton than you were last year in Devonshire. Before I went to Spain I spent several weeks there [1]—certainly not

Fleetwood Parkhurst, Landor's schoolfellow at Rugby. Mr Rosenhagen always believed that the letters of Junius were written by his father. Landor wrote some verses on Mrs Rosenhagen's marriage, and others on her death. See Works, 1876, viii. 97, 98.

[1] This was just before Landor's Spanish expedition. "I am going to Spain. In three days I shall have sailed. At Brighton, one evening, I preached a crusade to two auditors. Inclination was not wanting, and in a few minutes everything was fixed. . . . May every Frenchman out of France perish! May the Spaniards not spare one!"—Landor to Southey, 1808.

very miserably. I had then four capital horses, two for riding and two for the carriage. At present I should drive a hard bargain for a donkey. Nevertheless I do assure you I am really and truly a rich man —rich enough to give four or five pounds a week for lodgings. Now if you hear of any robbery do not have me taken up on suspicion. . . .

My friend Ablett has given twenty acres of fine land adjacent to Denbigh, for the site of a lunatic hospital. I assure you he made the donation before my arrival, so you may be satisfied it is an act of pure charity and without any reference to friendship. There exists no similar constitution in the whole extent of the Principality. It is my intention to write an appeal[1] to the Welsh in order to awaken their generosity. Because my friend has done so munificently, the gentry are inclined to do nothing, since they would not appear to be *less* generous : and hence they pretend to raise objections. Some however have come over to Llanbedr for the purpose of engaging me to write the appeal : and this I promised them I would do. I am not quite idle, you see—whatever you might have imagined from my rambling letter. With Julia's love,

Believe me ever, Dear Rose,
Affectionately yours,
WALTER LANDOR.

[1] It was published in the *Examiner* of August 16, 1843.

To Miss Rose Paynter.

LLANBEDR HALL, *July* 18 [1843].

DEAR ROSE,

. . . Delightful as this place is, I have always been on the look out for Devonshire. As you and Mrs Paynter are not to be there, neither shall I. Julia says she shall be quite as happy at Bath. We return to our old residence on the twentieth of August, at the latest. . . . We wish you were here for ten thousand reasons, and among the rest because the flowers are both profuse and choice. No grounds can be kept more neatly. The climate is very mild at all seasons. Walter, who ought to be very proud of your enquiries, went out a fishing this morning with perfect innocence. . . . Do you happen to remember the game which puzzled so many wise men, young and old, in Great Bedford Street? I mean the game played with ivory letters. I have been exerting the whole of my genius in the composition of a charade.

> What three letters make the word
> Which expresses, first, a bird,
> Then a thing for milk or cream,
> Then what *all* do when they dream.

Now King Edipus was far more celebrated for his riddle than for his royalty. How greatly then must *my* riddle place me above any station I may have hitherto attained. . . . I leave Llanbedr the first of

H

August. Rose says " I never take hints, Mr Landor," and Mr Landor says he would willingly be an *exceptionable* man on this occasion. Julia tells me she will be too late for the post, but there is time I think for a line or two, *addio*. . . .

To Miss Rose Paynter.

WARWICK, *July* 24 [1843].

DEAR ROSE,

. . . Yours are the only letters I run over again and again. My eyes have very much suffered by poring over my own illegible hand—for such it is, if not when I write to you, yet when I write in pencil or in small characters what I dispose for publication. Hundreds of sentences and of paragraphs I have transcribed from the backs of letters and from old pocket books, with great difficulty, and sometimes with great doubt in regard to certain words. Forster tells me he never saw such extremely small characters as I have employed in my interlining. . . .

Ever and everywhere faithfully yours,

W. S. L.

To Miss Rose Paynter.

BATH, *Saturday* [*August* 19, 1843].

DEAR ROSE,

We returned last evening from Plymouth, where we have been spending the week with

Colonel Hamilton Smith,[1] a man of more extensive and more accurate information than any in existence. There was a regatta on Thursday—which of all uninteresting things is to me the most uninteresting. However I thought my dear Julia might be amused by it, but she understood as little of the matter and enjoyed it as little as myself. She did not receive your letter until she reached the rectory at Colton. You may fancy that either I am or am about to be a bishop by my visitations among the clergy. We proceeded from Colton to my brother Robert's at Birlingham, and after resting at Bath for a day or two hurried again into Devonshire. . . . Colonel Smith tells me that I am expected by Sir Samuel Meyrick [2] at Goodrich. He possesses you know the finest and most complete collection of ancient armour, &c., &c., of any in the world. It is more authentic

[1] The joint author, with Sir Samuel Meyrick, of "Costume of the Aboriginal Inhabitants of the British Islands, &c." London, 1815.

[2] Sir Samuel Rush Meyrick, of Goodrich Court, Herefordshire, was the author of "A Critical Inquiry into Ancient Armour, as it existed in Europe, but particularly in England, from the Norman Conquest to Charles II.," a magnificent and learned work published in 1824. On his death, in 1848, his collection of armour became the property of a cousin, and was sold, mostly to M. Spitzer, the English Government having declined to give £50,000 for it. Landor's verses to "Meyrick, surrounded by Silurian boors," are printed in his Works, 1876, viii. p. 176. In another poem there is mention of

> " The treasures round each trophied wall,
> Where armour of past ages shows
> How brave were some whom no one knows."

—Works, 1876, viii. 319.

than that in the Tower. His uncle General George Meyrick is an old friend of mine. But I think I shall not quit Bath again this autumn for any greater distance than Clifton. I am bringing up a myrtle for you. Its mama was given to my sister by General Maister who lately had the command in the West Indies. This species of myrtle is in blossom the greater part of the year and is remarkably broad leaved. The three letters of my Charade are A. P. N. A *pea hen, pan, nap.*

In regard to verses[1] I never have any of my own worth sending you, but perhaps you may never have met with these. *Le duc de Nivernois ayant demandé à la Duchesse de Mirepois une boucle de ses cheveux, elle la lui envoya avec ces vers :—*

Les voilà ! les cheveux depuis longtemps blanchis !
Je ne regrette rien de ce que m' ôtât l'âge,

---

[1] The Duc de Nivernois, "celebrated for his graceful manners and his pretty songs," came to England as Ambassador from France in 1762. Lord Chesterfield respected him as the model of a perfect gentleman. His verses to Madame de Mirepois are quoted in his " Œuvres Posthumes," Paris, 1807, but I do not know where Landor found the lady's. Madame la Maréchale de Mirepoix had also been in England, where, she declared, her hair began to turn grey from drinking too much tea. Besides pretty songs, the Duc de Nivernois translated a book of Milton's " Paradise Lost" and Pope's " Essay on Man " into French, his version of the latter beginning—

" Reveille toi, Mylord, laisse aux rois ces chimères
De leur petit orgueil jouissances si chères."

He also wrote Imaginary Conversations between Cicero and Fontenelle, Alcibiades, and the Duc de Guise, the younger Pliny, and Mme. de Sévigné, Pericles and Mazarin, &c. M. Lucien Perey has published two interesting volumes on the Duc de Nivernois and his times.

Il m' a laissé de vrais amis.
On m' aime jusqu'autant, et j'aime d'avantage.
L'astre de l'amitié luit dans l'hiver des ans,
Fruit precieux du goût, de l'estime, et du temps
On ne se meprend plus ; on cède à son empire,
    Et l'on joint sous les cheveux blancs
Aux charmes de s'aimer le droit de se le dire.

LA REPONSE.

Moi ! vous parlez de cheveux blancs !
Laissons, laissons, courir le temps
Que vous importe son ravage ?
Les tendres cœurs en sont exempts,
Les Amours sont toujours enfants,
Et les Grâces sont de tout âge.
Pour moi, Thémise, je le sens,
Je suis toujours dans mon printemps,
Quand je vous offre mon hommage
Si je n' avais que dixhuit ans
Je pourrais aimer plus longtemps ;
Mais non pas aimer d'avantage.

I hope you may receive the same sort of verses at the same time of life. In English we find a few tender ones but none more graceful; and even the tender ones are heavy and breathe hard. There is something of the languid in the best of them. Even the passionate have more of the lucifer match-box than pure flame. I can speak only of those that I have seen : perhaps you may have seen some that I have not. How beautiful is " L'astre de l'amitié" in the former, and " Je pourrais aimer plus longtemps," etc., in the latter.

Julia talks of writing to you now she is once more fixt in Bath again. She is become a little less brown than she was, and looks much better for it. I was quite surprised and a little vext and grieved at seeing her so tanned. Last week I desired Forster that he would forward to Mrs Paynter the next *Examiner.* I hope you will receive it to-morrow. It will contain, I trust, a severe reproof and castigation which I have given to Lord Brougham[1] for his manifold sins and iniquities. . . . You see I have taken a larger sheet of paper than has been seen anywhere out of the public offices for several years. But I do assure you Sir Robert Peel has bestowed no employment on me, and that the letter is not written on government paper. . . .

I remain, dear Rose,
Ever affectionately yours,
W. Landor.

To Mrs Paynter.

[Bath,] 20th September [1843].

Dear Mrs Paynter,

. . . I went to the regatta at Plymouth, which was amusing to Julia and Walter. Yet both of them were glad enough to return to Bath. Walter rides and walks occasionally with Captain Roberts, and Julia is delighted with his daughter. . . .

---

[1] Published in the *Examiner*, August 26, 1843. See Part II.

I send you, together with these stupid and troublesome and rambling lines, the two *Examiners*,[1] one
containing my letter on Lord Brougham, the other
an appeal in favour of the Greeks against King Otho.
This has been translated into the Attic language, and
will appear in every part of Greece.   I hear also that
it will be (perhaps is) translated into the Turkish.
Yesterday I sent another to the *Examiner* containing
a series of charges which the noblest subjects of King
Otho bring against him.   I rejoice in being chosen
their interpreter and advocate.   I am, however,
damped a little in inflicting any chastisement on Lord
Brougham from the certainty that it will be displeasing to Mrs Meynells, to whom he was an unsuccessful suitor, but whose friendship (in spite of his un-
steadiness) he has retained.   She has fifty-fold the
sense and judgment that he has, and writes as gracefully as he writes vilely.

The moment I had received your last, I went to
Great Bedford Street and inquired for Daisy.[2]   She
was not come nor to come.   How does she do?   Poor
dear Daisy.   I hope at least she does not suffer pain
—for she cannot assuage it by writing to a friend.

---

[1] The *Examiner* of August 26, 1843, contains Landor's letter on Lord
Brougham.   His first letter on "Greece and King Otho" was in the
Examiner of September 16.   A second letter with the same heading was
published in the *Examiner* of September 23.   See Part II.

[2] Miss Paynter's spaniel, mentioned more than once in these letters, as
well as in Landor's published verse.

Julia and Walter must leave me in the first week of October. They promised to be absent from Italy no longer than six months at the farthest. My heart sinks within me at the thought of their departure. The happy days of my existence are all past. They send their kindest love to you and Rose. I hope dear Rose will bring back all her bloom *this* time, I wish to see it contrasted with the orange flower.

Ever yours,

W. S. L.

To Miss Rose Paynter.

BATH, *September 21st* [1843].

DEAR ROSE,

. . . It delights me to know that you have been so well amused in Lancashire. You did right in not killing the grouse. Let men do these things if they will. Perhaps there is no harm in it—perhaps it makes them no crueller than they would be otherwise.[1] But it is hard to take away what we cannot give—and life is a pleasant thing—at least to

---

[1] A short passage from this letter is quoted in Forster's "Life of Landor." Something has been said in the Introduction about Landor's attitude in regard to field sports. He told Dr de Noé Walker that he once found a partridge still alive, which he had fired at and only wounded the day before ; and that after this he would never go out shooting again. The reader may recollect what Byron wrote :—" The last bird I ever fired at was an eaglet, on the shore of the Gulf of Lepanto, near Vostitza. It was only wounded, and I tried to save it—the eye was so bright. But it pined and died in a few days, and I never did since, and I never will, attempt the death of another bird."

birds. No doubt the young ones say tender things to one another, and even the old ones do not dream of death. Talking of old ones, I come naturally to say a little of myself. I am an absolute cripple with the rheumatism. Perhaps a gallop round Doncaster race-course would do me good, but I doubt my elasticity in springing to the saddle. I thought old age a fable until now : I now find it a serious and sad calamity.

It is no wonder to me that you were enchanted with York Cathedral. Whatever is excellent raises your admiration and enthusiasm. In how deplorable a state was architecture throughout the whole of Europe, until these last thirty years, ever since the death of Wren. And he undervalued and misunderstood the marvels of the Gothic. I can hardly imagine that even the Athenians heard such music in their chaste and beautiful temples as you heard in the Cathedral at York.[1] . . .

Mrs —— tells me she and her family went over to Weston Super Mare. Of all the places on the earth or the waters, this is surely the most muddy and miser-able. She found it so, although her voyage was not made in search of the picturesque. I have no other Bath news to offer you. I have exhausted my genius

---

[1] " Grecian architecture does not turn into ruin so grandly as Gothic. York Cathedral a thousand years hence, when the Americans have conquered and devastated the country, will be more striking [than the ruins of Pæstum]."—Landor to his sister, Nov. 1827, Forster's " Life of Landor," ii. 137.

in the long letter I wrote to Mrs Paynter this morning. Luckily she asked me for two *Examiners*. The best of me was in them. If you happen to receive them do not think me spiteful because I am severe. It devolved on me to punish two evil-doers. I was called to it by many loud voices, and some of them from afar. I do confess to an intolerance of baseness, but I am very tolerant of the most adverse opinions on all subjects whatsoever.

> Believe me, dear Rose,
> Ever affectionately yours,
> W. S. LANDOR.

To Mrs Paynter.

[BATH, *Sept.* 30, 1843.]

DEAR MRS PAYNTER,

I have this morning received your kind letter, and that *Examiner* which contains my first on Greece. But the second which I sent to you last Sunday never came back, and I have been asked for it by many. . . . In to-morrow's *Examiner* [1] there will be a third letter of mine. I did not expect the most glorious (because the most bloodless) of revolutions to have taken place so soon. My advice, *hinted* only in the *Examiner*, was to wait quietly until the

[1] Landor's letter on " The Revolution at Athens" was published a week later in the *Examiner* of October 7th. See Part II. On Sept. 14 the Revolutionary party at Athens established a new Ministry, and invited the National Assembly to prepare a new constitution.

explosion at Warsaw—for that whether it succeeded or not, it would fully occupy the attention of the Russians. My letter was written but about a week before the Insurrection at Athens, which Otho precipitated by ordering a set of military commissions, to try and hang his subjects, in every part of Greece. . . . I now come to what pains me most bitterly. Julia had promised, I find, to be absent only six months. This being the case, I have never uttered one word, much less one complaint, against it. . . . She [Julia] and Walter send their love. Julia will express to Rose, before she leaves England, her regret at losing so soon so kind a friend. . . .

Ever most truly yours,

W. S. LANDOR.

Saturday, Sept. 30.

To Miss Rose Paynter.

[Oct. ? 10, 1843.]

. . . My Julia went by the steamer on Sunday. The weather was very boisterous. I rose several times in the night and attempted by putting my hand out of window to ascertain in which point was the wind. . . . My dear Julia wished not only to be with me but alone with me as much as possible. We parted in unutterable grief, but youth and fresh scenes will soon assuage all hers. That is enough.

Adieu, dear Rose.

To Miss Rose Paynter.

DEAR ROSE,

I think your verses on the " Bride of
Death "[1] very beautiful.   Perhaps I should if they
were less so.   Frederick's pleased me so much that I
read them over twice.   They want compression—as
nearly all modern poetry does, particularly Byron's.
Cowper, Crabbe, and Moore run the least into this
fault since the time of Goldsmith.   There is much of
the superfluous even in Gray's beautiful Elegy.[2] . . .

I had seven lines from Julia on Thursday.   She
reached home on the 26th, at 4 in the morning, tired
to death.   Old Walter wrote a long scrawl on various
things—all more than pardonable in him, but not all
quite pleasing to me.   He is a dear, good creature

---

[1] This was a picture by Thomas Barker (the younger) of Bath, painted
for Princess Clementina, Louis Philippe's daughter.   Mr Barker died in
1882.

[2] " Gray's Elegy will be read as long as any work of Shakespeare, despite of its moping owl, and the tin kettle of an epitaph tied to its tail.   It
is the first poem that ever touched my heart, and it strikes it now just in
the same place."   Landor to Forster (Life, ii. 422).   In the Imaginary
Conversations Landor makes Horne Tooke say:—" Expunge from his .
Elegy the second and third stanza, together with all those which follow
the words—
          ' Even in our ashes live their wonted fires,'
and you will leave a poem with scarcely a blemish : a poem which will
always have more readers than any other in any language " (Works, 1876,
iv. 192.)   Landor said he would rather have written the ninth stanza of
the Elegy—
          " The boast of heraldry, the pomp of power," etc.
and one of George Herbert's, than any other in poetry.

nevertheless—and I told him so without the nevertheless. . : .

Affectionately yours,

W. S. LANDOR.

To Mrs Paynter.

BATH, *Dec.* 5, 1843.

DEAR MRS PAYNTER,

We are now beginning to have such
weather in Bath as makes it undesirable to walk out.
. . . I had formed the resolution to abstain from parties
for the future.   But as all my resolutions, or nearly all,
are either weak or unwise, I broke it—and went to
hear music at Mrs Yeate's, whose pretty daughter
played admirably.   Now be cautious never to enter a
wheel chair in damp weather.   It was by doing so that
I caught as severe a cold and fever as ever befell me.
Bread and butter pudding, seltzer water, and strawberry jam have been my only sustenance.

I am vext that I cannot pay my usual visits to poor
Daisy.   But I trust you receive the daily bulletins
from Miss Reade, and that they are such as remove
all inquietude about her.   Our balls commenced on
the fourteenth.   A few days ago I had the honor of
escorting the Miss Woodwards from the pumproom
home again. . . .

Yours very sincerely,

W. S. L.

To Miss Rose Paynter.

BATH, *Dec.* 6, 1843.

DEAR ROSE,

Entertain better hopes of dear little Daisy.
The first thing I did when I awoke this morning (I keep
London hours) about one o'clock—was to order a
neck of mutton for Daisy.   Challon on going to Great
Bedford Street, found that the medical adviser had
prescribed the identical thing, and that it was already
in the house.   The scientific are of opinion that warm
baths, completely so, are injurious, but order the feet
and legs to be put in hot water.   Never will I recommend anything again—but I once had a valuable and
most beautiful greyhound in the same condition—
occasioned by putting a sack over her to protect her
from the rain or mist.   She was rubbed with the hand
for two hours morning and evening, and recovered—
but never ran so well as before.   While Daisy was
under my care her exercise was gentle, and only for
about an hour.   I then brought her into the house,
spunged her feet dry, and made her lie down upon the
sofa—not very reluctantly.   She had an excellent
appetite, which I treated as I do my own, leaving
a part of it.   I owe something of my health to this.
Health, indeed, where is it gone ?   However, my cold
is no worse than in most other years : but the fever is
only to be conquered by the most rigid abstinence.
Strawberry jam and seltzer water are my medicines.

If you can think of anything for Daisy tell me. . . .
Ah! these pets! these pets! Is there no song upon
them, too? There should be. When I lost my
marten, I foreswore all other *delizie*—and yet if Julia
sends me a yellow *can* Pomero[1] I shall just live long
enough (perhaps) to grieve over another broken
resolution.

Addio.

[BATH] *Saturday Night, December* 23 [1843].

DEAR ROSE,

You fill me with delight by your generous and just remarks on Dickens. No mortal man
ever exerted so beneficial and extensive an influence
over the human heart. Very much private and still
more public good will have originated from his genius.
From the midst of adventurers, shufflers and im-
postors of all parties, just Posterity will place high
apart the names of Dickens and Lord Ashley.[2]

What a shock it would give to Marlborough Build-

---

[1] The exact date of " Pomero's " arrival in Bath I have been unable to
fix. Mr Forster says it was in the Autumn of 1843 ; but if this letter was
written in December, it must have been later. Landor's dog, Pomero,
canem amicum suum egregie cordatum, was a character almost as well
known in Bath as Landor himself. " Everybody knows him," Landor
wrote, " high and low, and he makes me quite a celebrity."

[2] Afterwards the Earl of Shaftesbury.

ings if it were known that Mary Boyle[1] dined alone
with me yesterday—with me! so dangerous and dis-
solute a man! Sir Courtenay left her under my care
in the morning.   He returned to Marston, so extremely ill, that I expect to hear of his death to-
morrow.   What a house.   Poor Lady Cork in her
coffin, Lord Cork struck with blindness, Lady Boyle
incurable, Sir Courtenay hopeless.   Lord Dungarvan
and his brothers have come from Eton for the holi-
days.   What amusements can they find in a house
at all times the most melancholy in the world, and
now hung with mourning all around.

Mrs Marlow has mellowed down into a rich austerity but well flavoured.   Mrs Layard thaws.   She
was so gracious as to invite me to a musical party;
and I went.   I hear that James's[2] "Arabella Stewart"
is admirable.   On Monday I shall begin to read it.
I wish he could be persuaded to live in this part of
the world.   There is a little of stiffness in his manners,

[1] Some very interesting letters from Miss Mary Boyle to Landor were
published in the *Century Magazine*, February 1888, with an introduction
by J. Russell Lowell. Her father, Sir Courtenay Boyle, died May 21,
1844. Lady Cork, wife of the eighth Earl of Cork and Orrery, Sir Courtenay's brother, had died on November 29, 1843. Lord Dungarvan, now
Earl of Cork, was fourteen in 1843.

[2] G. P. R. James had been Landor's neighbour and friend in Florence,
and Landor was an enthusiastic admirer both of the man and his works.
"You cannot overvalue James," he wrote to Miss Boyle; "there is not
on God's earth (I like this expression, vulgar or not,) any better creature
of His hand, any more devoted to His highest service, the office of im-
proving us through our passions." His verses on the death of James at
Venice, in 1860, were printed in "Heroic Idyls," &c., pp. 213 and 223.

but he is courteous and deferential. Formerly such qualities were agreeable to the ladies; they appear to be superseded by the higher accomplishments of *baffi*[1] and cigars. I do not believe you have given in your adhesion to this party. . . .

Remember the fourteenth of January is Colonel Jervis's ball. He will be sadly disappointed, and God knows how many more, should you be absent. I still enjoy the privilege of seeing you dance, which was always one of my greatest pleasures. In Devonshire you will probably have had enough of it—but as the philosopher said, " We do not live for ourselves alone." Be equally wise, and generously tell him in reply, " It is not for ourselves alone that we dance." Julia has written twice since you left Bath. She sends her love, and begs you will thank Lady Caldwell on her part for the beautiful present from Canada. . . . Let me wish you a merry Christmas. The word sounds like distant bells and chimney piece holly berries. Many happy returns my dear, good Rose, and may the coming one be the prime of them. So long as there are any for me, happy or unhappy,

Believe me,
Ever Your's Affectionately,
W. S. L.

[1] Italian—whiskers.

I

CHAPTER IV

1844—1847

Sophy & Miss Rose Paynter.

CHAPTER IV

1844—1847

In Landor's eyes, one can scarcely doubt, by far the most notable event of the period now to be explored was the marriage of his fair correspondent. At the end of the chapter, he looks forward, with pleasant anticipation, to seeing the young couple in their beautiful Cornish home. His annual excursions have included visits to his brother Robert, whose "Fawn of Sertorius" was published in 1846, to Lord Nugent, and Archdeacon Hare; as well as a trip to Devonshire, where he met the future historian of the Crimean war. In the summer of 1846 he changed his lodgings, moving to Rivers Street; and it may be that one good lady in Bath watched the departure of a guest not always placable, with something like a sigh of relief. The same year was also marked by the publication of a collected edition of his works in two stout volumes, which the *Athenæum* received with the comment that "the literature of the nineteenth century has long since numbered Mr Landor among its representatives to posterity." This was followed in 1847 by the publication of a volume of "Hellenics, enlarged and completed," but to be again enlarged in 1859, and a choice collection of Latin verses. Political affairs at home and abroad were discussed in letters to the *Examiner* and other papers. Landor wrote a petition to Parliament against British intervention in Portugal, which was signed by over a thousand of his fellow citizens. He also joined in the movement for purchasing Shakespeare's house at Stratford-on-Avon.

To Miss Rose Paynter.

[BATH] *Tuesday morning* [*Jan.* 1844].

DEAR ROSE,

Never in future seal with a black seal any letter you write to me. You know how suddenly the most irrational thoughts seize upon me, and how I live and have my being among impracticable and impossible things. No man beyond the walls of a madhouse could have been so terrified as I was. It is true, a moment was quite sufficient to assure me that the writer was alive when it was written: yet what a chaos was generated during that moment, in my uncalculating and unreflecting head. I opened the letter—and joined the hunt and the dance. In the hunt I was not very much amiss : in the dance but so so. People (not many, it is to be hoped) even doubted my juvenility.

A thousand thanks for your kind recollection of my

dear Julia.   She is better. . . . Carlino[1] has gone into the Maremma for a month's shooting: grave good Walter stays quietly at home and studies drawing.   Arnold has bought a beautiful mare, he tells me.   I had interest enough with the trustees to get him an additional fifty pounds a year to support his dignity as Signor Conte Arnoldo.   As the two *poderi* are worth (being 100 acres) pretty near £30, the deuce is in it if he cannot maintain his state.

My Niece Teresita[2] had a son born on the 2nd. She is doing well.   The Baroness Browne-Mill[3] is about to marry the Rev. Mr Seymour.   The angelical does not espouse an evangelical as people thought she might.   Another old bridegroom is departed and another young widow left : Mr Brooke[4] of the Crescent, but he was only half a century older than the lady, and only seventy-five when Hymen scattered the first blossoms of felicity on the nuptial couch.

If it should snow as it seems likely to do, nobody will be able to present to you such a boss of violets as I carried down to the station for you *yesterday*.   Here they are—still fresh—but violet-life is brief.   Alas !

---

[1] Landor's son Charles, the father of Mr A. H. Savage Landor, the Tibetan traveller.

[2] According to Burke, the Hon. W. de Vere Stopford Beauclerk was born Jan. 3, 1844.

[3] The Baroness Browne-Mill married, secondly, the Rev. M. Robart Seymour.   See p. 109.

[4] Mr Robert Brooke, late of the Bengal Civil Service, died Dec. 10, 1843.

how many things are—beside violet-life and human
life too.   Adieu, dear Rose.

Believe me,

Ever affectionately yours,

W. S. LANDOR.

To Miss Rose Paynter.

BATH, *Saturday* [*Sept.* 14, 1844].

DEAR ROSE,

. . . Pray tell me how it happens that
your stay at Brighton is protracted beyond the first of
October. . . . I have been passing two [days] at
Clifton with the Cowells, who made many kind
inquiries how you and Mrs Paynter are, and when
you return. . . . They and Fonblanque,[1] who dined
with us, come over in the course of the week to lunch
with me, attracted by the report of a certain lobster
whose apparition I have promised to set before their
eyes, as clearly as any in the ink of the Egyptian boy,
and quite as substantial to say the least.   I came back to
Bath to avoid several invitations which were sent to me
by very kind and amiable friends.   I become less and
less fond of society ; not from any unconsciousness of
being less fit for it as far as spirits and such things are
concerned.   Perhaps these are too exuberant for a
time of life which ought to be more grave.   Dickens
has written eight letters to Forster, which Forster is

---

[1] Mr Albany Fonblanque, editor of the *Examiner*.

bound to come and read to me. I have desired
Forster to insert in the *Examiner*¹ some lines I
addressed to Dickens at Genoa, which you will receive
at the same time as this.   They are good for little but
to commemorate our friendship which would be remembered by him and me, and possibly by some few
more, without them.

Believe me,

Ever affectionately yours,

W. S. L.

To Miss Rose Paynter.

Friday Night [*Dec.* 1844].

Dear Rose,

. . . Dance away this horrible weather. What
must it be in London, when even in our genial and
almost tropical Bath this very morning I had been
sleeping in an ice-house. . . .

Have you any old pensioners who are looking out
for you? If you have, appoint me your almoner. I
have kept some money on purpose. This month and
the next, I am resolved to spend on myself only half

¹ Landor's verses to Charles Dickens were published in the *Examiner*,
Sept. 21, 1844, and are reprinted in Works, 1876, viii. 144. Here occur
the lines :—

"Ah! could my steps, in life's decline,
Accompany or follow thine!
But my own vines are not for me
To prune, or from afar to see."

my large income. My heart sinks and aches every time I go out of doors, such is the misery of the poor.

Ever yrs.,

W. L.

To Miss Rose Paynter.

[*Dec.* 26, 1844.]

How many regrets have you softened, my dear Rose, by the new purse [1] you have sent me to replace the lost one. But do not desire me ever to wear it. I shall be worn out myself before that is. I shall carefully place it in the treasury which contains so many gems from the same mine. . . . Last night I attended our oratorio. The room was crowded, the music excellent. . . . Yesterday I received General Napier's "Conquest of Scinde."[2] That is, the first volume : there will be two more. He writes with his usual spirit, but I sadly fear his health is declining. What a man the world will lose if it loses him. God avert so great a calamity from his friends and his country. This morning I was answering a letter I received from Dickens[3] when yours was brought me.

[1] A netted, silk purse was found the other day among the keepsakes in Landor's writing desk.

[2] The first part of "The Conquest of Scind" by General Napier was published in November 1844.

[3] Charles Dickens, who had taken up his abode for a time in the Palazzo Peschiere, Genoa, paid a flying visit to England, early in December 1844.

Can you believe it! he was a week in England and neither he nor Forster told me anything about it. His letter as usual is a delightful one, enough to bring you back to Bath for the sake of reading it. He is starting from Genoa for Tuscany ; thence to Rome, Naples and Sicily. I hope you have enjoyed his " Chimes." Wonderful man! Everything he writes is in the service of Humanity. His Genius was sent from Heaven to scatter good and wisdom upon the earth.

Believe me, dear Rose,

Your obliged and affectionate,

W. S. LANDOR.

To Miss Rose Paynter.

[BATH, ? 17 *Jan.* 1845.]

DEAR ROSE,

It occurs to me that your birthday falls on Sunday, on which letters are not delivered in London. You will receive then, on Saturday, my usual congratulations, warm and cordial as ever. . . . I had lately a delightful letter from your friend, James FitzGerald, but it was written before yours. Whatever is amusing to you is interesting to me—for which reason I am confident you will always let me hear this much, leaving the rest to my powers of divination.

The ancients were assisted in this art by certain birds, great and little. We have only birds.

Dickens wrote to me about a fortnight ago. He sends his compliments to Mrs Paynter and yourself. It is his intention to proceed to Florence, Rome, Naples and Sicily. I wish he were again in England. But it neither is nor ever will be my destiny to see much of those I love most. Keene and his wife are here. The Boyles, I mean Sir Courtenay Boyle's daughters and their young cousin, Lord Dungarvan, dine with me to-day and then go to the theatre. . . . I think there must be some mistake in regard to one of the party : for the Maid of Honor[1] told me in a letter I had a few weeks ago that she should be in waiting all this month. Last evening there was a ball and supper at the Hawkesleys. They did me the honor to invite me but I declined it. In the morning I met Lady Stewart[2] at the Pumproom. . . . God grant you favourable weather for your passage to Ireland—it must be propitious for your return.

I remain, dear Rose,

Yours affectionately,

W. S. LANDOR.

---

[1] The Hon. Caroline Boyle, for many years Maid of Honour to Queen Adelaide.

[2] Lady Aylmer's niece, and sister to Miss Rose Bathurst. She was married to the Earl of Castle Stewart in 1830, and after his death to Signor Alessandro Pistocchi.

SENT WITH FLOWERS.[1]

Take the last flowers your natal day
  May ever from my hand receive!
Sweet as the former ones are they,
  And sweet alike be those they leave.

Another in the year to come
  May offer them to smiling eyes ;
The smile that cannot reach my tomb
  Will add fresh radiance to the skies.

———

To Miss Rose Paynter.

[BATH, *March,* 1845.]

DEAR ROSE,

  . . . Last evening I spent in Great Bedford
Street. Lady Stewart was there looking very
brilliant. I think her handsome. . . . The Miss
Bathursts, serious good girls, propending a little to
the heavy, played at letters. I have been doing it
all my life. But here, I mean the puzzle of words—
for instance I. C. C. R. U. X. &c. In my humble
opinion this is the department I excell in. And now
on the other side I will write out for you a couple of
verses, containing twenty syllables, in which there is
only one vowel.

PRSVRYPRFCTMNVR
KPTHSPRCPTSTN

[1] Published in the " Keepsake" for 1845.

I do not envy you Dublin, but I envy Dublin you. Pray do not make the two countries quarrel worse than they are quarrelling at present.

Believe me, dear Rose,

Ever affectionately yours,

W. LANDOR.

To Miss Rose Paynter.

[BATH, *May 14th 1845.*]

DEAR ROSE,

. . . You forgot to return me *Hood's Magazine*,[1] in which was inserted a poem of mine to Napier. Nothing very extraordinary. It will seem very odd to me to write not a line on your next birthday. But long ago I formed the resolution to write neither verse nor prose after I had reached seventy.[2] I can hardly believe that I have attained that boundary line of human life, so little do I feel changed. But were I to continue the sin of writing, some Gil Blas without my bidding might remind the archbishop that

---

[1] *Hood's Magazine*, vol. iii., p. 329 (1845), contains Landor's verses to Major-General Sir William Napier—

"Napier ! take up anew thy pen."

Reprinted in Works, 1876, viii. 148.

[2] "Once beyond seventy, I will never write a line in verse or prose for publication. I will be my own Gil Blas. The wisest of us are unconscious when our faculties begin to decay. Knowing this, I fixed my determination many years ago."—Landor to Lady Blessington, Nov. 1844. He was seventy on Jan. 30, 1845, but the resolution was broken.

languor was creeping over him. . . . The lilacs venture out : the laburnums wait for you.

Believe me, dear Rose, with kindest regards to all your party,

Ever affectionately yours,

W. S. L.

To Miss Rose Paynter.

[BATH] *Sunday Morning, 25th April*[1] [1845].

DEAR ROSE,

A letter from you always brings back to me many happy hours. . . . You sometimes have told me that I was "fishing for compliments." I do not think I ever was. But how far beyond all compliments is the idea that you will one day regret me. May the day be distant and the regret be brief. I will never speak or write again on this subject. Daisy is looking up into my face, with one foot upon my knee. Before I could write the last word, she removed it. I do believe she is fonder of me than anyone. We talk a great deal together, but not more nonsense than is usual with me. I have just opened a letter from Lady Blessington, who tells me that Lady Canterbury[2] is with her, extremely ill, and that she is at this moment putting a new roof on her house,

[1] The date of this letter is uncertain. April 25, 1845, fell on a Friday. Perhaps it should be May.

[2] Lady Canterbury died November 16, 1845.

to the great annoyance of the inmates. She wishes me to come in June, and to stay much longer than I intended my present visit to have been. However, I shall now defer it until another year. I hope you will enjoy the Opera, indeed I am sure you will. In three weeks I shall expect you here again; and if Lady Caldwell should forget to invite me to her picnics, pray remind her. Already I have formed a plan of my station—not exactly opposite to you, but almost— near enough to see you distinctly—not near enough to overhear a single word. . . . When you meet Mr St John [1] pray offer my kindest remembrances to him. He is an excellent scholar—which is little—but he is also an excellent man. You will often see our friend James FitzGerald. Tell him that among my regrets at not being in town this season is losing the pleasure I should have enjoyed in meeting him. . . .

   Believe me, dear Rose,
     Ever affectionately yours,
       W. S. Landor.

To Miss Paynter.

[Warwick, ? *June* 18, 1845].

Dear Rose,

   . . . The Percys, the only people I know well in this quarter of the world, returned on

---

[1] In a footnote to Landor's "Pericles and Aspasia," there is a reference to "The History of the Manners and Customs of Ancient Greece," by

Saturday, and I dined with them at Guys Cliffe on Tuesday. Lord Leigh, Mrs Clive, Mr Dugdale, were invited. But *the* person was Mrs Somerville, the most wonderful woman the world ever saw.[1] Her philosophical work is the admiration of all the scientific. I need not tell you I am not one of these. But her modesty is equal to her information.

I have been invited both in Staffordshire and Cheltenham. My sister goes and wishes me to accompany her—but I am more disposed to return to Bath at the end of the present month. . . .

To Mrs Paynter.

WARWICK, *Aug.* 3 [1845].

DEAR MRS PAYNTER,

This morning I received Fred's poems. They are as I expected to find them, spirited and energetic; but there are some few places which would have profited by your correction or Rose's. He said that he had begun to lose a little

James Augustus St John, London, 1842—"The most learned, the most comprehensive, and the most judicious work ever written about the manners, the institutions, and the localities of that country."—Works, 1876, v. 474.

[1] "The Connection of the Physical Sciences," by Mrs Mary Somerville, was first published in 1834. In the memoir written by her daughter, there is reference to a visit to Lord and Lady Charles Percy, at Guy's Cliffe, and to the pleasantness of the society, but whether she was there in 1844 or 1845 it is difficult to say. Mrs Archer Clive, the "V" of *Blackwood's Magazine,* became better known, perhaps, as the author of "Paul Ferrol" and other novels. She died in 1873.

K

of his admiration for Byron.   In Byron there is much to admire but nothing to imitate : for energy is beyond the limits of imitation.   Byron could not have written better than he did.   Altho' he seems negligent in many places, he was very assiduous in correcting his verses.   His poetry took the bent of a wayward and perverted mind often weak, but oftener perturbed. Tho' hemp and flax and cotton are the stronger for being twisted, verses and intellects certainly are not. . . . It is unfortunate that Ariosto did not attract him [Byron] first.   Byron had not in his nature amenity enough for it, and chose Berni in preference, and fell from Berni[1] to Casti.[2]   But his scorching and dewless heat burnt up their flowery meadows.

. . . The farmers here are crying out about their hay.   Lord Leigh told me he had near a hundred acres cut and spoiling.   The corn in many parts is mildewed.   I hope Ceres and Crœsus are reigning in Carmarthenshire.

Believe me, dear Mrs Paynter,

Very truly yours,

W. S. Landor.

---

[1] Berni (*ob.* 1536), an Italian poet, "partly known for his ludicrous poetry, which has given that style the appellation of *Poesia Bernesca,* rather on account of his excellence than originality ; but far more for his *rifaccimento,* or remoulding of the poem of Boiardo."—*Hallam.*

[2] John Baptiste Casti (1721-1803).   Landor makes Metastasio say to Alfieri : "I am afraid our Italian band of poets is neither so brilliant nor so numerous as you could wish.   Casti is at the head of them."

To Miss Rose Paynter.

[RUGELY, ? *August* 26, 1845.]

DEAR ROSE,

Your letter has followed me to Colton Rectory, and it appears to have brought fine weather with it. Here I have been ten days without a ray of sunshine. To-morrow I start for Bath, where I shall remain about a week, waiting to hear from Bezzi and Kenyon. It was my intention to have been at Linton in the last week of the present month. You alarm me lest lodgings may be difficult or impossible to procure. However, I will attempt it at Budleigh Salterton before I go to Linton. . . . Yesterday I had a letter from Forster telling me that I must be in London on the 20th of September, and with Dickens [1]—that they are about to act one of Ben Jonson's comedies. . . .

Affectionately yours,

W. S. LANDOR.

To Miss Rose Paynter.

BATH, *Sept.* 3 [1845].

DEAR ROSE,

. . . I am reading " Mount Sorel " [2] at your recommendation. Think me not vainer than

---

[1] "Every Man in His Humour," with Dickens as Bobadill, was acted at Miss Kelly's theatre in Dean Street on Sept. 20, 1845. A bill of the play is preserved in the Forster Library at South Kensington. A second performance was given at the St James's Theatre on Nov. 15, when Dickens, Mr Greville says, " acted very well indeed."

[2] " Mount Sorel : or the Heiress of the De Veres," a novel by Mrs (Anne) Marsh. London, 1845.

I am when I declare to you that there are sentences in it which I could almost swear I myself had written. I did not however : that is certain.   There are a few inaccuracies and inelegancies.   She talks of Higgins being called a Jacobin in 1788.   The Republicans had not met in the hall of the Jacobin monks (whence the name) until the next year; nor indeed was there until then, the convocation of the States General.   I wish she had never used the vile Americanism of *realize* for comprehend or conceive.

If there is a lodging cheap or dear to be procured at Budleigh I will take it from the eighth of September, the day of the Blessed Virgin, as I find it in the almanack, until Monday, the twenty-second, which I find in the same authority is the flight of Mahomet. My lodging must be open to the sea, and have good water, my only beverage.   I intend to be at church on Sunday, and may reach Budleigh that evening. . . .

Affectionately yours,
W. S. L.

To Miss Rose Paynter.

[BATH, Nov. 30, 1845.]

DEAR ROSE,

On Monday poor Daisy was removed from under my guardianship—I mean on Monday night soon after nine.   Mr A—— had the care of her subsequently, and took her out with him on his ride on Tuesday.

On Wednesday, yesterday, I spent the day at Clifton, and heard on my return that Daisy was afflicted with her old disease. The first occupation of this morning was to visit her. She is very unwell. Your servant had not given her the medicine that was left for her in case of illness. I waited at your house till he came, and rated him severely for his negligence. Poor Daisy crept up from her mat and came toward me, looking most piteously in my face, but not whining. While she was with me she often whined, and I think the most when she was most happy. I pretended to be asleep on the sofa. For a long time she stood upright with her feet upon it. Then she crept on the other side of me and licked my cheek. The moment I smiled, she knew I was awake, and put her foot on my mouth. I took her a walk in the Park every day, and gave her only one thin slice of bread and butter, and three biscuits of the finest flour morning and evening. This regular and spare diet brought her into the best condition. I saw that she was too fat to run fast or long together, therefore, when she had taken a short run upon the grass, I called her back again. When we had walked an hour, I took her home and left her on the rug before the fire, with a basin of fresh water under the sideboard.

Mr A—— is as fond of Daisy as I am—and perhaps he thought it would do her good to give her a gallop for an hour or two. Even his horse's trot would require her gallop. I will go and see her every day, and will immediately take the remainder of her biscuits up to her. If she does not get better, I will consult the most scientific in these cases. Whatever care can be taken of her shall be taken. So do not vex yourself, nor let Mrs Paynter be too anxious about her. . . .

Believe me, dear Rose,
Affectionately yours,
W. Landor.

Death of Daisy.[1]

Daisy! thy life was short and sweet;
Who would not wish his own the same?
And that his hand, as once thy feet,
Were claspt in hers whose vocal name
Awakes the summer, and the bird
That sings so lonely and so late;
A song these many nights I've heard,
And felt, alas, it sang my fate.

To a Bride, Feb. 18, 1846.[2]

A still, serene, soft day; enough of sun
To wreathe the cottage smoke like pine-tree snow,

[1] These verses are printed in " Dry Sticks," page 26.
[2] On Feb. 18, 1846, Miss Rose Paynter was married to Mr, now Sir Charles Brune Graves-Sawle, *Bart.*, of Penrice, in Cornwall. The following is from the *Times* of Feb. 19, 1896 :—" Sir Charles and Lady Graves-

Whiter than those white flowers the bride-maids wore;
Upon the silent boughs the lissom air
Rested ; and, only when it went, they moved,
Nor more than under linnet springing off.
Such was the wedding-morn : the joyous Year
Lept over March and April up to May.
    Regent of rising and of ebbing hearts,
Thyself borne on in cool serenity,
All heaven around and bending over thee,
All earth below and watchful of thy course!
Well hast thou chosen, after long demur
To aspirations from more realms than one.
Peace be with those thou leavest! peace with thee!
Is that enough to wish thee? not enough,
But very much : for Love himself feels pain,
While brighter plumage shoots, to shed last year's ;
And one at home (how dear that one!) recalls
Thy name, and thou recallest one at home.
Yet turn not back thine eyes ; the hour of tears

Sawle were the recipients yesterday, at Penrice, Cornwall, of many congratulations on the celebration of their golden wedding. A deputation
from their tenantry presented them with an illuminated address, together
with a clock and a pair of vases. Subsequently representatives of the
county magistrates were received, and the Earl of Mount-Edgcumbe,
lord lieutenant of Cornwall, in their name presented a pair of gold Queen
Anne cups. Sir Charles, who is eighty years old, has just retired, on
account of advancing age, from the chairmanship of the Cornwall Quarter
Sessions, which he has held uninterruptedly for forty years." The verses
printed above were published in Landor's Works, 1846, ii. 674, the date
being wrongly given as Feb. 17. In my copy of the book, which contains
several of the author's manuscript corrections, it is altered to Feb. 18.

Is over ; nor believe thou that Romance
Closes against pure Faith her rich domain.
Shall only blossoms flourish there? Arise,
Far-sighted bride! look forward! clearer views
And higher hopes lie under calmer skies.
Fortune in vain call'd out to thee ; in vain
Rays from high regions darted ; Wit pour'd out
His sparkling treasures ; Wisdom laid his crown
Of richer jewels at thy reckless feet.
Well hast thou chosen. I repeat the words,
Adding as true ones, not untold before,
That incense must have fire for its ascent,
Else 'tis inert and cannot reach the idol.
Youth is the sole equivalent of youth.
Enjoy it while it lasts ; and last it will ;
Love can prolong it in despite of Years.

———

To Mrs Graves-Sawle.

[BATH], *March* 15, 1846.

. . . Is it possible that I appeared to you sad and
sorrowful on your wedding day. . . . I am convinced
you have chosen the man most certain to make you
happy for life. . . . I shall be delighted to see you at
one more Master of the Ceremonies Ball. It is the
only one I shall attend this season. And after this
season I shall give up balls and all other amusements.
It is time I should begin to feel the effects of age, and

I think I do.   Let me fold my arms across my breast, and go quietly down the current until where the current ends. . . . Adieu, my ever dear friend, and believe me, your husband's too,

W. S. LANDOR.

ON A PRIMROSE PUT INTO A BOOK OF POEMS.[1]

Umile fior! dono di Rosa! mai
Agli occhi mici men bello tu sarai
Quando Io sia con la terra mescolato
Te, qual che d'uno troverà servato,
Ed "Abzati" dirà.   'Su! fior de' fiori!
Sei preferito ad elleri ed allori.

TRANSLATION.

Humble flower! the gift of Rose!
If to-day thy life must close,
Yet for ever shalt thou be
Just as fair and fresh to me ;
And when I am underground
Shalt among these leaves be found,
And the finder shall exclaim,
" Up! arise! awake to fame !
He who gave thee length of days
Held her flower above his bays."

[1] These Italian verses, dated April 12, 1846, are in Lady Graves-Sawle's album.   The translation was printed in "Last Fruit."   I found a dried primrose among the odds and ends in Landor's writing-desk.

To Mrs Graves-Sawle.[1]

[*July* 6, 1846.]

. . . Between the hay-harvest and the corn-harvest, there is a lull of nature, a calm and dull quiescence. Autumn then comes to tell us of the world's varieties and changes.   At last the white pall of Nature closes round us.   In the last seven or eight years I seem to myself to have passed through all the seasons of life excepting the very earliest and the very latest.   I doubt whether I have ever been so happy in any other equal and continued space of time.   Italy would sometimes flash back upon me; but the lightnings only kept the memory awake, without disturbing it.   How much, how nearly all, do I owe to your friendship, to your music and your conversation.

To Mrs Paynter.

BATH, *August* 26, 1846.

DEAR MRS PAYNTER,

Yesterday evening I returned to Bath again, after a visit of a fortnight at Lord Nugent's, a very quiet and delightful place, when I met the brother of General Riego.   Let me congratulate you on the recovery of the Admiral, after what I

[1] This extract from a letter to Mrs Graves-Sawle, the year after her marriage, was printed by Mr Forster, to whom one or two letters were lent when he was writing his Life of Landor.   The originals are now missing.

hear was a very serious illness. . . . Last evening, when I attempted to open my writing-desk,[1] I found it quite impracticable. I do not believe the people of the house are capable of any kind of dishonesty, but it appears that my landlady was afraid of leaving it in my room, and took it into hers. So it got shaken and a good deal injured. She is unwell, and wrote me a note telling me that her nerves will never be right again while she has the charge of such precious things in her house, and that (at my convenience) she hopes I will resign her lodgings. On this, I went instantly and engaged rooms at No. 2 in this Square,[2] where I go the first of September. I hate to move, and I never can hope to live again in any Square. This grieves me. It is now eight years within a month that I have resided in St James's. I have a cat-like attachment to places. Talking of cats I must not forget to mention a couple of dormice given to me by Mrs Ravenshaw[3]—playful pets and dear delights to me. . . .

Believe me,
Sincerely yours,
W. S. LANDOR.

---

[1] Landor's writing-desk, made from the wood of an old cedar tree at Ipsley Court, and given to him by his sister Elizabeth, is now in the editor's possession.

[2] This may be a *lapsus pennæ* for street. Landor moved to 3 Rivers Street.

[3] Mrs Landor's sister, the wife of an Indian civilian.

To Mrs Graves-Sawle.

BATH, *Sept.* 26, 1846.

DEAR MRS SAWLE,

It was only on Friday night that I returned from a visit to Crosse, not having gone at all into Devonshire. Kenyon was with me. His conversation and Crosse's made four days pass away delightfully. At Taunton I met Mr Kinglake the author of "Eothen," and dined at his mother's. Never was a day spent more to my satisfaction. Indeed I may say that in seven years I have not passed seven consecutive days so pleasantly as those seven. I find on my table a great number of gift books. Among the rest Lord Nugent's "Lands Classical and Sacred."[1] I am reading it with much interest. I think you will do the same. Miss Garrow has also sent me her translation of Niccolini's "Arnold of Brescia."[2] Niccolini is more like Alfieri than Sophocles, and more like Sophocles than Shakespeare. . . .

Believe me,

Ever your affectionate friend,

W. S. LANDOR.

[1] "Lands Classical and Sacred," by George Grenville, Lord Nugent. London, 1845. Lord Nugent, grandson of the Lord Clare to whom Goldsmith addressed "The Haunch of Venison," was an old friend of Landor's, who often visited him about this time at his place near Aylesbury. He died November 26, 1851. See "Dry Sticks," pp. 18 and 161; and "Heroic Idyls," p. 242.

[2] "Arnold of Brescia, a Tragedy, by Gio. Batt. Niccolini; translated by Theodosia Garrow." For an anecdote about Niccolini, "as modest a man as he is a distinguished poet," see Landor's Works, 1876, vi. 223.

To Mrs Graves-Sawle.

[BATH, *June* 2, 1847.]

. . . Lambe has just met me in the street giving me the most favourable intelligence of all my friends in Cornwall. . . . Before next month is over I hope to visit the *graziosissima sposina* and the *imparagonabble sposo.* Do not let fishermen catch all the trout, for they are pretty creatures, and I am delighted to see them playing on the surface of the water. The very oldest of them may sometimes be detected in this idle occupation—so there is a sort of sympathy between us.

I know not whether the pleasures of your country life allow you any leisure for reading. If they do, let me recommend to you Lady Georgiana Fullerton's last novel, " Grantley Manor." I have reached only as far as the seventeenth page, in which I find a piece of eloquence such as I never found in any other novel for the sublimity of the thought and for the purity of the expression—

"Whatever was the spirit that had moved her soul erewhile, one mightier still had now gained the mastery. Whatever billows were gathering about her, she was treading them again with a firm step, and measuring them with an unshrinking eye." [1]

---

[1] " Grantley Manor, a Tale," by Lady Georgiana Fullerton, London 1847, vol. ii. p. 17. Lady G. Fullerton was the daughter of Earl Granville, Ambassador in Paris. Her first novel, " Ellen Middleton," was reviewed by Mr Gladstone.

It is impossible to think about oneself after reading
such admirable sentences.   But I began with the intention of saying how I had been occupied.   First in
eating strawberries and cream, with an interlude of
ices, all day long.   Then several people have called
to see me, some known, some unknown.   Yesterday
Sir Samuel Meyrick[1] came out of his way to dine
with me and went again this morning.   Yesterday
was also made memorable by the marriage of Miss
Gregory.[2] . . .   The crowd at the wedding was so
tumultuous that the bride's lace dress was torn in the
church.   Never have I seen in England a sky so blue
and cloudless as shone upon their espousals.   I hope
it may be emblematic.   On Thursday I go for a couple
of days to my brother Robert in Worcestershire ; and
then for three weeks or a month to my sister at Warwick.   I hope you will find a moment's leisure to write
to me while I am there.   We old men want cordials—
and I more than the oldest of them—but only in the
form of a letter from Restormel.   With kind regards
to Mrs Paynter and *l'ottimo*.

Believe me,

Ever your affectionate,

W. S. LANDOR.

[1] Sir Samuel Meyrick died April 2, 1848, aged 65.

[2] "June 1, 1847.   Frederick H. Peat, Esq., late 97th Regiment, to
Frances Jane Isabella, daughter of Lt.-Colonel Gregory, and grand-
daughter of the late Hon. John Forsyth of Montreal."—*Bath Chronicle.*

To Mrs Paynter.

[? *June* 1847.]

DEAR MRS PAYNTER,

Lambe came to me yesterday and brought the most desirable intelligence that you are all well at Restormel. The loveliest of mansions and the sweetest of *bambini* must occupy all your thoughts otherwise I would recommend your reading the poems of Aubrey de Vere.[1] Nothing of our days will bear a moment's comparison with them, nor indeed do I find anything more classical among the best of the ancients. I have not the honor of knowing the author, but he sent me this little volume with a prose work entitled "English Misrule and Irish Misdeeds." A work which unites the wisdom of Bacon with the eloquence of Burke. Speaking of Ireland, James FitzGerald has sent me a serious project for transferring all the Irish, gentry as well as commonalty, to Vancouver's Island, on the continent nearest to it. Nothing is wanting but to lay down a railroad across the Atlantic, and about two thousand miles of lake,

---

[1] A second edition of "English Misrule and Irish Misdeeds," by Aubrey de Vere, was published in 1848. A volume containing "The Search after Proserpine and other Poems," was published at Oxford in 1843. "Have you the 'Masque of Proserpine'? He has raised her not only up to earth again, but to heaven. It is delightful to find one figure who has escaped the hairdresser and milliner." Landor to Forster, Oct. 23, 1848. Verses addressed by Landor to Mr Aubrey de Vere are printed in his Works 1876, viii. 244 and 256. Both poems had been printed in "Last Fruit."

mountain and snow, with a hundred or two of static
well provided for the accommodation of fifty or six
thousand persons in eatables.   As for sleeping, the
snow is soft, and the waves are softer.   They may
turn out *convanintly*.   In about a hundred turns and re
turns we might convey the desirable six millions, mer
women and children, within the moderate space of tc
or a dozen years.   The poorer have been taught tc
shoot flying, and the richer may amuse themselve
with their old practice of shooting one another.   I ar
sorry to see so many of the people turned into tigei
It would be better if they were turned into cats, ar
all of the Kilkenny breed.   The arts and sciences ।
that country seem now to be confined to the making
of pike heads and vitriol.   With kind regards to al
my hospitable friends,

Believe me, dear Mrs Paynter,

Very truly yours,

W. S. LANDOR.

To Mrs Graves-Sawle.

[? *July* 5, 1847.]

. . . How often, or rather how perpetually I askec
for your presence at the opera when Jenny Lind[1] wa

[1] Jenny Lind's first appearance in England was at Her Majest;
Theatre, on May 4, 1847, as Alice in *Robert le Diable.*   On May 13, ᵛ
18 and 25th, she appeared in *La Sonnambula.*

ᶜᶦᵘging. . . . Her acting was infinitely beyond any I
conceived to be possible. One night when she performed in the Sonambula, I had the good fortune
to occupy a front seat in the Russian Minister's box
just over the stage. Sometimes Jenny Lind came
within four paces of me. After a fortnight in London
I went to visit my old friend, Archdeacon Hare;[1]
but I could only stay a week with him. He has
married a sweet-tempered and intelligent wife, who
appears not only to reverence but to love him,
which is better. He might be a bishop, but he
will never leave his comfortable house and charming
country. His library contains ten or eleven thousand
books, and his conservatory is full of exquisite flowers.
Even *l'ottimo sposo* is only by a few degrees a happier
man, and no other on earth half so happy.

Think again before you invite me in the peach
season. The fattest black snail is less mischievous.

The people here are very busy about the election.[2]
I am outrageous against the ministers for their expedition against the Liberals in Oporto.[3] The Queen has

[1] Archdeacon Hare had married, in 1844, the sister of Frederick Deni-
son Maurice. Landor made more than one visit to Hurstmonceaux. In
1846 he had dedicated the two volumes of his collected works to Julius
Hare and John Forster.

[2] The general elections began on July 28, 1847.

[3] A British squadron under Admiral Parker had been sent to the Tagus
in November 1846, to support Queen Donna Maria, whose subjects had
broken into insurrection. In the following May, 1847, a Conference was
held in London, attended by the Representatives of England, France,
Spain and Portugal, to discuss the Portuguese Question. Lord Malmes-

broken her oath to the constitution, to which we were
guarantees.   I have written a petition to Parliament
that it will not (in its wisdom) commit so flagrant an
injustice.   I will send it you when it is printed.   I
wrote it yesterday, and several men have subscribed
their names.   I hear I treat the Parliament with little
deference ; and the ministers are informed to-day that
the Petition is drawn up by me.

I hope you are delighted with every number of
Dombey and Son.[1]   Dickens looks thin and poorly.
Forster fat and ruddy as usual.   Macready[2] gave a
grand dinner to grand people to meet Jenny Lind.   I
was the only unimportant person invited, and probably
the only one who declined.   I wanted quiet and
country air and the sight and conversation of an old

bury wrote in his diary on June 18, 1847 : — " Lord Stanley's motion con-
demning the Government for their intervention in Portugal ended very
unfortunately, owing to Lords Ellenborough and Brougham not choosing
to speak in support of it ; the consequence being that the division took
place much earlier than was expected, and most of our men were absent
at dinner, so we were beaten by twenty.   In the House of Commons the
debate came on the same night, but the House was counted out.   In the
meantime the English fleet has taken the Portuguese ships, and made
two thousand prisoners."—*Memoirs of an ex-Minister.*

[1] " NEW WORK BY BOZ.   On the 30th instant (June 1847) will be published, price 1s., the tenth number of ' Dealings with the Firm of Dombey
and Son, Wholesale, Retail, and for Exportation,' by Charles Dickens, with
illustrations by Hablot K. Browne."

[2] " May 30, 1847.—The Lord Advocate and Mrs Rutherford, Mr and
Mrs Dickens, Mr and Mrs Carlyle, Panizzi, Eastlake, Rogers, Miss
Jewsbury, Edwin Landseer, and Jenny Lind came to dinner."—
Macready's " Diary."   On May 15, Landor, Forster, Maclise, and M.
and Mme. Regnier dined with Macready.

kind friend. My week at Hurstmonceaux has thrown
several years off my shoulders. The last made me
feel its weight, and perhaps the next will be as heavy
or heavier. It is unwise to look forward quite so far.
My vision rests on Restormel. There is nothing on
this side or beyond half so pleasant to dwell upon.

Believe me,
Ever your affectionate,
W. S. L.

To Mrs Paynter.

[BATH, *July* 13, 1847.]

DEAR MRS PAYNTER,

. . . People here are very busy about
the election. I take no part whatever in politics ; but
the folly and wickedness of the Ministry in attacking those of Portugal, who defend the Constitution
of which we ourselves are trustees have excited me
to a Petition which is printed in the *Examiner.*[1]
Both parties have signed it quite unsolicited. The
next name to mine is the great Tory, Caldecot's.

We have no reason to complain of the heat in Bath.
Since I left London there have been only four warm
days, and I hear that even in Cornwall you enjoy

---

[1] There is a letter from Landor on "Portugal and Spain" in the
Examiner of July 3, 1847. (See Part II.) A petition against intervention in Portugal was presented to Parliament from Bath, with 10,033
signatures, in July 1847 ; but I can find no copy of it.

fires in the evenings.   I continue to walk a couple of hours in the morning, and as many after dinner, but I begin to discover that the vale of years is the least pleasant of walks and the least adapted to walk in. . . .

Believe me, dear Mrs Paynter,

Very truly yours,

W. S. LANDOR.

CHAPTER V
1848—1857

CHAPTER V

1848—1857

THE letters printed in this chapter cover the last ten years of Landor's life in Bath. Shadows were deepening round him. Some of his oldest and best friends died within the decade: Ablett, Lady Blessington, Countess de Molandé (the Ianthe of his verse), D'Orsay, Mr Rosenhagen, Miss Caldwell, Julius Hare, John Kenyon, his brother Charles, and his sister Elizabeth. Yet he bore up bravely against sorrows and losses. He could thoroughly enjoy a visit to Restormel, and was gladdened by occasionally meeting his correspondent, now Mrs Graves-Sawle, in Bath. There also he welcomed other guests, amongst them Thomas Carlyle, who found the unsubduable old Roman a man altogether to his liking, and Dickens who loved and respected him. Once he visited Llanthony: "Sad scene!" he wrote, "sad remembrances! Forty-three years have passed since I saw the place, and never had I wished to see it again." He went about less than formerly; but he still wrote and published. "The Last Fruit off an Old Tree" came out in 1853; followed and preceded by various pamphlets and letters to the newspapers, especially during the Crimean war. "The

Letters of an American" were dedicated to Mr Gladstone, whom Landor had forgiven for his "Homeric
Studies." Then came that unhappy volume "Dry
Sticks fagoted by Walter Savage Landor." It contained much that was interesting, not a little that one
can read with delight; and one or two things which
any publisher possessed of moderate intelligence must
have seen ought not to be printed. There were other
printed leaflets which should never have got abroad.
But the whole subject is inexpressibly painful, and one
shrinks from repeating the story. It need only be
said that, not without good grounds for taking offence,
Landor found himself indicted for libel, and had to
leave the kingdom. He was never to see England
again; nor were his bones to be laid in the resting-
place he had chosen in Widcombe Churchyard.

To Mrs Graves-Sawle.

BATH, *Jan.* 18, 1848.

. . . Death last year took aim at *me* but missed me.
Let him take another as soon as he pleases, but pass
by those I love. I have lost my kind friend, Joseph
Ablett.[1] He died on the ninth after a relapse. My
sister too has been seriously ill for several weeks, but
her day is not yet come, and I hope it may be yet

[1] "Poor dear Ablett, at whose house we were to meet in the spring,
died on the 9th (January 1848), and I can remember few things that have
caused tears to burst forth from me as this did. . . . Good generous
Ablett! One more tear for thee!"—Landor to Mr Forster.

far distant.   Poor Forster too has been confined
to his bed for several days.. . . . If ever you see
the *Examiner* [1] you will see what an enthusiast
he is about me and my old nonsense of poetry.
He threatens to be still more extravagant next
Saturday.   I believe in his sincerity—but when
others praise me, I no more heed them than I
heed a plaisterer who praises the Elgin marbles.   I
send you what has already been printed in Italy—
my dedication to the Pope and my Preface. [2]   Among
the poems there is one which you never have seen—it
is my best—you and nobody else will perfectly understand it.   You must come to Bath for it.   Until then,
my dear friend, adieu.

Ever affectionately yours,

W. L.

To Mrs Graves-Sawle.

THURSDAY NIGHT [*Feb.* 1848].

. . . I always like your recommendation of a book.
Long ago I read " Monte Cristo " in French — cer-

---

[1] The *Examiner* of Jan. 8, 1848, gives the text of Landor's dedication
of his " Hellenics " to Pope Pius IX.   A long review of the " Hellenics "
was published in the *Examiner* of Jan. 22.

[2] The dedication prefixed to the " Hellenics " had been printed in the
Tuscan Athenæum, a journal published at Florence.   It was there described as being written by " one of the wisest, most learned, and noble-
hearted of Englishmen."   In the preface to the " Hellenics " Landor
says :—" It is hardly to be expected that ladies and gentlemen will leave
on a sudden their daily promenade, skirted by Turks and shepherds and
knights and plumes and palfreys, of the finest Tunbridge manufacture,
to look at these rude frescoes, delineated on an old wall high up, and
sadly weak in coloring."

tainly the most powerful work of fiction in that
language. Collings had not "The Girondins."[1] I
therefor have ceased my subscription to his library.
This very evening I sent up to Mrs Paynter the
" Reminiscences of Talleyrand."

When I was a very young man I met him once in
London, but he conversed only with the lady of the
house—Mrs Knight—a lady silly enough in speech
but sillier in conduct. She was the daughter of Lord
Dormer, and had been educated in France. Ten
years afterwards she was divorced from her husband
in consequence of her preference for Lord Middleton
—a swain of sixty-five. She was then about thirty-
one. . . . Her half brother who succeeded to the
title was my friend. . . .

Believe me affectionately yours,

W. S. L.

To Mrs Graves-Sawle.

[BATH, *June* 3, 1848].

DEAR ROSE,

. . . To show you I do not spare
my fingers—for head is but little in requisition—I

---

[1] "Lamartine's 'Histoire des Girondins' is the most successful book
that has been published for many years. He is the Jenny Lind of
Literature."—" Greville Memoirs," Dec. 26, 1847. It was said afterwards
to have been the prime cause of the Revolution of 1848. Mrs Graves-
Sawle had asked Landor if he had read the book. He hurries to the
Circulating Library, and cannot obtain it. With the impetuosity of his
nature, he stops his subscription !

transcribe two small pieces which Forster and Dickens overrate. One was written in the first year of this century while I lay half on the sand in a little grotto at the Petit Trianon.[1] The other is more recent. Both are placed far remote from those on you—but you may find them if you think them worth looking for.

Yours, Dear Rose, affectionately,

W. S. LANDOR.

To Mrs Graves-Sawle.[2]

EXETER, *Wed. eve*
[*Aug.* 16, 1848 postmark]

MY DEAR KIND HOSPITABLE FRIEND,

Here I am until to-morrow. The coach started at eleven. I reached Exeter after one.

[1] I think these must be the lines to Marie Antoinette :—

"O gentlest of thy race !
How early do we trace
    The wrath of Fate on thee !
Not only that thy head
Was hurl'd among the dead,
    The virtuous, wise and free,
O Marie Antoinette !
Do generous souls regret
    Thy sceptred destiny, &c.
                    —Landor's Works, 1876, viii. 61.

[2] This was written just after Landor's visit to Mr and Mrs Graves-Sawle at Restormel, thus recorded in Lady Graves-Sawle's Diary :—
"*Aug.* 7, 1848.—Mr Landor arrived. *Aug.* 8.—We started a carriage full for the flower show at St Austell's, lunched with Sir Joseph and Lady Graves-Sawle at Penrice, and returned home by moonlight. *Aug.* 9.—Walked about Restormel and showed the place to Mr Landor ; a happy,

I had no other accident but leaving my guide-book
and gold spectacles. I must disburse half my patrimony for another pair! Vexat ous as I have six or
seven pairs already, but at Bath, . . .

Believe me

Ever yours most affectionately,

W. S. LANDOR.

RESTORMEL.[1]

Known as thou art to ancient fame,
  My praise, Restormel, shall be scant;
The Muses gave thy sounding name,
  The Graces thy inhabitant.

To Mrs Graves-Sawle.

January 19 [1849].

. . . There is one day in the year in which I have
reserved to myself the ancient privilege of saying
" Dear Rose." I hope this day may recur to me
another and perhaps another year yet; and that you
will hear it from many friends another half century.

merry party. *Aug.* 10.—A splendid summer day ; we drove to Pencarrow
(Sir W. Molesworth's) and lunched with them. . . . *Aug.* 14.—Went up
to the Castle and got soaked through. *Aug.* 15.—Went to Lanhydrock
[now the residence of Lord Robartes]. *Aug.* 16.—Dear Mr Landor left
us by the Plymouth coach at seven."
  [1] From Lady Graves-Sawle's album. The verses were afterwards
printed in " Last Fruit."

. . . If you see the Duc de Guiche[1] offer him my compliments on his marriage.

Believe me,
Ever affectionately yours,
W. S. Landor.

To Mrs Graves-Sawle.

My Dearest Kind Friend,

May 7 [1849].

. . . In no time of my illness did I think so much about it as about you, however well I knew I had nothing to apprehend. " Hope told a flattering tale," which mama's next letter and a gracious Providence will confirm.

Good Luisina [2] has been very attentive to me. She is like her dear mother in all things but consummate beauty, and loves me affectionately. I hope I may live to see her well married. Eliza Lynn [3] comes to see me on Saturday. What a charm it is even at the close of life to be cared for by the beautiful and gentle, and to see them come out from the warm sunshine and the sweet flowers toward us in the chilliness of our resting place. This is charity, the

[1] The marriage of the Duc de Guiche with Miss Mackinnon took place on Dec. 27, 1848.

[2] The granddaughter of Landor's old friend, Countess de Molandé (Ianthe).

[3] The late Mrs Lynn Linton. Landor's verses to the authoress of " Amymone, a Romance of the Days of Pericles," were published in the *Examiner* of July 22, 1848.

charity of the Graces. They are fond of walking where Love has walked before, altho' they are certain they shall not find him there again. . . . Let me commend you with my whole heart to God's especial care. . .

W. S. L.

To Mrs Graves-Sawle.

[*June* 27, 1849.]

My dear Friend,

. . . Julia writes from Florence that all are quite gay there. Austrian uniforms, no doubt, produce this effect on the ladies. Hamilton[1] has given a grand entertainment to the officers. This has brought several censures on him, not only from the Liberals abroad, but also from Lord Palmerston I hear. Never was anything so atrocious as the conduct of the French Government towards the Italians generally, but more especially towards the Romans.[2] I hope my old friend Louis Napoleon will meet with the deserts of his villainy, and that all the

[1] Sir G. B. Hamilton, Envoy Extraordinary and Minister Plenipotentiary in Tuscany.

[2] "*May* 10, 1849. The French expedition left Civita Vecchia on the 28th, and reached Rome on the 30th ultimo, expecting to be received with open arms; but instead of that it seems they got a good beating. . . . *June* 29. The French have taken possession of a portion of the outer walls of Rome, but have not yet entered the city. . . . *July* 12. The French entered Rome on July 3, and the same day Garibaldi left the city with his corps unmolested."—*Memoirs of an ex-Minister.*

French may fall under the popular vengeance or
Heaven's. They have entered the walls, nothing was
easier; but the conflict is hardly yet begun. I enclose the last thing I have published on this subject.[1]
With every blessing on your two darling children,

Believe me ever,

Yours most affectionately,

W. S. LANDOR.

To Mrs Paynter.

[RHYL, *Sept.* 10, 1849.

DEAR MRS PAYNTER,

Your letter followed me from
Warwick to Llanbedr, and gave me, as all yours do,
great pleasure. I am for a fortnight on a visit to the
widow of my old friend Ablett. He left her his large

---

[1] Two letters by Landor on "France and Rome," were printed in
the *Examiner* of June 9 and June 23, 1849. See Part II. Landor also
expressed his indignation in another way at the proceedings of the
French in Italy. The incident may be told in his own words : "When
the French general [Oudinot] landed at Civita Vecchia, with a lie in his
mouth thrust into it by the President [Louis Napoleon], an English gentleman [Walter Savage Landor] sent back the work on artillery, ['*Etudes sur
le Passé et l'Avenir de l'Artillerie*'] which the President had given him.
This gentleman was in the habitude of meeting the Prince at Lady
Blessington's, under whose roof a greater number of remarkable and
illustrious men assembled from all nations, than under any other since
roofs took the place of caverns. When he returned to London from
his captivity at Ham, he was greeted by Lady Blessington's friend, 'as
having escaped the two heaviest of misfortunes—a prison and a throne.'"
Landor's Works, 1876, vi. 582. How the identical book came into Mr
Forster's possession I cannot say, but it is at South Kensington.

property for life, and afterwards to a very distant relative. By a strange oversight the will authorises him to remove the books, pictures, and a noble statue by Gibson. I know it was not so intended, and he himself declared that he never would remove them in her lifetime; but all last week was spent in their removal. He says he is one of the elect, no doubt he is, but who is the elector? Poor Mrs Ablett is sadly hurt. . . . I have raised her spirits a little, and she wishes me to prolong my visit, but go I must, for I shall have only three days to spend with my brother Robert, with whom I promised to stay a fortnight.

Little did I think my brother Charles[1] would have died before me. He seemed to have life enough in him for fifty men and fifty years. He was the finest man and almost the wittiest and most spirited I ever knew. To lose so early a companion as Charles, and so kind a friend as poor Lady Blessington[2] within so short a space of time bore heavily on my spirits. . . . Walter, who is much gratified by your kind remembrance is going to spend a few days at Llanthony. We shall meet again only a day or two before he returns to Italy.

Believe me, dear Mrs Paynter,

Very sincerely yours,

W. LANDOR.

---

[1] The Rev. Charles Landor died July 1849.
[2] Lady Blessington died at Paris, June 4, 1849.

To Mrs Graves-Sawle.

Jan. 19, [1850].

Once more I am permitted by the kindness of Providence to offer my felicitations on your birthday. Three years have elapsed since a rose or a lily of the valley or a violet came along with them. I will however now look out for the least perishable of them, and I defer the sealing of my letter until I can enclose it.

Here it is at last. . . . Dear Restormel! its hanging woods, its sheltered gardens, its warm summerhouse; in all these my past comes back to me. . . .

Mr Sandford,[1] who has travelled much in Hungary, called on me a few days ago and told me I might expect a visit from Teleki, late Ambassador from Hungary to France. Lately I have been reading the May and June numbers of *Blackwood,*[2] in which are many interesting facts about the war. Kenyon has written me a very laudatory letter on the Epitaph.[3] Shall we ever walk up and down the Pump Room again? The music is as good as usual. Scarcely a soul of my old acquaintance is left in Bath; some are gone to London, some to Paris, and some to that country where there neither are nor ever will be railroads. I

[1] Landor's verses to William Sandford—"Sandford! the friend of all the brave"—are printed in "Heroic Idyls," p. 119.

[2] *Blackwood's Magazine* for May and June 1849; articles on "Austria and Hungary."

[3] The Latin Epitaph on Lady Blessington, see "Last Fruit," p. 330.

M

was very near taking my ticket a little while ago, and now stop only in the waiting-room.—Adieu my dear friend, and believe me

Faithfully yours,

W. S. Landor.

To Mrs Graves-Sawle.

BATH, *Sept.* 22 [1850].

. . . If I deferred writing for two days, it was because I could not see Howell.[1] This evening, my dear friend, I have spent entirely in Gt. Bedford Street, and am most happy in assuring you that he appears to me better and better every time I see him. . . . Miss Caldwell is once more at home after that little wandering which all young persons are fond of. I have not heard of any myrtle crown brought home from the sea-side, and I am afraid the orange flower is yet to blossom. . . . Before long you shall see that I have not been quite idle ; meanwhile I enclose what I have last published in the *Examiner.* . . . [2]

Ever affectionately yours,

W. S. Landor.

[1] Colonel Howell Paynter, R.A., Mrs Paynter's brother. He died of wounds received at the battle of Inkerman.

[2] In the *Examiner* of Sept. 14 there was a lettter from Landor on "the reception of Haynau." See Part II.

To Mrs Graves-Sawle.

[BATH, *Dec.* 1850.]

Christmas must not pass over without a letter to my dear friend at Restormel.   I have not the heart to wait till the first day of the New Year : my wishes fly in bright clouds before it.   I had not been in Gt. Bedford Street since you left, nor anywhere else. . . . During the winter I do not even leave my card at houses, liable as I am to take cold by standing a few moments at the door.   Within the last fortnight I have walked twice in the Crescent, never beyond. And now about another person much more interesting and important.   My friend Mr Sandford, the friend also of Klapka[1] and all the other chief Hungarians, met me at the station. . . .

W. LANDOR.

REPROOF OF THANKS.[2]

Nay, thank me not again for those
Camelias, that untimely rose ;
But if, whence you might please the more
And win the few unwon before,

[1] General George Klapka, one of the foremost leaders of the Hungarian Revolution, died in May 1892. His book on "The War in the East from 1853 to 1855," was translated into English, and was referred to by Landor in a letter to the *Examiner* of Oct. 13, 1855.

[2] These verses were printed in *Leigh Hunt's Journal*, March 1, 1851.

I sought the flowers you loved to wear,
O'erjoy'd to see them in your hair,
Upon my grave, I pray you, set
One primrose or one violet.
Nay, I can wait a little yet.

To Mrs Graves-Sawle.

[BATH, *Jan.* 17, 1851.]

Lest my letter should come "a day after the fair,"
I write to the fair a day before.   Many, many happy
birthdays, my dear friend.   I shall keep it alas! quite
alone. . . . God bless you all, says the old man.

W. S. L.

To Mrs Graves-Sawle.

[BATH, *Jan.* 21, 1852.]

A Monsr. Sohier is about to translate my Imaginary
Conversations.   Some of them several years ago were
translated by another Frenchman and inserted in the
Revue des Deux Mondes.   Louis Napoleon has accomplished my prophecy; he will be a worse scourge to
the world than his uncle, for he has double his wisdom
and the same [*illegible*].   But Louis' cunning is im-
penetrable.   The other thief was fond of showing his
picking-lock keys, and how cleverly he entered his
neighbours' houses.

Now blessings on you and yours,
my ever kind friend,
W. S. L.

To Age.[1]

Welcome, old friend!   These many years
　　Have we lived door by door :
The Fates have laid aside their shears
　　Perhaps for some few more.

I was indocil at an age
　　When better boys were taught,
But thou at length hast made me sage,
　　If I am sage in aught.

Little I know from other men,
　　Too little they from me,
But thou hast pointed well the pen
　　That writes these lines to thee.

Thanks for expelling Fear and Hope,
　　One vile, the other vain ;
One's scourge, the other's telescope,
　　I shall not see again.

Rather what lies before my feet
　　My notice shall engage,
He who hath braved Youth's dizzy heat
　　Dreads not the frost of Age.

[1] Published in the *Examiner*, June 5, 1852, in "Last Fruit," and in Works, 1876, viii. p. 221.

To Mrs Graves-Sawle.

[? WIMBLEDON, *July* 10, 1852.]

Let me congratulate my very dear friend on Mr Sawle's success.[1] I do not mean his greatest. . . . With sincere and hearty congratulations, believe me

Ever yours most affectionately,

W. S. L.

I am at Kenyon's : next week I shall be at Archdeacon Hare's, Hurstmonceaux, near Lewes.

To Mrs Paynter.

WARWICK, *August* 7 [1852].

DEAR MRS PAYNTER,

The death of poor, dear D'Orsay[2] fell heavily tho' not unexpectedly upon me. Intelligence of his painful and hopeless malady reached me some weeks before the event. With many foibles and grave faults he was generous and sincere. Neither spirits nor wit ever failed him, and he was ready at all times to lay down his life for a friend. I felt a consolation in the loss of Lady Blessington in the thought how unhappy she would have been had she survived him. The world will never more see united such graceful minds, so much genius and pleasantry, as I

[1] Mr Charles Graves-Sawle was elected M.P. for Bodmin in July 1852.
[2] Count Alfred D'Orsay died in Paris Aug. 4, 1852. He was born in 1798.

have met, year after year, under her roof.   Since she was [? intercepted] from me by the shadow of death, I never have enjoyed society, and have rarely and reluctantly entered it.   Age has perhaps something to do in this change of temperament and disposition, but not very much.

I have been spending a fortnight with Kenyon who will let nobody be dull.   Afterwards I went to visit my old friend, Archdeacon Hare, at Hurstmonceaux. His Rectory is beautiful in itself, and the gardens and scenery are most delightful.   I had the pleasure of meeting there the Chevalier Bunsen,[1] one of the most learned men in Europe.   The Ministers that Prussia sends to foreign Courts are usually men of intelligence. England has sometimes broken her etiquette by doing the same.   My friend Julius Hare has the best library of any private man in England, and also many admirable pictures, and among them a Virgin and child by Raffael. . . . You are fond of flowers; I wish you had been with me on a visit I made to Mr Richard Cavendish[2] at Eastbourne.   The house belongs to his brother, Lord Burlington, who keeps up the gardens admirably.   I came to Warwick on Thursday and shall remain here about five weeks and

[1] Afterwards Baron Bunsen, Prussian Minister in London. He was an intimate friend of Archdeacon Hare's.

[2] Afterwards Lord Richard Cavendish, brother of the seventh Duke of Devonshire, at this time Earl of Burlington. Lord Richard Cavendish died in 1873, his brother the Duke in 1891.

then to Burlingham and Cheltenham for a few days.
Heartily glad shall I be to see Bath again, and you
and Lady Caldwell and Rose. With compliments to
Lord Aylmer,

I remain, dear Mrs Paynter,

Very sincerely yours,

W. S. LANDOR.

Pomero never writes to me but sends kind regards.
In my last verses *coast* should be *strand*.

WRITTEN AT HURSTMONCEAUX.

ON READING A POEM OF WORDSWORTH'S.[1]

Derwent! Winander! sweetest of all sounds
The British tongue e'er utter'd! lakes that Heaven
Reposes on, and finds his image there
In all its purity, in all its peace!
How are your ripples playing round my heart
From such a distance? While I gaze upon
The plain where William and where Cæsar led
From the same Gaulish strand each conquering host,
And one the Briton, one the Saxon name,
Struck out with iron heel. Well may they play,
Those ripples, round my heart, buoyed up, entranced.
Derwent! Winander! your twin poets come
Star-crown'd along with you, nor stand apart.
Wordsworth comes hither, hither Southey comes,

[1] These lines were printed in the *Examiner*, July 31, 1852. The
"Julius" of the last line but one is Archdeacon Hare.

His friend and mine, and every man's who lives,
Or who shall live when days far off have risen.
Here are they with me yet again, here dwell
Among the sages of Antiquity,
Under his hospitable roof whose life
Surpasses theirs in strong activity,
Whose Genius walks more humbly, stooping down
From the same highth to cheer the weak of soul
And guide the erring from the tortuous way.
Hail, ye departed! hail, thou later friend,
Julius! but never by my voice invoked
With such an invocation. . . . hail, and live!

To Mrs Graves-Sawle.

BATH, *Nov.* [1852].

DEAR ROSE,

Ha, you see by these two words that
I have not forgotten you. My memory is indeed
become very imperfect; but what is wonderful, my
imagination is quite as vivid as ever. It is a sad disappointment to me that I shall not see you before
February. Do not tell me that either of your boys is
to be the genius of the family. It must go in the
female line. . . . Boxall is coming shortly to finish a
picture of me begun in January.[1] You must not think
me vain enough to desire a portrait of myself. My

[1] This is no doubt the painting by Sir William Boxall, R.A., now at
South Kensington Museum.

vanity—pride, rather—is already in one portrait, or rather in the place it occupies. Forster has so urged me to let him prefix one to my forthcoming edition of Imaginary Conversations, which I gave unreservedly to him, that I could not well refuse his importunity. However I hope I may be able to persuade him to defer this idle decoration until after my death. I have heard from Mr Henry, son of the American Chief Justice, that two editions have been printed in his country. The price of Boxall for a portrait I believe is high, but he is incomparably our best painter. I have seen pictures by him which would have done honor to Titian. His hands are full at present.

There is in the last *Examiner* a graceful letter to me from Lord Dudley Stuart.[1] In the next will be my reply. I will send you copies when I can get them. . . .

To Mrs Graves-Sawle.

[BATH, *August* 1853].

MY VERY DEAR FRIEND,

Last evening I spent in Gt. Bedford Street, in the hope that a letter might possibly come from you. How kind it was to think of me again so soon! I never see your handwriting without a strong

---

[1] Lord Dudley Stuart's letter to Landor was printed in the *Examiner* of Nov. 6, 1852 : Landor's reply in the *Examiner* of Nov. 13. See Part II.

sensation of delight. To hear that you returned safe to Restormel and that your dear children are full of enjoyment leaves nothing in mine incomplete. A few regrets at losing you all will now and then over-shadow it—but when I see before you so much present and future happiness, my heart expands with the fulness of its content. . . . How often shall I think of you within the short space allowed me! And you will sometimes think, even when he is furthest absent, of

Your affectionate
W. Landor.

To Mrs Graves-Sawle.

Bath, *Nov.* 28 [1853].

My dear Friend,

If the weather permits I will carry down to the Post Office for you my new book[1] I presented a copy to Mrs Paynter, who did me the honor to desire I would write my name as the giver. Such a ceremonial seemed to me quite unnecessary in regard to the volume which you will receive. More than one page exhibits my sentiments towards you, and such as they were, they are and always will be. . . .

Your old friend,
W. S. L.

---

[1] "The Last Fruit off an Old Tree," by Walter Savage Landor. London, Edward Moxon, 1853.

To Mrs Paynter.

[BATH, *Jan.* 20, 1854.]

DEAR MRS PAYNTER,

This morning I receive not only your congratulations on my birthday, but Mrs Sawle's. This is anticipation. Mine is on the 30th. Before my breakfast-cloth is removed, I write a quatrain to her which you will see on the other side.

Sir Roderick Murchison[1] has made me several visits with his lady. The world owes to his inductive reasoning the discovery of gold in Australia and California. Twelve years ago he found that the same strata which form the Ural Mountains ran throughout the Cordilleras of America and Australia. The Emperor of Russia was intimate with him alone. Had he been sent to Petersburg, he would have averted a war which will be more devastating than any since the creation. It will, however, end well for humanity.

Ever truly yours,

W. S. LANDOR.

---

[1] Sir Roderick (then Mr) Murchison was introduced to Landor at Tours, in 1815, by Francis Hare. See the verses to Sir Roderick Murchison in "Heroic Idyls," p. 112 :—

"O Murchison !
Why hast thou looked so deep into the Earth,
To find her treasures ? Gold, we thought, had done
Its worst before," &c.

To Mrs Graves-Sawle.[1]

No leaves adorn my writing-screen,
And no more sunny days are mine ;
Your bays are fresh, your myrtles green,
And gracefully they intertwine.

Jan. 20, 1854.

Blackwood,[2] who always abused me, has said something grand about me, I hear. I always have abstained from reading what is written for or against me.

To Mrs Graves-Sawle.

BATH, *August* 2, [1854].

. . . So you and Mr S[awle] are going up the Rhine. . . . Let me commend a morning's or evening's walk up the Moselle. The scenery is here very different from that along the Rhine—it is more pastoral. I walked up the beautiful river six or seven miles quite by myself. I remained two entire months at Heidelburg.[3] The ruins of the palace there are incomparably the most picturesque I ever saw, and the small garden is a perfect paradise. The river Neckar is worth the trouble of ascending. There is a

[1] These lines are not printed elsewhere.

[2] *Blackwood's Magazine* for January 1854, contained a long and sympathetic review of " Last Fruit off an Old Tree."

[3] Landor was at Heidelburg in the autumn of 1836. He had gone there in the hope of meeting his sons, Arnold and Walter. See Forster's " Life," ii. p. 317.

good, clean hotel near the bridge. I tried another, it would not do. Bad smells are death to me. . . . Before you leave England you will certainly see Mrs Paynter. Present my kindest remembrances to her and Lord Aylmer, and believe me ever,

Your affectionate old friend,

W. S. LANDOR.

To Mrs Graves-Sawle.

BATH, [*Feb.* 1855].

DEAR ROSE,

You know I never delay for an hour answering your letters. This before me gives me pain. "In a few weeks I hope to be in Bath." A few weeks! It was a few weeks many weeks ago. Then it was to be toward the end of January, then before the end of February, and now February has only three weeks left. However, when you come at last you will remain until the London season hurries you away. My Lord the Admiral[1] says you are too fond of fashion. My reply to him is that fashion is too fond of you, and that you think it a duty to return the fondness.

My birthday was as happy as friends and relations could make it; never was it joyous to me. Yours alone had that effect on my spirits, and the last had not. How I desired to see you and your children, the

---

[1] Admiral Lord Aylmer.

Rose with the violets and primroses at the stem. Winter has been variable and severe, two equally bad things, and not in climate only. You may easily imagine it has left no verdure on me, but it has not quite dried up the sap. And now I must express my regret that I have scarcely any autographs[1] of memorable men. Forster, who will write my life, took possession of all my correspondents' letters. A few of Sir W. Napier and of Kossuth are remaining. These are the greatest men of our age; the one the greatest historian, the other the purest statesman. These you shall have when you come for them.

Ever yours affectionately,

W. S. Landor.

To Mrs Graves-Sawle.

March 16, [1855].

My dear Friend,

If this letter should come a few days after date, it will be because I shall defer sending it until I can enclose a few verses. I hear that many of my writings get into newspapers, etc., of which I know nothing. In the beginning of next month Kossuth will contribute to the *Atlas.*[2] Thinking he

---

[1] In reply to a letter asking for autographs.
[2] Kossuth's first article was published in the *Atlas* of April 17, 1855.

had begun to do it I sent a couple of articles,[1] and
entered my name as a subscriber.   The world has seen
only one man in two thousand years so eloquent as
Kossuth.   I have a letter from him [2] which I trust my
grandchildren will value as the highest honor that
could be conferred on the best of them, and the most
imperishable part of their heritage.

Never was book so negligently printed as Lady
Blessington's Life and Correspondence.[3]   In regard
to myself, I was obliged to remark through the *Athenæum* [4] that my godfather, General Powell, never was
in London when I was, that he offered my brother a
commission, on my refusal to dissemble my political
opinions.   My brother did not accept the commission,
because the Rectory of Colton, worth £1000 a year,
was always given to the second son.   Again, my
wife's ancestor, Baron Jean Thuillier Malaperte de
Nieuville, was not First gentleman of the Bedchamber
to Charles the Eighth, but only one of them.   The
family left France for religion and settled at Geneva.

---

[1] The *Atlas* of March 17, 1855, contains two letters from Landor, on
"The False Politics of the War," and "The King of Prussia." See
Part II.

[2] A letter from Kossuth to Landor, dated Winchester, October 24, 1851,
was printed in the *Examiner* of November 1, 1841, together with Landor's
reply.

[3] "The Literary Life and Correspondence of the Countess of Blessington," by R. R. Madden. 3 vols. 1855.

[4] Landor's letter was published in the *Athenæum*, March 3. See
Forster's "Life."

My wife's grandfather was general in the Austrian service; his son was a republican and *ultra* even at Geneva. He placed his money in a mercantile house at Cadiz; he lost part, but going over there took possession of the whole concern, and left his nine children about £1500 each. I refused to touch a penny of it. L. Napoleon is master of the world, England excepted! Julius Cæsar, Gustavus Adolphus, and Cromwell are the only three princes that ever equalled him in political sagacity. If we are weak or false (and the people in power are likely to be both, and seem to be one), he will probably make his own terms with the new Tzar. Of course, whatever happens, he will have the Rhine and be protector of the Rhenish Confederation—Italy, Turkey, and Poland. God grant it may end there. Could any man less of a fool than Lord J. Russell think Prussia so mad as to join our alliance, so contrary to her interests. Even if you live to my age you will not see a peace honourable and lasting. . . . Every good wish to the whole of your circle from the old man.

WRITTEN IN SICKNESS.[1]

Death of the year! wilt thou be also mine,
  O Winter! never must I catch again
  The virgin breath of mountain cyclamen,
Pushing aside the wayward eglantine?

[1] These verses were published in the *Examiner*, March 17, 1855, and afterwards in "Dry Sticks."

N

Such were my phantasies not long ago,
  Ere thou wast nearer : I had thought once more
  To ramble as of old along the shore
Of Larius, now indeed with step more slow :

And thence, if such a scene the heart can bear
  To leave behind, Sorrento's cliffs along,
  From that old terrace-walk guitar and song
(Spectres ! away with ye !) again to hear.

To Mrs Graves-Sawle.

[*July* 1855.]

. . . I found my old friend[1] in better health than I
expected.   He had never seen the Crystal Palace.
Lame as he is, he came over the following day with
Lady Napier, and we went together over the whole of
it. And only fancy, the great fountains were set playing for me !   The beautiful N.[2] showed me her little
girl, who was very amiable with me, as little girls
always were : I mean the very little ones.   I was
obliged to declare to Lady Napier that if she spoilt
her grandchild I would never make her a proposal.   I
spent some hours too with Kossuth, who could not
dine with me and Forster, because he had to receive a

[1] In 1855 Landor visited London, and he never went there again,
except when he passed through on his journey to Italy in 1858. The
above letter was published in Forster's "Life." His "old friend" was
General Sir William Napier, then living in Clapham Park.

[2] Miss Nora Napier had married Sir Henry Bruce, afterwards Lord
Aberdare.

deputation quite unexpected; and by no means the smallest part of my pleasure was the introduction to me, on the following day, of Mr Lytton.[1] None of the younger poets of the day breathes so high a spirit of poetry. Of what impressed me most in the palace itself I should tell you that I saw the statue of Satan by ——, and the wonderful picture of Cimabue and Giotto by ——. Alas! alas! every name flies off from my memory when I would seize it. Leighton,[2] I should have said, is the painter; the sculptor is Lough.[3]

To Mrs Graves-Sawle.

[1855.]

DEAR ROSE,

Ever since I received your commands I have been looking over parcel after parcel of my letters to find any autograph worthy of your notice. It occurred to me, before I went to bed last night, that Forster had carried all such away with him. He will write my life in another year or two. I hope he is in no hurry. I am in none. I have never known more

[1] Afterwards the Earl of Lytton, writing at this time under the *nom-de-plume* of Owen Meredith. The following passage is from an unpublished letter of his, dated Florence, Jan. 7, 1854 :—"I have read the *critique* upon Landor's new work, and like the extract there given exceedingly. God bless him for what he says about the Madiai. That is a man I should greatly like to know."

[2] The late Sir Francis Leighton, President of the Royal Academy.

[3] Mr John Graham Lough, who died in 1876. Perhaps his best known statue is that of Her Majesty the Queen, in the Royal Exchange.

than two *great* men, although many good ones—
Napier and Kossuth. I have only seen and once
conversed with Kosciusko. Of Louis Bonaparte I will
say nothing. He is the greatest and most powerful of
living potentates—but a scoundrel like the rest. . . .

Ever affectionately yours,

W. S. LANDOR.

To Mrs Paynter.

January 1 [1856].

DEAR MRS PAYNTER,

When you write to Rose send her the
verses I shall transcribe on the other side. She
has kept alive in me the spirit of poetry, such as it is.
I shall miss her sadly on the 19th. I never drink a
health on a birthday without a sigh after it. My own
interests me little, hers greatly. How much happiness lies spreading before her. May the most affectionate of mothers live long to see it.

Your old faithful friend,

W. S. LANDOR.

———

To Rose.

I was not young when first I met
That graceful mien, that placid brow :
Ah! twice ten years have past, and yet
Near these I am not older now.

Happy how many have been made
    Who gazed upon your sunny smile!
I sate as happy in the shade
    To hear the voice that could beguile.

My sorrow for whate'er I left
    In bright Ausonia, land of song,
And felt my breast not quite bereft
    Of those home joys cast down so long.

W. S. LANDOR.[1]

———

To Mrs Graves-Sawle.

[*Jan.* 1856].[2]

MY DEAR FRIEND,

If you can suggest to me a single new thought of affectionate regard, I promise I will invest it with verse. Believe me I retain all the old ones. Instead of lines addressed to you I am constrained to send a few very different. Those to a Lady at Malvern I found accidentally as I was about to burn a packet of letters. I felt great pity, no great love, for this lady, long since dead. On the other side are a few verses on our old friend Barry's marriage. I doubt whether I myself should not be about as good a

———

[1] Printed in Works, 1876, viii. 287. The original manuscript is in Lady Graves-Sawle's Album.

[2] I am indebted to Mr John Enys of Enys, Cornwall, for a copy of this letter.

bridegroom. But he has youth on his side. I am quite delighted to receive so excellent account of you and your dear children. There is nothing I look forward to with more pleasure than to see you all once more at Bath.

I retain my health and am stronger than I was two years ago. My portrait has just been taken by Mrs Campbell at the desire of Mrs Paynter and Lady Aylmer, as I had resolved, long ago, to sit no more for it. I have been working out a list, and found that twenty-two have been taken. What have you ladies to answer for! I can hardly believe that at the end of this very month I am 81 years old. I hope that for at least one more I may tell you how truly I am

Your affectionate old friend,

W. S. LANDOR.

[*Enclosure.*]

ADVICE TOO LATE.[1]

My dear friend Barry!
Think ere you marry
That "Time is on the wing."
Do you not fear
That you may hear
A bride with laughter sing
Fa! la!

[1] These verses were afterwards printed in "Dry Sticks."

[BATH, *Jan.* 18, 1856.]

Confinement by a troublesome cold has not made
me forget the 19th Jan.   On more than half your
birthdays I have had the pleasure of drinking your
health.   On this one, so near, I think I may indulge
in the hope of doing so.   Alas! I am gone very far
down the vale of years, a vale in which there is no
fine prospect on the other side, and the few flowers
are scarcely worth gathering.   But it is pleasant to
turn round in the midst of one's weariness and to look
on the verdant declivity behind; pleasant to see pure
white images on either hand, and to distinguish here
and there a capital letter on the plinth.   Dim as my
eyes are become, I do think I can peruse the letter R
on the one nearest to me.   Old people, it is said, are
apt to be verbose, so I must not authenticate it. . . .
My dear friend, I beg you to believe me,

Your ever affte. old friend,

W. S. L.

[*Oct.* 5, 1856.]

DEAR ROSE,

Do not attempt a version of Dante
nor anything else in which others can excell you.   I

will not take you by the hand over a bridge like
Mahomet's of razor edge. Dante has been well
translated already, best by Cary,[1] whose version
contains a selection of useful and instructive notes.

Lady Dacre[2] has given us some fine specimens of
Petrarca. In his vast volume he has given us nearly
or quite a dozen of Canzoni or sonnets worth reading.
On the other side I will transcribe a few verses,
which, however, I think are printed in my works.
Were they addrest to you?[3]

I wished to escort Mrs Paynter as far as Restormel,
where I would have spent a week or nearly with you,
but she could not come now.

Ever afftly. yours,

W. S. LANDOR.

[1] The Rev. Henry Cary, the translator of Dante, had been in the same
form with Landor at Rugby. Four years after the date of this letter,
Landor wrote to Mr Robert Lytton (afterwards Earl of Lytton) :—" Do
not despise Cary's Dante. It is wonderful how he could have turned the
rhymes of Dante into unrhymed verse with any harmony : he has done
it. . . . He was a learned and virtuous man. Our Ministers of State were
never more consistent than in their neglect of him." Landor's verses to
Cary are in " Heroic Idyls," p. 122.

[2] " Le Canzoni di Petrarca, &c., Tradotte in versi Inglesi," by Miss
Wilmot, afterwards Lady Dacre, first published about 1815.

[3] Landor had transcribed the verses sent with Petrarch's sonnets—

> " Behold what homage to his idol paid
> The tuneful suppliant of Valclusa's shade "—

for Lady Graves - Sawle's album. But they were first printed in
" Simonidea " (1806), and were then addressed to Ianthe.

To Mrs Graves-Sawle.

Dec. 1856.]

DEAR ROSE,

       Did I ever send you a bit of poetry beginning

> " My little kid [1]
> If I forbid
> Your access to my tender trees."

If I did it is possible you may have thought it worth keeping.   I can find no copy and I quite forget in what periodical or other paper it was printed.   I sadly want it. . . .

            Affectionately yrs.,

               W. S. LANDOR.

THE LAST GIFT. [2]

Jan. 12, 1857.

The shadows deepen round me ; take
   I will not say my last adieu,
But, this faint verse ; and for my sake
   Keep the last line I trace for you.

The years that lightly touch your head
   Nor steal away nor change one hair,
Press upon mine with heavy tread
   And leave but barren laurels there.

[1] The beginning of a poem afterwards printed in "Dry Sticks," for which Landor seems now to have been collecting material. There is also a Latin version of the piece.

[2] From the original MS. in Lady Graves-Sawle's album. The verses were printed in " Dry Sticks."

To Mrs Graves-Sawle.

[BATH, *Feb.* 4, 1857.]

DEAR ROSE,

I trust I have never been so forgetful as to have omitted sending you any passable poetry of mine. If you have the meeting of " Achilles and Helena on Ida,"[1] pray send it to me. I never wrote anything so good and cannot find it. Good bye.

W. S. L.

To Mrs Graves-Sawle.

[BATH, *Feb.* 14, 1857.]

DEAR ROSE,

I ought always to have sent you whatever poetry I had written. We, of course I mean we men, are apt to fancy that we *have* done what we ought.

" My Kid " is come back to me this morning. It was published in the *Morning Star.* I had forgotten this. Mr Linton,[2] who is to marry Eliza Lynn early in next year, was desired by her to look for it—which he did and found it. . . .

W. S. LANDOR.

[1] This dialogue in verse was published in the enlarged edition of " The Hellenics," 1859. A prose version had appeared in the " Imaginary Conversations of Greeks and Romans," 1853.

[2] Mr William Linton, artist and writer, at one time a Chartist leader, and a friend of Garibaldi, died in New York, Dec. 30, 1897.

To Mrs Graves-Sawle.

[BATH.]

DEAR ROSE,

It appears to me an age since I wrote to you or you to me. Mrs Paynter had proposed to visit you this autumn. If she had, I certainly should have been of your party at Restormel. Lord Aylmer, I trust, will be happier in her company than any other. I thought him looking very well when he was here; but he could not be prevailed upon to prolong his stay. Clubs are the curse of families. Mr Sawle requires no such distraction, and never will. It never suited my pursuits and habits, as you know. They continue to be such as they were formerly.

Your affect. old friend,

W. S. LANDOR.

To Mrs Graves-Sawle.

BATH, *Sept.* 24, 1857.

DEAR ROSE,

Half the pleasure I anticipated is swept away by hearing that you are coming out of health. Bath is the only place to restore you. . . . There is a report of a contested election in Bodmin. Were you able to canvass, Mr Sawle's success would be certain. If he goes out, let me advise you to accept the title of Viscountess Restormel.

I have a good mind to write an address to the electors—yes I will. Look on the other side—find it and improve it.

> Ever faithfully and affectionately yours,
>
> W. S. Landor.

"My friends and constituents! Five years ago you elected me as your Representative in Parliament. I humbly hope that I have performed my duties to you and to the people at large : certain I am that I have done it to the best of my ability. Should you again deem me worthy of your favor I shall continue in the same unalterable course : but I would not by encountering a contest, disturb the harmony now prevailing in the Borough."

To Mrs Graves-Sawle.

[BATH, *Oct.* 23, 1857.]

DEAR ROSE,

Your last letter was greatly more satisfactory than the former. Often did I wish that your rheumatism could be removed to me. My shoulders have borne heavier and more irritating burdens, and your presence has made them fall off. Now will you believe that I was seized last Wednesday by the most inflammatory pains in the shoulder and right side. If I were half as pious as I ought to be, I should believe that my interior prayers were heard. I was recommended to apply a mustard poultice. I never do things by halves. I kept it about me from 8 at night till 11 next day.   My patience and perseverance were rewarded.   I am now like one of those saints who were flayed alive and I am somewhat more of a lobster color than a man's.   I am told that in a fortnight I shall be as white as ever.   We "ugly men" have not the privilege to be *décolletés* as you ladies have.   I never had rheumatism since the year I left College.   I caught it lying in a damp bed after hunting.   Surely I must be made of iron all but the heart. What that is made of must be decided by those who have best examined it.

Your Mama has been specially kind to my nieces and drank tea with them on Friday, when she met their brother and his pretty, ladylike wife, sister to Brigadier-General Stanton, who commanded very ably and successfully a Brigade in the Crimea.   Perhaps you may remember how bravely and calmly he acted against the popish rabble in Ireland three years ago.

I do not venture out of doors.   No warning shall restrain me on the 19th Jany. if I live.   Your birthday always makes me joyous.   I was always melancholy on my own.   In future I shall be less so.   I have nothing to hope or fear, God will do the best for us all.   Adieu, dear Rose, till *mi vien da ridere.*

W. S. L.

To Mrs Graves-Sawle.

BATH, *Tuesday* [*Oct.* 27, 1857].

DEAR ROSE,

I keep only one other birthday, which happens on the nineteenth of January. I have engaged at present no other visitants but a small party of flowers. I am no botanist but have learnt by heart the name of one, after frequent repetitions. Two days ago there left me a great florist, the Principal of the College at Calcutta.[1]   I wish he could have protracted his stay. We heard this morning that Delhi[2] is taken. They talk of six hundred of our men fallen. God grant there may not be three thousand at the least. The wisdom of one man would have prevented all these horrible murders of women and children. Men must fall. Sir C. Napier was the only truly wise general of our times. Even Wellington did not see so far nor conciliate so many. Havelock has done wonders. Surely the miserable fool who gave a command to Anson, on which a surprise depended, ought to be shot. Our most dangerous enemies are in our public offices. Tell Francis and Charles[3] unless they

[1] Professor E. B. Cowell, a botanist as well as an accomplished Oriental scholar.

[2] News of the fall of Delhi (Sept. 20, 1857) reached London on Oct. 26.

[3] Now Colonel Francis Graves-Sawle, Coldstream Guards, and Captain Charles Graves-Sawle, R.N.

come speedily and help me to recover my Latin and Greek, I must give it up.

Good bye,

W. S. L.

To Mrs Paynter.

DEAR MRS PAYNTER,

I send you a curiosity. Charlotte Philipps gave me a lump of some mineral, which was afterwards stolen from me, and I wrote these lines at St Clair's.

Do me the favor to accept some classical Designs by Gibson. They may perhaps find room on your drawing-room table.

Very truly yours,

W. S. L.

[*Enclosure.*]

ST CLAIR.[1]

Of all the saints of earth or air
What saint was ever like St Clair!
'Twas she herself who crost my way,
And thunderstruck me yesterday.
In simple vest she stood array'd,
To mortal eyes a mortal maid,

---

[1] The original manuscript of these lines, over a hundred years old, has been preserved by Lady Graves-Sawle among Landor's letters. The poem was printed in "Dry Sticks."

And in her dexter hand she bore
A shining mass of shapeless ore.
My courage, voice, and memory gone,
I bow'd and kist the magic stone.
I urged attendance ; she complied ;
And now behold us side by side.
I speak ; the country people stare . . .
"The Saxon speaks to empty air."
When all but lovers long had slept,
I tost and tumbled, fretted, wept,
To Love himself vow'd endless hate,
Renounced my stars and curst my fate ;
When, lo! in pity to my tears,
In sleep an angel form appears ;
"Subdue," she says, "regrets like these,
We angels vanish when we please."
    My curtains, starting, I undrew ;
The Morn appear'd, the Vision flew.

Oct. 5, 1796.

To Mrs Paynter.

[BATH, *Nov.* 1857.]

DEAR MRS PAYNTER,

                    The verses I sent to you are
in the earliest of my handwriting. So far they are
curious, but your kind acceptance of them makes them
of value to me. Pray keep them until the paper,
which is now literally in the yellow leaf, utterly gives
way. Few are living who have written verses sixty-

one years ago, and this is the sixty-first anniversary
of mine. . . .

Ever yours sincerely,

W. S. L.

To Mrs Graves-Sawle.

December 1 [1857].

DEAR ROSE,

You observe that my old friends see
little of me.   Never was I ungrateful and never will
I be.   To those old friends I owe the recovery of my
spirits and happiness on my return from Italy.   I do
not venture to say who may fairly claim the greater
part of it.   Perhaps I may have said it often, both
asleep and awake. . . . In fifty-one days I shall hope
to hear you sing again *mi vien da ridere* and *mi vien
da piangere* . . . that music so dear to me from a
thousand recollections.   Lady Castle Stewart has
become a Catholic.   This is now quite the fashion.
Unless you become one, I verily believe I shall never
be a convert.   Lady Caldwell looks almost as young
as you do.   God bless you all.

Your affte.,

W. S. L.

To Mrs Graves-Sawle.

[BATH, *Dec.* 30, 1857.]

DEAR ROSE,

To-morrow comes *Capo d'anno.*   May
he make you many visits full of gladness.   He will

o

never see another verse of mine on any occasion
whatsoever.   It is right and proper that my last verse
should be on you, and when your company is gone,
and you are kept in the house by a rainy or snowy
or windy day, you may find them toward the close
of my volume, beginning—

" Few the years," &c.

There are very many things which I wrote early in
life and never thought of publishing.   My reason for
doing so now is to be found in the preface.   Do not
accuse me of vanity in sending you Forster's note.
If I ever was vain, you made me so, and will never
cure me. . . . Kindest regards to every soul at
Restormel.

Ever yours,

W. S. L.

———

To Rose.[1]

Few the years that wait for me
Rounding my centenary ;
But my latest wish shall be
Health and happiness to thee.

Years in age are apt to grow
Crabbed ; all the rest may go
Ere another fall of snow
Fill the furrow on my brow.

[1] These verses were printed in " Dry Sticks."

We shall see thy face again
When despotic winter's chain
Clanks upon the pallid plain.
Let him rave ; he raves in vain.

Not a floweret fears the cold
In thy presence : we are told
That the bravest men enrol'd
In Fame's record were less bold.

———

CHAPTER VI

1858—1863

CHAPTER VI

1858—1863

"I THINK I will go and die in Italy, but not in my old home. It is pleasant to see the sun about one's death-bed." So Landor had written to Mr Forster in the autumn of 1856. The intention was fulfilled, but under the pressure of misfortune. Rightly or wrongly, Landor's legal advisers declared that the libel suit brought against him would infallibly result in an adverse verdict, coupled with heavy damages ; and they suggested that he should sign a deed transferring all available assets to his son, and leave England before the trial. It is futile to ask now whether a more skilful defence might have served to obtain, at any rate, a mitigation of the penalty. There is more pleasure in recalling the glimpse we get of the old man's meeting with Dickens, when he stayed a night in London on his way to Italy. One may find it in a letter from a friend of Mr Forster's, who wrote :—
"I thought that Landor would talk over with him (Dickens) the unpleasant crisis ; and I shall never forget my amazement when Dickens came back into the room laughing, and said that he found him very jovial, and that his whole conversation was upon the character of Catullus, Tibullus, and other Latin poets."

And Dickens himself wrote :—" I would not blot him out, in his tender gallantry, as he sat upon his bed, at Forster's that night, for a million of wild mistakes at eighty-four years of age."

The first of Landor's letters printed in this chapter was written six months before his flight ; the fifth one just after he had left England for ever. All that he says about the trial is eliminated. Quite enough, and perhaps more than enough, is told by Mr Forster. Nor has it been thought necessary to throw further light on whatever was sad and painful in the few remaining years of his life ; but rather, where possible, to show that happier reflections were still left. If memory failed him at times, he could still write with something of the force and freshness that mark all his best compositions. Unequal to his best, the Conversations of Virgil and Horace, Milton and Marvel, Macchiavelli and Guicciardini, are yet unmistakably Landor's. And when the lately-discovered Savonarola Conversation was printed, a year ago, competent critics saw in it signs of "undiminished grace and vigour." But the present letters, of course, will be taken rather as testimony that, nearer ninety than eighty, the old man's disposition was curiously unchanged. Strange fits of passion might still move him to fierce wrath and implacable resentment of real or imagined wrongs ; but his friends were as dear to him as ever, his heart as full of tenderness and affection.

To Mrs Graves-Sawle.

[BATH, *Jan.* 17, 1858.]

. . . The day after to-morrow I shall celebrate your birthday quite alone, for my nieces will have gone into Warwickshire. I can offer you no new wishes, no fresh flowers, and only one glass of wine for libation. I was deplorably stupid in sending you Forster's letter instead of Napier's, where I am "among the first Greek tragedians," with "Achilles and Helena." I always had thought my poetry at its best when inspired by you. The next effusion will be at the gates of Paradise, half a century hence, or soon after. I would not fix the hour, for I never disappointed a lady, and I must confess I shall be willing to wait for you. Confess that you have never heard any man say the same here on earth. And now continue to believe me, what I have always been, and always shall be,

Your affcte. old friend,

W. S. LANDOR.

To Mrs Graves-Sawle.

'[BATH, *Jan.* 1858.]

MY DEAR FRIEND,

I would not be behind my usual congratulations on your birthday. I did hope to have been able to send you with them a few lines of better poetry than usual, I mean usual with me. When you

come to Bath, I do trust that I may be able to do it.
Until then and ever after,

> Believe me, with all my old faith,
>> Yours,
>>> W. S. L.

To Mrs Graves-Sawle.

[BATH, *Feb.* 1, 1858.]

DEAR ROSE,

Of all the letters I have received on my
birthday yours is the most precious to me. I am
unworthy of your prayers and almost of your thoughts.
But God will grant your prayers that the children may
soon be restored to health. . . . Dr Watson tells me
that he sees no reason why I should not live another
ten years, and that he does not remember my looking
better than I do now. A lady would equivocate and
say, " I do not see much difference."
Entreating the Almighty to protect you all,

> Believe me, dear Rose,
>> Yr. ever affte. friend,
>>> W. S. LANDOR.

To Mrs Graves-Sawle.

[BATH, *Feb.* 8, 1858.]

DEAR ROSE,

For all my pride, and there is no little of
it, you alone are accountable. Praises for my writings

I have received more than I can digest or swallow. For the greater part of my last poems I want pardon rather than praise. Most happy shall I be to subscribe to the *Codex Augiensis*,[1] the labour of so eminent a scholar and so virtuous a man. I wish I myself partook of either quality. I have forgotten my Greek, of which I had formerly as much as boys of fifteen have now. Butler,[2] afterwards Bishop of Lichfield, and myself were the first at Rugby, or, I believe, at any other school, who attempted a Greek verse. His was the best. Latin I still possess a small store of. I will enclose the prospectus to my nephew, and request him to forward it to my brother Robert. . . .

Ever most afftly. yours,

W. S. LANDOR.

BOULOGNE, HOTEL DE LONDRES, *July* 23 [1858].

DEAR ROSE,

In leaving England for ever, the heaviest of my sorrows is that I shall never see you again. I shall retain in my inmost heart the grateful memory of your kindness and compassion. How is it possible that I could ever forget the comfort you gave me, when circumstances made it impossible for me to remain in Italy. How often have I listened to

[1] Edited by the Rev. F. H. Scrivener, 1859.
[2] The Right Reverend Samuel Butler, Bishop of Lichfield, died in 1839.

a voice sweeter if possible in conversing with me than in singing at my request. Well do you remember the interest I took at all times in your welfare. The most affectionate of an affectionate family could not more heartily rejoice in your happiness. I regret my misfortune in the impossibility of my seeing Francis, and helping him a little way over the thorns of Latin and Greek. It might have caused me some vexation to part with my pictures. But my legal friends tell me that it is necessary. . . . I am going to Genoa in another fortnight. May God continue to you every earthly blessing, for you deserve them all. Think sometimes of your faithful old friend,

W. S. LANDOR.

To Mrs Graves-Sawle.

[FLORENCE] *Sept.* 8, 1858.

. . . In your letter to Julia you give me a hope, altho' a faint one, of seeing you in Italy. Feeble as I am, I will attempt to meet you in any part of the Continent at any season. If it never should be, perhaps in your walks you may take the road to Widcombe.[1]   There

---

[1] Landor, either before or after he left England, arranged that a space for a grave should be reserved for him in the churchyard at Widcombe, near Bath. I have the manuscript of his verses :

> "Widcombe ! few seek with thee their resting place ;
> But I, when I have run my weary race,
> Will throw my bones upon thy churchyard turf," &c.

His purpose, however, was unfulfilled. He lies in the English cemetery in

I intend to be buried. Such was my promise in my early days to one who could not make the same, but whose last words pronounced my name with faithful and fond remembrance. So did my sister Elizabeth, as Kitty tells me. I never have forgotten those who loved me, even a little. . . . I have received a very kind note from my old friend Lord Normanby [1] who is paralytic. Lady Normanby wrote it. . . .

To Mrs Graves-Sawle.

FLORENCE, VIA NUNCIATINA 267, *December* 23 [1859].

DEAR ROSE,

A happy Christmas to you and all dear to you. Included in this wish is a happy new

Florence, where a flat stone marks his grave. A monument to his memory has been erected by his sons in St Mary's Church, Warwick.

[1] Can this have been a reply to the letter which Landor is said to have written to Lord Normanby, and which, according to Lord Houghton, ended as follows ? :—

"We are both of us old men, my lord, and are verging on decrepitude and imbecility, else my note might be more energetic. I am not observant of distinctions. You by the favour of a Minister are Marquis of Normanby, I by the grace of God am
WALTER SAVAGE LANDOR."

The story is that Landor on his arrival at Florence was aggrieved by the Marquis's cool reception of him, and thus expressed his resentment of the affront. Yet here we have him writing kindly enough of his old friend to whom, when Earl of Mulgrave, he had dedicated " Pericles and Aspasia." The accuracy of the anecdote and the supposed date of the angry letter are not easily reconciled with the fact that Landor did not leave England till July 1858, and Lord Normanby had ceased to be Minister in February, having been recalled by Lord Malmesbury.

year and many of them. Wish me one; this will be
quite enough. I mean the Christmas, not the entire
year. I never was desirous of a long life. You
have greatly contributed to the happiness of nearly a
quarter. . . .

When I left Fiesole I went to Siena with my friend
Browning. Mr Story,[1] the son of Judge Story, the
celebrated American jurist, most hospitably received
me into his villa until a smaller one was prepared for
my reception. The good Sandford is gone to Egypt.
He often came to visit me. Also the Bishop of
Jamaica;[2] he sent to me his poetry, and his lady
wrote me a most flattering note on the eve of his
departure. He is dead since. Poor man! he smiled
when I told him I was once a poacher on his grandfather's grounds at Blenheim.

I have lately been confined to my room and am
still very weak. I begin to sleep about six in the
morning and again take my siesta as usual. On the

[1] Mr W. W. Story, the American sculptor, died in Rome, where he
had resided for the past forty years, on Oct. 6, 1895. His statue of
Peabody, the philanthropist, stands in front of the Royal Exchange. He
was the friend of Thackeray, Hawthorne, Browning and Tennyson. His
father, Judge Joseph Story, was Chief Justice of the United States
and a distinguished jurist. See Landor's verses in " Heroic Idyls,"
p. 268.

> "Story ! whose sire maintained the cause
> Of freedom and impartial laws," &c.

[2] The Right Rev. Aubrey George Spencer, Bishop of Jamaica, was
the son of the Hon. William Spencer, the poet (see p. 85), and grandson of the second Duke of Marlborough. But he did not die till
1872.

other side I will transcribe a few lines written when I thought I was about to die.   Surely they will be my last. . . .

[*Enclosure.*]

" The grave is open, soon to close
    On him who sang the charms of Rose,
    Her pensive brow, her placid eye,
    Her smile, angelic purity,
    Her voice so sweet, her speech so sage
    It checkt wild Youth and cheer'd dull Age
    Her truth when others were untrue,
    And vows forgotten.
                                    Friends, adieu !
    The grave is open. . . . O how far
    From under that bright morning star."

To Mrs Graves-Sawle.

[FLORENCE] *January* 30, '60.

DEAR ROSE,
            Your letter was brought to me on the evening of your birthday and I am writing to you on the morning of mine.   How delightful is it to me, to whom scarcely anything else is, to receive such an account of your lovely children.   Alas ! that there is little chance that I should ever see them again.   The present day was always a melancholy one to me, and yours was always a happy one until the present. Three glasses of Chianti to your health have been

insufficient to dispel my gloom. Twenty years was the nineteenth of January kept as a holiday by me, and in almost all of those years in Great Bedford Street . . . I am better than I was two years ago, yet I hope Doctor Watson's prognostication may not be accomplished, that I am "good for another ten years." I was stronger at sixty than many are at forty. I can hardly think that I have entered on my eighty-sixth year. Altho' I am unable to alight from a carriage without help I will exert my best powers to join you in any part of Italy. But surely you and Mr Sawle will travel on as far as Florence. The Gulf of Spezia is quite as well worth seeing as the Bay of Naples, and Florence is richer in works of art than any other city in the world, and you shall carry back with you any one of the five pictures which were sent to me here from England.

Tell Rosina I send her a kiss thro' a beard as long as a Jew's ; and you know, dear Rose, how faithfully

I remain yours,

W. S. L.

To Mrs Graves-Sawle.

[FLORENCE] *January* 24 [1861].

DEAR ROSE,

I have always kept your birthday sacred, usually with joy, but this time with a tear in each eye. It is a great happiness to hear that you and all yours enjoy your usual health.   Here in Florence we have suffered as severe and comfortless weather as there can have been in England.   To-day there is a deep fog.   Among the kind letters I have received, one is from Mrs Burton Borough of Chetwynd Park.   Perhaps you may remember her at Bath as the daughter of Admiral Gawen, an old friend of mine.   In six days I shall have entered my eighty-seventh year.   I can stil write a little.   You will see I have been rubbing up my Italian with the pen.   Fifty-five years ago, when my cousin, Sophia Shuckburgh, was going to Paris, she told me she must *rub up* her French a little.   I told her not to rub it too hard, for fear of rubbing it all away.

I wish I could hear once more an Italian song of yours.   I hope Rosina will sing. . . . The ugly old man has grown uglier since she saw him.

Yr. affte. old friend,

W. S. L.

To Mrs Graves-Sawle.

FLORENCE, *Jan.* 14 [1862].

DEAR ROSE,

It gave me about as much pain as an old withered heart can feel, to be sensible that your approaching birthday will probably be the last on which I shall be living to congratulate you.   In a few days I shall have entered my eighty-eighth year.

P

What is become of the gay youth you saw at Florence, not blooming quite like Spring, but very like Spring in the vicissitude of sunshine and shower?

Sandford wrote to me lately and told me of your being at the seaside, and an older friend, Admiral Erskine, gave me a good account of himself. The India Station has been offered to him, which I hope he will refuse. We dined together several times here in Florence.

All my former friends have left this country. Most of them are dead. Mrs Browning among these; and Browning has gone to England, probably never to revisit Florence. There stil remain Kirkup, Mrs Trollope and the Countess Baldelli [1] née Walker. She brought her sister and two children to see me a few days since. She often shows me the same kindness since I have been unable to get so far as to her house. . . . My grave is already made in Widcombe Churchyard, where I proposed it should be sixty years ago. Do you remember our walk there with Napier on the way to Prior Park? Dear, good Napier! he thought of me in his last painful days. Stopford sent me a most affte. letter from his wife who is coming to England. She has been staying with the Countess de Montejo, mother of the Empress, whom she knew intimately. My sons Walter and Charles visit me almost daily. Arthur Walker writes to me

[1] To whom Landor's verses in " Heroic Idyls," p. 274, were addressed.

every week, and a few friends in England have not forgotten me. Do not you.

Believe me ever, dear Rose,

Yr. affte. old friend,

W. S. L.

To Mrs Graves-Sawle.

[FLORENCE] *January 19,* 1863.

DEAR ROSE,

You see just above that I have not forgotten the nineteenth of January. May you have many such birthdays, all as happy as any of the past. In ten days more I shall enter my eighty-ninth year, and I have already lost, what people generally lose earlier, much of my eye-sight and hearing, and my two front teeth. Do not laugh at this, it is quite as grievous as the other! . . . Few of the friends I knew here formerly are here now. Kirkup, the Trollopes, Count Coterell come to me occasionally and some from abroad. Seymour,[1] as you know, is now Ambassador in Germany. He came frequently to see me, and his father, Lord George with him once or twice. He was about my age and died lately. It is high time for me to go too. Nothing I wish more. Countess Baldelli often comes to relieve my solitude and brings her children.

[1] Sir George Hamilton Seymour had retired from the diplomatic service in 1858, and his visit to Landor may have been paid some time ago.

. . . I have not left my room these four months. My
sons Walter and Charles are very attentive to me.

My friend Mrs West[1] of Ruthin Castle has sent me
her "Garibaldi's March" which she composed. Alas!
I shall never hear it, which I might hope were I again
in Great Bedford Street. I have given a parcel of
poetry to my friend, Arthur Walker, to do with it
what he pleases.[2] I had no time or inclination to
arrange it. The books I have lately been reading are
the works of Washington Irving. None of our present
writers write such pure English; he reminds me of

[1] Mrs West, wife of the late Frederick West, grandson of the 2nd Earl
de la Warr, died in 1886. Her grand-daughter is Princess Henry of
Pless. Among the manuscript verses which I found in Landor's desk
were some lines addressed to "the Lady of Ruthin Castle," and referring
to her musical composition "Garibaldi's March." As they have never
been published, I append them here. They are among the very last
he wrote :—

> " Stiffly I rise from this arm-chair,
> Even to greet the wise and fair,
> Who daily, one or other, come
> To cheer me in my dressing-room.
>   " I have but thanks to pay for song,
> And March the brave will march to long.
> Rejoice : Caprara has receiv'd
> Him o'er whose wound pale Europe griev'd.
> Again his spirit breathes in all
> That host which Death could ne'er appall,
> Until he stood above the head
> Of one they deem'd already dead.
>
>   " The laurel planted for your crown,
> Altho' no moderate breeze shake down,
> You must *refreshen* day by day,
> Or leaves of it will drop away."

[2] "Heroic Idyls," by Walter Savage Landor. London: T. Newby, 1863.

Addison, but has more genius and a richer invention. Perhaps on the whole he is more like Goldsmith. I have not time enough before me to learn our new English.

Who knows but at this very hour I am detaining you from attending to Rosina's lessons. I must not hazard it any longer. This is probably the last tidings you will receive from

Your affectionate old friend,

WALTER LANDOR.

This is the last letter in Lady Graves-Sawle's album. Nor is there anything here to add to the story told by Mr Forster and Mr Colvin. Walter Savage Landor died in Florence on September 17, 1864.

PART II

PUBLIC LETTERS

CHAPTER I

1838—1840

WALTER SAVAGE LANDOR
ABOUT 1840
From a Sketch by W. Fisher

CHAPTER I

1838—1840

DURING his last residence in Bath, Landor was perpetually addressing letters to the *Examiner*. A few of them were reprinted in pamphlet form, and afterwards in "Last Fruit of an Old Tree," but the greater part have never yet been retrieved from the limbo of old newspapers. In addition to signed letters and articles, and occasional poetry, he also contributed anonymous reviews, portions of which were subsequently incorporated in "Imaginary Conversations"; but to these it is seldom possible to discover a clue. In the following selection an endeavour has been made to put together all his more important writings on political and literary subjects.

The following letter was addressed to Daniel O'Connell, and was printed in the *Examiner* of September 30, 1838. Mr Forster in his "Life of Landor" quotes O'Connell's reply, but he does not give the letter which evoked it.

To Daniel O'Connell, Esq., M.P.

BATH, *Sept.* 25, 1838.

SIR,

There are so many of all conditions who take the liberty of writing and appealing to you, that you hardly can wonder if another, whose name is unknown to you, should offer a few reflections. The only thing at all extraordinary is, that he abstains from eulogy or invective.

To come at once to the point.

No question has been more agitated or less sifted than the question what is conducive and effective to the pacification and prosperity of Ireland. The debaters on this subject have usually been hot-headed and ignorant men, who delivered such opinions as they fancied most agreeable to their party. I speak of those whose opinions are likely to gain attention, the members of Parliament. With your experience and acuteness, have you really been deceived by expectations and promises? If so, and you are disappointed in past hopes, beware of what you cherish for the future. Above all, do not believe that by reconstructing a House of Commons in Ireland you will obtain your object. Recollect the last. Was there ever so desperate a gang of scoundrels united in one confraternity? How few abstained from the open sale of their constituency! and how many of the other House are at this moment in the full enjoyment of their prostitution! We disfranchise a miserable town for ever, where a few drunkards are instigated to bribery, for one vote, on one occasion; yet do you not every day see Irish Lords, with foreheads unbranded, and with ears unslit, who sold the fee-simple of their votes for ever? How happens it that you never have risen from your seat and demanded, if not judgment on these traitors, at least a final cessation of such infamous hush-money, and an instant abolition of their pensions? The law empowering them to receive from the country the wages of iniquity would be repealed with unanimous approbation: any supporter of it would expire under the vengeance of the people. With all our reforms and regulations, and alphabetical schedules, and stringent tapes, the most zealous partisans of good house-wifery, having stripped the first skin off the onion and blown it away as unserviceable, come to the second and find it tough and intractable. They must bring it over the coals and keep it stewing, if they expect from it any nourishment. They begin to think it as impossible for a public man to be an honest man, as for a public woman to be an honest woman; and they see this only difference, that the public woman may keep her appointment, which the public man of late is never found to do. A fine bill of fare was laid before us;

but at last we are reduced to our old regimen : the ministers find *bubble*, and the people *squeak*.

When you pluck and pinion your own defaulters, all that was granted to them in any shape ought to be applied to the comforts and instruction of your poor. No doubt you smile at so inadequate a project ; and well you may, if nothing lies beyond it. This was only suggested as the most obvious, and the first and foulest stumbling-block of offence. Furthermore, then, let every diocese in Ireland have both its Protestant and its Roman Catholic bishop. Let each enjoy the ample pay of twelve hundred pounds a year; a larger sum than is the average stipend of the bishops in France and Italy; a larger sum, by more than double, than is granted to our generals and admirals after a half-century of service, after a life of danger, after a separation from friends and families, after a loss of health and limbs. Let the total of church lands be sold in small divisions, year after year, to supply a fund for schools and colleges, in which morality and religion shall be taught more effectually than invidious wealth can teach them ; these being the objects for which all forms of worship were established. Thereto might be added whatever is above five hundred a year in church livings. I see no more injustice or hardship in this curtailment, than in reducing to half-pay the officers of the army and navy. We do not say to them, "You shall enjoy your full pay during your lives; but your successors shall receive only half-pay " : why should we then to another profession, as much under the head of the church as these are under the head of the army? Is it because the one is re-munerated in silver and gold, the other in corn and cattle? Who-ever is paid by the nation may lawfully be paid in such proportions as the nation shall appoint.

Livings have been subdivided; why may not bishoprics? In fact, the only reformed church is the Papal; and thousands are daily taking refuge with her, from the avarice, fraud, and hypocrisy of her blustering, bloated sister-in-law ; from the sale of whose false curls and pigments and perfumery, not only might enough be added to schools and poorer benefices, but much would remain, which might be applicable to noble plans of colonization. No doubt can be entertained that our gracious Queen would joyfully contribute to them her extensive possessions in Ireland, from which Majesty derives but small revenue, and Industry no advantage. Enough might be sold by auction every year to conduct into Canada and Australia twelve thousand men, women, and children; to supply each labourer with an axe and spade, with clothing for two years, and with sixpence daily to both old and young, for the first eight months. Would not this be better than to immure the healthy, although within sight of home; and if beyond sight of their friends, by no means beyond the hearing of their voices? Doubtless these are benefits, gratuities, blessings : but can we invent none greater? none more congenial? If such questions are vagaries, quite unworthy of the politician, let us consider whether nothing can be thought of more convenient and serviceable to ourselves.

Is colonization less advantageous to us than the same expenditure of our wealth in workhouses, which some of the Irish will look upon as prisons, and others as the outworks of fortresses, ready to be voided of their inmates and to be converted into barracks at the first panic of an irresolute Ministry? The money destined for this unpopular scheme will be much better expended in canals and railroads, on which a large proportion of the same poor people may be employed, whom our legislators are preparing to immure. Let ten acres in Canada and Australia be allotted to every man, woman, and child who emigrates. In a very few years our remaining colony in America will support a population quite adequate to counterbalance the French inhabitants. Hence a third of our customary force will be sufficient to maintain the tranquillity of the country. These considerations alone, leaving aside humanity, would have their weight, were any consideration so weighty as power and patronage; and I address them, sir, to you, as able to force our Administration on the line of duty, or to crush and scatter it if refractory.

You will find that, if the system of colonization is carried on for twenty years, your country, instead of losing in population, will much increase in it: poverty alone will diminish: crimes will grow less atrocious: political and religious differences will be forgotten in the circle of domestic comforts: new interests will spring up between man and man, visibly and tangibly: and old animosities will subside and cease. Indeed I am convinced that, at the expiration of twenty years, not only will your numbers be much greater, but that your wealth and prosperity will advance in a still higher degree, by the perpetually moving current of well-regulated colonization. The blood-suckers of stagnant Ireland will no longer be able to derive forty or fifty shillings a year from a solitary acre of potato ground : for, suppose that *regrating* of land is not represt by law (as it ought to be) like *regrating* in the market, yet such will be the quantity brought into cultivation at home, and such the facility of obtaining it abroad, that middlemen will be found only in your circulating libraries, and their suzerains must return from England and learn arithmetic and humanity in your parish school rooms.

I am, Sir, &c., &c.,

WALTER SAVAGE LANDOR.

In an Imaginary Conversation published in 1829 (Nicholas and Michel) Landor suggested the possibility of the Pasha of Egypt, Mehemed Ali, being permitted to extend his authority over Syria and Arabia. In 1833 Syria was made over to the Pasha, in accordance with the Treaty of Kutajah ; but six years later the Sultan attempted to recover the province. The defeat of the imperial troops and the desertion of the Turkish Navy would have left Mehemed Ali master of the event, but for the interference of the Powers. In July 1840, a Treaty was signed by England, Russia, Austria, and Prussia, France dissenting, by which the Pasha was required to restore Syria and be content with the government of Egypt. Ultimately this decision had to be forced by arms.

Mr Greville says that the humiliation of Mehemet Ali had for years been one of Lord Palmerston's favourite projects. The *Examiner* of Sept. 8th, 1839, contained a short letter from Landor, headed

"Mehemet Ali and the Five Powers"; but it will suffice to give a later and more elaborate dissertation on the subject, printed in the *Examiner* of Dec. 15th, 1839.

Egypt and the Eastern Question.

Nov. 18, 1839.

SIR,

When I addressed to you, several weeks back, my observations on the imprudence of our Ministerial threats against the Autocrat of Egypt, I scarcely expected that he, consummate politician as he is, would so speedily have demonstrated, to those who govern in Constantinople, their true, prime and vital interests. It now appears, however, that Mehemet Ali has persuaded his late adversaries, under the banner of the same prophet, that the safety of the Ottoman empire depends on peace and union with him. Nothing would so certainly and instantaneously have dismembered it as the attack of England on Egypt. I say of England; for neither France nor Russia would have co-operated to a larger extent than a sheet of paper. But each would have awaited the crippling of our inadequate fleet; the one to seize on Constantinople, the other on Rhodes and Cyprus, forming such an alliance with Mehemet Ali as should exclude us from the Red Sea and the Euphrates.

We are rather too presumptuous in our contempt of Asiatic politicians. In private life we have always been among the most prudent and honest of nations : in public we are very far from the most prudent; and if there be one behind us a few paces in the path of honesty, thanks are due to Louis Philippe, who certainly has the graciousness not to outstep us . . . somewhat such thanks indeed as

"T. Annæo Lucano beneficio Neronis fama servata."

The perfidy of the French Government, throughout the civil war of Spain, could leave on the mind of no wary politician an idea of sincerity in the alliance; and its late impudence in demanding the evacuation of Passages shows only an inclination for a momentary quarrel. No other answer ought to have been given than this brief one :—" *Whenever Spain requires it, we evacuate the village ; not before.*" It became the French Government, the same under Louis

Philippe as under Buonaparte, and conducted by men whom both in turn have stigmatised, to abandon to its fate that glorious nation to which France owed a great part of her victories both in spain and Germany. But it never was incumbent on us to advance in the cause of Poland, otherwise than with appeals to the sanctity of treaties. The expense must have been great, the success uncertain. For never will our nation and France co-operate long together with cordiality. She thinks we would cheat her because we look gravely and earnestly at her ; and we will not drink her wines because they sparkle.

But we may act by ourselves, and without any reference to her, in regard to Russia, although the French people and soldiery would simultaneously cry out for war against their conqueror at the first cannon fired. We may act in regard to Russia as Russia has been acting in regard to us. Furthermore, we may do lawfully and rightly what she has been doing disloyally and traitorously. We may secure the Turkish empire by aiding the Circassians ; and we can do it effectually by no other means. Our great object, we at last are made sensible, is to establish our preponderance in Persia : and this also is to be done by it, and alone by it. Long before the present day, we ought to have had a fleet in the Euxine. All that the Circassians want from us may be supplied at a less expenditure than a single month's in the last war. Russia would not openly resent it : she could not : she has the gout in one leg for five months in the year, and cannot limp up to us with the other : we are beyond the reach of her snow-balls. She knows that she extorted from Turkey a nominal thing, and that she has vainly attempted to found a real one on it. Turkey did not, either at the commencement or close of the war, or at any time previously, occupy Circassia. She neither had troops nor civilians in that country. She was about as much the sovran of Circassia as George the Third was sovran of France : not indeed quite so much ; for he at least held France upon his coins. Neither of them could cede more than the title. George the Third, who was always ready to warm his hands at a war, would not, however, have engaged in hostilities with Russia, for having carried stores and munition into his kingdom of France : neither do I conceive that Russia will deem it expedient to engage in hostilities with us, for aiding to this extent a nation not even in titular subjection to her, and never in her occupancy. But, whatever be her will, she has neither the right nor the means. It is only in peace and by diplomacy that she can injure us; and she already has injured us all she can.

If we take the vantage-ground of Circassia, we may cripple her for ever: if we neglect to take it, we, instead of procrastinating hostilities, only accelerate them, by multiplying the means of her annoyance, expediting the facilities of her aggression, and clearing the field for her attack. On the European side of Turkey the interests of Austria stand prominently forth against her ulterior encroachments; and within seven years, Austria will probably, with the consent of England, take under her protection the ill-governed and long-suffering Greece, which, ever since the battle of Navarino, has been Russian. But policy requires that neither Austrian nor other arms occupy that country, of which the various population always has been, and always must be, virtually republican and confederate. We must look to this, before we sanction, what we now perceive to be necessary, a new order of things. We are strictly, by the nature of our position, conservative, corrective, and controlling. We cannot with advantage to ourselves, increase our territory in Europe to the disadvantage of any neighbour. This alone would designate us, to the impartial of all nations, as the fittest arbiters of justice in their territorial disputes: and our power, which equals the united power of any two continental states, will uphold us on our high tribunal. In order to be the worthier of it, we must be somewhat more liberal in imparting the blessings and privileges we enjoy.

The great and prevalent fault of all governments is shutting out the light from those who are restless, instead of opening their eyes, calling them up, and exciting them to walk abroad. To the utmost of our abilities, we ourselves have pursued this system. While we wanted to share duties, we held rights behind our back, raising a suspicion that we were at best half-wise and very much less than half-honest. The cajoleries of Russia are concocted with more heat into greater potency. Her royal hand drugs the posset with costly and far-sought ingredients, and administers it among the grooms on enchased and resplendent salvers. Whoever has travelled much and observantly on the Continent, must necessarily have heard and noticed to what an extent, and into what ramifications, the Russian influence is perpetually running on. The smallest states in Italy and Germany contain some imperial agent. If there are two presses in any town, one is worked by Russia. Professors are invited from every foreign university: even they who decline the offer are proud of the distinction, which ribbands and rings and snuff-boxes materially enhance: one unbroken line of conduct, ministry after ministry, age after age, is pursued invariably; and there is always a Philip of Macedon on the throne of Muscovy. Gold moulds intellect, intellect moulds policy, and policy holds back or precipitates the march of war. Incorruptible as we boast to be, is there any man who believes that our press, our parliament, our privy council, will remain for ever, or for long, uncontaminated by Russia? We consider the Germans honest; and they are so; certainly no less than ourselves: yet in every city of Germany, royal, imperial, or free, but in the free particularly, the principal trade is *mask-making* for Russia. She stands already at our door in a flimsy domino, which it behoves us to strip off before she cross the threshold. I do not say *Delenda est Carthago*: I do say *Servanda est Caucasia*.

WALTER SAVAGE LANDOR.

Lord Brougham's "Sketches of Statesmen in the Reign of George III.," First Series (London, 1839), provoked a series of criticisms from Landor. One of them, originally published in the *Examiner*, May 19, 1839, was reprinted in the 1846 and 1876 editions of his works;[1] but the others have till now been overlooked. They illustrate, however, in an interesting way, Landor's critical methods; and are not without instruction for careless writers. The first letter here given, appeared in the *Examiner*, June 16, 1839.

Lord Brougham's "Sketches of Statesmen."
[SECOND NOTICE.]

SIR,
       When I sent to you, a fortnight since, my remarks on the judgements of Lord Brougham, in those passages of his writings

---

[1] Landor's Works, 1846, vol. ii. 457; and Works, 1876, v. 553.

where he speaks of Cesar, of Buonaparte, and of Milton, it wa:
not my intention to notice him again.   But hearing that he i:
about to be appointed Minister of Public Instruction, I hope t(
remove from his mind any little displeasure he may have receivec
from my animadversions, by offering him a few brief notices anc
references for his new Portfolio.

Since all knowledge must be conveyed by language, and since :
Minister of Public Instruction ought to be accurate and correct in it
I will take the trouble, for his benefit, to mark some blemishes o
style and some distortions of thought, which I confidently hope h(
will correct in future.

The commencement of every work should be simple and brief
Involutions and intricacies are, in all cases, much to be avoided
but particularly in the first sentence.   It is in vain to say, "*I ped*
fausto," where you are heaping up loose briars about a man, anc
pushing him into the dark.   Now the very first sentence in Lor(
Brougham's Treatise on the Statesmen of the last Century is encum
bered with repetitions, and intractably prolix.

"The affairs of men, the interests and history of nations, the relative *value* o
institutions, as *discovered by their actual working*, the *merits* of different system:
of policy as *tried by their effects*, are all very imperfectly examined without :
thorough knowledge of the *individuals* who administered the systems, and pre
sided over the management of the public concerns."

Here the word *systems* is idly repeated: *value* and *merits* ar(
opposed: *discovered by their actual working* and *tried by their effect:*
are nearly the same: *individuals*, always a bad expression, always
used in a sense contrary to the real meaning, signifies here, no!
single and separate persons, but men united in number, less o!
greater, and constituting an administration, or a part of one.

So much for the first sentence.   Now for the second—

"Sensible influence over the *destinies*," &c.

$This Gallicism of novel introduction deforms our language.   Men
cannot exert a sensible influence *over* the destinies: they may exert
it in accomplishing what is here denominated so: but this is *under*,
not *over*.   By *destinies* I presume are meant the *decrees* of Divine
Providence.   Now, *over* these there can be no human agency.

Third—

"This *kind* of inquiry, this *species* of record."

You may invert the words *kind* and *species*; you may employ or omit either.

"*Undeviating candour*" is a false metaphor.   The last sentence in the same page is excellent.   But let me ask whether the author is quite sure that he himself holds up to veneration "the votaries of duty, of peace, of freedom"; whether, on the contrary, he never has acted contemptuously and superciliously in regard to those "votaries," men who have disdained the clamorous of all parties, the distribution of all honours and emoluments, men whom no elevation to the woolsack could exalt, and no expulsion from it depress or irritate.

P. 5. "*Both* to himself personally, to the order in which his lot was cast, and to the rest of mankind."

Both is applicable to *two* and no more.

P. 5. " "*Unhappily* he took the wrong direction."

Did any man ever take it *happily*?

P. 6. " A narrow understanding, which no culture had enlarged."

Culture may *improve*, but not *enlarge*.

P. 7. "Defects eradicated."

Defect is the same as *deficiency* or *failing*.   You cannot *eradicate* what is *deficient* or *absent*.

P. 7. " Neither knowledge, accomplishments, nor abilities."

Neither is the opposite of *either*: one or other ; not two or more.

It is painful to revert to anything, much beyond the commencement, in the dismal and disastrous reign of George III.   But here is a sentence worth transcribing.

" The different orders in the State have a right to look *forward towards* that high quarter, all in their turn, for support, when their rights are invaded by one another's encroachments, or to claim the Royal umpirage when their *mutual conflict* cannot be settled by mutual concessions."

Instead of animadverting on such an inelegance as *forward towards*, I hasten to look at the *mutual conflict*.   Let nobody call its propriety in question.   Usually, when there is a conflict, proof enough is given that *two can play at that game*, as school-boys say, and sometimes several take a part in it : but Lord Brougham, like the Romans after their triumphs, has exhibited the most stupendous games at his own expense, himself the combatant with himself. The sentence I have just quoted is true. Moreover, the King could have given the elective franchise to as many and as great masses of the people as he thought convenient, without the enactment of that sorry farce, entitled the *Reform Bill.* He could not take away, as that bill did, the elective franchise from any man. Unless bribery and corruption had been proven against a constituency, the united power of the three Estates can no more take it away than it can take away freehold. But to every rotten borough the King alone, by his own authority, could have added as many fresh voters, from the neighbouring towns or hundreds, as would give them soundness and constituency. He can as constitutionally grant new charters for such purposes as for fairs and markets ; and I wonder that, in his Royal wisdom, he did not save Parliament the trouble of taking any part in the discussion of Irish Municipalities, and of some other matters concerning Canada and Jamaica. In the two greatest of all free nations, England and America, the executive power is too feeble. In our country, as now united, it was needless to make more representatives : we did not want more ; we wanted truer and better. . . .

"The same *want* of enterprise and of pirit *prevailed.*"

Now, enterprise and spirit may *prevail,* but want of them never can. Why not use the plain, simple expression, " *There was* the same want of enterprise and of spirit ? " . . .

P. 30. "There is, indeed, hardly any eloquence of ancient or of modern times, of which so little that can be relied on as authentic has been preserved, unless perhaps that of Pericles, Julius Cesar, and Lord Bolingbroke."

It would indeed be fortunate, if we had as much of Chatham's eloquence as of Cesar's : but surely Lord Brougham can never have read his Commentaries. They contain many of his speeches, some of which are very simple and comprehensive. Lord Brougham doubts the authenticity of that grand Oration, preserved by Sallust, on Cataline's conspiracy. Sallust, I think, would hardly have dared to substitute words of his own under Cesar's name, knowing how tender and jealous of his literary character was that most eloquent and graceful writer. It appears to have escaped the learned lord's recollection, that we not only have " nothing which can be relied on as authentic," but nothing even supposititious, of those several great orators who contended with Pericles, and those others who were thought by their contemporaries to have been the rivals, the equals, and, in many parts of eloquence, the superiors of Demosthenes. We have nothing of Cleon, nothing of Demades, nothing of Phocion. I could here insert many more names, but these are enough in numbers to show the hastiness and inaccuracy of Lord Brougham. The style of Cato and of Cesar was very similar; of rich austerity, of unsparkling purity, of unsuspected strength. I cannot think it possible that Sallust, although, if he had any virtues, modesty was not among them, would have ventured to impersonate such men as Cato and Cesar in the midst of their friends and adherents. He would greatly have offended the more ambitious of the two if he had given a worse speech than his own, and grievously if he had given a better. Has Lord Brougham forgotten the treatise of Cicero, *De Oratore*? Is there any authentic page extant of the illustrious orators he mentions in it? What is there of Marcus Antonius? What is there of Hortensius? his contemporaries. What is there of Pollio and Messala? . . .

Of what consequence is it whether such men as Castlereagh and Canning have, or have not, "a right to blame Lord North" (p. 65).

Certainly he is less blameable than Pitt and Fox; less blameable than men coalescing with one whom, a week before, they had denounced as a traitor, and had threatened with the scaffold. Nevertheless, he acted both against his country and his conscience, when he pandered to the malignant passions of an obstinate madman, and persisted, year after year, in the dishonest labour of sawing and sundering one half of the British Empire from the other.

Why is the question of Parliamentary reform—

" A question which, in any other age, perhaps in any other country, must have been determined, not by deliberations of politicians or arguments of orators, but by the swords and spears of armed men " (p. 64).

What great antagonistic power was interested in coming forward with such violent opposition? A part only of the peers, and not at all the king. He was holden in thraldom by that body as much as ever his predecessors were by the contumacious old barons. A thraldom the more odious and intolerable, as the principal of these revolters was created by his father, and were not descended, as those old barons, from ancestors of valour and note, but were lawyers, and scriveners, and stock-jobbers, and had risen into wealth by the cunning of such vocations.   The same people were most strenuous against the improvement and enlargement of municipal institutions. I would not willingly try experiments upon health, much less upon vitality : but here was unsoundness and contraction.   Municipal institutions are the earliest that are found in the aggregation of society; and it is by their violent disruption that tyranny has succeeded.   Civilization and all the higher humanities must arise from them, and never can long exist without.   A fire-place may be ornamental in the centre of a large room, but cannot warm it like flues running all the way round and penetrating upward from the floor.   By centralization, and by the abolition of municipal powers, Napoleon utterly subverted the little that was remaining of liberty in France.   Under the worst of the Roman emperors, all the towns of Italy were in the full enjoyment of civil freedom, unvext by arbitrary taxes and by magistrates sent from other places, because they retained their municipal institutions.   These have outlived the irruptions of barbarians and the changes of dynasties; and the title of the chief magistrate is still the same as Horace found it on the road to Brundusium.

"Fidenarumque potestas,"

continues in the office of *podestà*.   Hence it is that the States of Italy, and particularly the upper and central, are better adapted than any other on the Continent of Europe, excepting the most virtuous of men, the inhabitants of Biscay, to that form of government towards which all are hastening.

In the *Examiner* of June 30, 1839, Landor returned to the charge :—

Lord Brougham's " Sketches of Statesmen."

[THIRD NOTICE.]

P. 65. "When the *senseless folly* was stated of clinging by colonies wholly useless and merely expensive, [which all admit must sooner or later assert their independence and be severed from the Mother Country, none of all this was denied, nor indeed could be ; but the answer was, that no government whatever could give up any part of its dominions without being compelled by force, and that history afforded no example of such a surrender without an obstinate struggle. What more did Lord North, and the other authors of the disgraceful contest with America, than act upon this bad principle?] "

The American colonies ought to have been "clung by"; but as a mother clings to her child, and not as a rattle-snake to its prey. We lost America by arrogance and injustice: we attempted to retain her by violence; we might have conciliated her by equitable concession. She was unprepared for the separation which we forced upon her; and nothing but the divine mission, of the greatest man whom God ever sent for the salvation of his creatures, could have released her from the worse than Egyptian bondage of a wretch more obstinate and more blind than Pharaoh. Had we been willing to retain the affections of America, had we granted to her the same rights and immunities as we ourselves were enjoying, the French Revolution would never have subverted all social order, and Freedom would have walked in quiet procession through Europe, no phantom, no exterminator. The better half of our navies would have been of American growth and guidance: and if we never should have needed the vigilance and energy of a Nelson, we never should have blushed at the somnolence and the nakedness of a Glenelg. The whole of our American policy has been absurd from the very beginning. In regard to Canada, we should have introduced our own laws and language: the laws instantly; the language after twenty years from the conquest. Language is more efficient than religion itself in the cement and consolidation of a people. Encouragement and allotments of land should have been given to as many Scotch and Irish as were disposed to emigrate. It is not yet too late to fill up this omission.

P. 66. "[No man ever till now had the assurance to put forward, as a general principle, so profligate a rule of conduct; amounting indeed to this, that] when any set of politicians find their avowed and recorded opinions inconsistent with the holding of office, [they may lay them aside and abdicate the duty of Government while they retain its emoluments and its powers]."

Is this an interpolation? If not, what phrenzy in Lord Brougham to utter such an outcry! In power he would snatch away from the hands of the Irish what, out of power, he thought insufficient for them. In power he would flog and fetter them for insisting on one-half of what his speeches had incited them to demand. What is right in a Canadian is wrong in an Irishman ; what was pleasing to the Gentleman of Cumberland is offensive to the Seigneur of Cannes.

P. 67. "Such are the points upon which the Ministers of the Crown are expected to have *exactly* no opinion ; alone of the whole community to stand mute and inactive, neither thinking, *neither* stirring, and to do just precisely neither more nor less than—nothing."

Sometimes a speaker or writer is allowed a superfluous word or two for euphony or ornament ; but this *exactly*, this *precisely*, this poor family of inoperative *neithers*, are as destitute of decoration as of utility.

P. 67. "Every man, be he Statesman or *individual*."

Iterum Crispinus ! But is not a Statesman what ladies and gentlemen are in the habit of calling an *individual*? No, no : I stand corrected. Lord Brougham himself has been two individuals, and very lately, and has shown us how wide is the difference between an *individual* and a *Statesman*.

P. 74. "The *effect* of his [Lord Loughborough's] eloquence upon a very favourable audience, certainly, and in a season of great public violence and delusion, for it was against the Americans, and before the Privy Council, at the commencement of the revolt, *are* well known."

What an excellent imitation of Burnet's style ! But Burnet had more respect for grammar than this Coryphæus of the *Edinburgh Review*. There is a chance that the Bishop would have written, "the effect *is*."

P. 75. "[When the ambassadors were met to sign the Peace of Versailles, by which the independence of America was acknowledged, Franklin retired, in order to change his dress and affix his name to the treaty in those very garments which he wore when attending the Privy Council, and which he had kept by him for the purpose many years], a little inconsistently, [it must be confessed, with the language of contemptuous indifference used by him at the moment.]"

Franklin *did* despise, as well he might, the impudence and ribaldry of Wedderburn. Nor was there any *inconsistency* in his retiring to change his dress at Versailles. Forty-four years ago, I heard from Mr Kempson, who accompanied Lord Auckland on his mission to the Hague, what Franklin had related to that diplomatist. He went in a court dress to attend the Privy Council, on which occasion he was called a *hoary traitor* by the shameless Scotsman. On his return he took off his coat, and folding it up carefully, thus soliloquized it. 'Lie there! I will put thee on again, when yon cock crows lower.' . . .

> P. 77. "[There can be no doubt that his object at all times was to gain]
> That great prize of the profession
> Which he at last reduced into possession."

Can we wonder that the best poets have been despised by such a poet as this? To "reduce a prize into possession" is far above the flights of Milton.

> P. 81. "[The Parliament of Ireland, it is to be remarked, did not, in the earlier case, pursue the same course with that of Great Britain.] Our fellow-citizens, although dwelling farther from the rising sun, are more devotedly given to its worship than ourselves. [They . . . at once addressed the Prince of Wales to take upon him the Government.]"

Here, in the first member of the sentence, the *rising sun* is really and truly that great luminary which we are in the habit of seeing, more or less, several days in the year; in the second it is a metaphor, in allusion to that effeminate and heartless wretch, whom, in scorn to antiquity, and in wrong even to profligacy itself, we call our Sardanapalus. Part of a sentence ought never to be composed of metaphor and the other part of that whence the metaphor is drawn. When we set the jewel we remove the plasma. . . .

> P. 83. "The marriage *de facto*, legal or illegal, which he [the Prince of Wales] had contracted with a Catholic lady, &c."

Mr Fox declared in the House of Commons that no such marriage was contracted. He knew the contrary; and Mr Errington, the relative of the lady, told Mr Fox that the Prince, and whoever else denied it, lied.

> P. 83. "[A disputed succession and] intestine tumults such as she [England] had not experienced since the days of the two roses."

Spain, I believe, is the only country in Europe in which such tumults as those under the *two roses* can be excited by a similar cause at the present day. And those are mistaken who imagine that a king or a queen is the object of contention in that country. The ancient rights of the Biscayans were violated by the central government, and an independence which had been acknowledged and respected by all the kings of Spain was declared null and void. Whoever has lived among that incomparable people will heartily wish them success, and confidently augur it, against the most degenerate of men, the slothful, worn-out Castilians. It would be well if all Spain were free ; but it is far more important that Biscay should remain so than that all the rest should become so. We know that Biscay, for thousands of years, has treated liberty as well as liberty has treated her; but we may shrewdly suspect from recent experience, that it will be long before the mass of Spaniards can be softened into humanity and moulded into freedom.

P. 87. "This wholesome lesson, and indeed useful warning, is above all required when we are called upon to *contemplate* a professional and political life so eminently prosperous as the one [Lord Loughborough's] which we have been *contemplating*."

The word *contemplate* was not used formerly on low and trivial occasions. No corruption of a language is so pernicious as the employment of such expressions on such subjects, by which they become unfit for the higher. *Gigantic, palmy, unearthly,* &c., are now the mode ; and we may expect a succession of annuals from the hot-houses and steam of our novelists. . . .

A specimen is given by Lord Brougham of Thurlow's wit. Another, I believe, constitutes all that ever was attributed to him. Bishop Watson, a great blusterer and boaster, and a defender of Christianity without a belief in it, had just presented his sermons to the King. He came to a dinner-party where Thurlow was, and began to expatiate on the freedom with which he had addressed his sovereign, when Thurlow turned suddenly round, and growled, "He said it ! G— d— him ; he no more said it than he said his prayers." Chancery wit assuredly is not borrowed from the theatre of Molière. . . .

P. 115. "Writing at a time when good or even correct composition was little studied, and in the newspapers hardly ever met with, his polished style [the style of Junius], though very far from being a correct one, and farther still from good pure English, being made the vehicle of abuse, sarcasm, and pointed invective, naturally excited a degree of attention which was further maintained by the boldness of his proceedings."

Surely so languid and so perplext a sentence ought not to come forward [from] the castigator of Junius. The style of this writer, it is true, has many faults, and grave ones. It has point without aim, and vigour without agility. Wit alone can long bear up the shafts of surcasm ; and the wit of Junius had only one leg to stand on, a stiff and swollen one. His flashy and figured invectives, like court-dresses, would fit half the court as well as they fitted the person they were made for; if, indeed, like the prefaces of Sallust and Cicero, they were not kept ready until the author had found or contrived a place for their exhibition. At the present day there are several newspapers, on both sides, written much more correctly than the letters of Junius ; but it hardly can be said that "correct composition was *little* studied," although it was studied by few, in the times of Bower, Johnson, Burke, Goldsmith, Shipley, Hurd, Inchbald, Carter, Harris, Lowth, and Blackstone. For one inelegance or incorrectness in the least excellent of these, I could easily find seven in the most popular of those who are, coarsely but aptly, denominated the *crack* authors of the present day.

We have seen, indeed, no great writer since the days of the *Commonwealth*, yet several have written correctly and eloquently. The subjects of these are not of extent and solidity enough to comprehend the present, the past, and the future, but occasional and transitory, and their march does not require the excitement of the full band. Why will not some powerful man stand up in the midst of us, with his eyes direct on Bossuet and Massilon, resolute to compete with, since it is impossible to excel them. After the reading of these authors, it must be acknowledged that Cicero himself, in many parts of his various works, appears—I dare not say frivolous, I will not say vainglorious—it is enough to say, rhetorical and scholastic. There are matters, not of religion or politics, of high and lasting interest, and such as would amply and becomingly occupy the most powerful genius. The highest rank, whether in prose or poetry, is not to be obtained by doing small things well, but great things worthily.

WALTER SAVAGE LANDOR.

On August 6, 1839, in the House of Lords, Lord Brougham moved five resolutions against the Irish policy of the Government, and made a long speech in which he denounced Landor's friend, Lord Normanby.

This irritated Landor even more than careless writing, and, with other utterances, incited him to address another letter to the *Examiner*, printed in its issue of October 6.

The Misconduct of Lord Brougham.

Sept. 29, 1839.

SIR,

In your *Examiner* of this day you have forestalled a few of the observations which I was about to send to you, in the evening, on the late conduct of Lord Brougham. The remainder of what I wrote on his "Statesmen," some months ago, would occupy too much of your paper, and shall therefore be published separately. There are several points on which we do not quite agree; and in these times of utter intolerance, I hold it very manly in you to grant admittance to the less congenial of my opinions. About Lord Brougham, however, no two honest men can differ, after your masterly exposure of his manifold contradictions. *You* speak out : *I* dare not say that I never found in any other author, ancient or modern, so much of insincerity and falsehood : I dare not say it, for Lord Brougham is a very great and a very choleric man ; and I am a very humble and a very timid one : but I will venture to affirm that in none whatsoever have I found so much which I am unable to reconcile, by any process of ratiocination, with what I believe to be sincerity and truth. Again, I dare not say I never saw in any one so much of arrogance, impudence, and presumption ; but with my hand horizontally above my eyes, and lowering them to the closest inspection, never have I descried what *appeared* to me so extremely like them. I may be asked if I think myself capable of setting right so great a personage. No, indeed. Great personages are never to be set right. This is the only criterion I know of greatness. Really and truly is it, like the globe we inhabit, *ponderibus librata suis.*

.   .   .   .

Had he been less mischievous, his abilities had been less noticed, although they have the pliancy and multiplicity of a polypus. But every man springs up from his seat to see an attack made against the first Governor[1] of Ireland who had pacified, by pacific means, that abused and indignant nation; and many find an original genius in him who chooses to assault, as the weakest point or the most offensive, an over-exertion of generosity and clemency. What is yet more stimulating to curiosity, is to witness a Lord Chancellor, with a mask over his face, but with robe and wig flying full behind him, and with innumerable nods to obtain the recognition of his party, run out of Parliament, dart across the Park, spring up the staircase of Buckingham House, and give a loud slap on the face—to whom? to a groom? to a valet? to a lord-in-waiting? No; to the Queen herself; to the Queen upon the throne; exercising the duties and exalting the dignity of her station.

Sir, I confess to you I find it difficult to disengage, in high life, the idea of *tory* from the idea of *gentleman*. Can Tories look on and see this? Can they receive with open arms, the outcast of the Whigs, the insulter—I will not say of a woman, I will not say of a young and high-born lady whom they universally call ill-protected and misled (a double claim on them), but of a Queen! an hereditary idol! And whence all this fury? Because her uncle fell asleep in the midst of the man's harangue, and, on awakening, rebuffed his familiarity. Lord Brougham has yet to learn many secrets of human nature: among the rest is this: that it is not every vulgar mind that is constant to vulgarity, nor every elegant one that at all hours is disposed to repudiate her. The first part of this lesson he might have learnt from William the Fourth, the latter he may collect from his admission to the society of Lord Wellesley.

WALTER SAVAGE LANDOR.

After all this denunciation of Lord Brougham's iniquities, it may be a relief to find Landor in a more benevolent mood. A note printed under the heading "Fine Arts" in the *Examiner* of August 16, 1840, gives an account of the discovery of Dante's portrait in the Palazzo Pretorio, generally known as the Bargello, at Florence, now the National Museum. A coloured

[1] Lord Normanby.

sketch and afterwards a tracing of the portrait was made by Mr Kirkup. Signor Aubrey Bezzi has been mentioned more than once in Landor's private letters.

Dante's Portrait.

A grand discovery has been made at Florence of some Frescoes by Giotto. They exist in a lumber-room, formerly the chapel of the *Palazzo del Podestà*, which became the residence of the Duke of Athens when he took possession of the republic. It was afterwards converted into a prison, and called the Bargello. In the year preceding the exile of Dante, the portrait of that poet was painted on the walls of this chapel, together with Brunetto, Latini, Corso Donati, and other illustrious citizens of the Florentine Commonwealth. Several coats of whitewash had covered them over, so that not a vestige was perceptible. The first who proposed to bring them into light again was the Canonico Moreni, a very distinguished antiquarian, now advanced in years. Cioni, professor of chemistry, discovered a mode of removing the lime and plaster, without injuring the solid *intonaco* underneath. But, as the modern artists of Italy, and particular the Florentines, entertain small reverence for their ancient predecessors, not even the majesty of Giotto was recognised by them; and Moreni found very few voices to second him in his application to the authorities. At last, after twenty more years, Mr Aubrey Bezzi, a gentleman no less intelligent than zealous in everything that relates either to the arts or to letters, presented, in the month of May 1839, his first petition to resuscitate the most illustrious of the Italians, their earliest great painter and their greatest poet. Several months elapsed; at last an answer, an evasive one, was given. It stated that "the Grand Duke would not be advised to undertake the restoration of the fresco, without ascertaining first the *exact* cost; and that his dignity prevented him from profiting by Mr Aubrey Bezzi's offer *of incurring the whole expense.*"

To overcome this difficulty, Mr Aubrey Bezzi sent in another memorial, offering to accomplish the undertaking for two hundred and fifty *francesconi*, or dollars, which the Grand Duke might re-emburse when the operation was completed. After a delay of many additional months, he obtained a decree, appointing him a commissioner, with two others, and limiting the expense to two hundred and fifty dollars; which moderate sum has actually sufficed. The figures are unimpaired. In one compartment is a Holy Family, with an angel, which those who have seen it, and are capable of estimating it, represent as of great beauty. It was offered by the authorities to Mr Aubrey Bezzi, who declined to mar the unity of the work by removing any part of it.

There are artists to whom the recovery of a painting by Giotto will be uninteresting: there are others, and some persons not artists, who will receive the intelligence of it with the same enthusiasm as of a hymn by Homer. To such, and such only, is this discovery announced. We now possess, what was wanting until now, a sure original portrait of Dante: and we, and our descendants all over the world, must own ourselves indebted for it to the indefatigable zeal of Mr Aubrey Bezzi.

WALTER SAVAGE LANDOR.

CHAPTER II
1843—1847

R

CHAPTER II

1843—1847

On August 4, 1843, in the House of Lords, Lord Brougham called attention to what he described as a libellous article in the *Examiner*, which charged him with insinuating that Cobden had recommended private assassination. He afterwards brought an action against the paper, employing artifices in support of his case which were stigmatised by Mr Greville as foolish and base. Landor seems to have thought that his own connection with the *Examiner* required him to join in the fray, and accordingly sent the following letter which was printed on August 26 :—

Lord Brougham and the Examiner.

August 17, 1843.

Sir,

The prosecution with which you are threatened by Lord Brougham might well be expected from every facette of his polygonal character. He began his literary and political life with a scanty store of many small commodities. Long after he set out, the witty and wise Lord Stowell said of him, that he wanted only a little law to fill up the vacancy. His shoulders were not over-burdened by the well-padded pack he bore on them ; and he found a ready sale, where such articles find the readiest, in the town of Edinburgh. Here he entered into a confederacy (the word *conspiracy* may be libellous) to defend the worst atrocities of the French, and to cry down every author to whom England was dear and venerable. A better spirit now prevails in the *Edinburgh*

Review, from the generosity and genius of Macaulay. But in the days when Brougham and his confederates were writers in it, more falsehood and more malignity marked its pages than any other Journal in the language. And here is the man who cries out he is wounded! the recreant who, screaming for help, aims a poisoned dagger at the vigorous breast that crushes him to the ground.

Had he no respect for the tenets by which he made his fortune? Has he none for a superiority of intellectual power which leaves to him superiority of station? This eminently bad writer and reasoner brings an action for slander on many counts, at the summit of which is "because it is *despicable*." Now did ever man or cat fly at the eyes for a thing *beneath his notice* : and such is the meaning of *despicable* among us who have learnt Latin and who write English. What other man within the walls of Parliament, however hasty, rude, and petulant, hath exhibited such manifold instances of bad manners, bad feelings, bad reasonings, bad language, and bad law? They who cannot be what they want to be, resolve on notoriety in any shape whatever. Each House exhibits a specimen of this genus, pinned to the last pages of its Journals. Such notoriety can in no manner be more readily attained than by suddenly turning round on one leg, showing how agile is old age in this step, and then appealing to you whether the Terpsichorist has ever changed countenance or colour, from youth upwards. Meanwhile the toothless jaws are dropping, on both sides, the slaver of wrath and dotage.

How many things are published with impunity which are more injurious to a man's character, more detrimental to his fortune and interest, than a great proportion of those which the law calls libellous! Suppose an author, who has devoted his whole life to some particular study, writes a book upon it; suppose it is in any manner displeasing to Lord Brougham, whether on its own account or the author's; would he hesitate, has he ever hesitated, to inflict an irremediable wound? Dexterity in mischief is applauded; the sufferer is derided. Easily may a weaker, who watches the opportunity, trip up a stronger. Similar feats are the peculiar gratification of coarse and vulgar minds. Has no virtuous man of genius bled to death under the scourge of such a critic as Brougham?

Years of application, if years were yet allowed him, would be insufficient to place him in the festive seat, which a crueller hand than a murderer's made vacant. On the contrary, the accusations brought against Lord Brougham, by the *Examiner*, could be shown by his Lordship to be true or false within a single hour, and the fact be rendered apparent to the whole nation before nightfall. But here no vindictive spirit can exert its agency : no lightning of phosphorus runs along the benches of the Lords ; no thunder as awful shakes the woolsack.

Wavering as he is by habit, malicious as he is by nature, it is evident that Lord Brougham says and does the greater part of his sayings and doings for no other purpose than to display his ability in defending them. He dazzles us by no lights of eloquence, he attracts us by not even a fictitious flue-warmth ; but he perplexes and makes us stare and stumble by his angular intricacies and sudden glares. Not a sentence of his speeches or writings will be deposited in the memory as rich or rare ; and even what is strange will be cast out of it for what is stranger, until this goes too. Is there a housewife who keeps a cupboardful of cups without handle or bottom ; a selection of brokages and flaws ?

I am, Sir, &c.,
W. S. LANDOR.

Within a week or two, Landor's attention was diverted to a matter of foreign politics. The affairs of modern Greece were only a degree less interesting to him than the glory of Athens in the age of Pericles. "The liberation of Greece is the heirloom of our dreams," he makes Horne Tooke say. Again, his imaginary Dr Johnson propounds something like a definite plan, however impractical, for securing the prosperity of the Greeks of to-day. " Greece ought to be preserved and guarded by the rulers of the world as a cabinet of gems, open and belonging to them all. Whatever is the fate of other countries, whatever

changes may be introduced, whatever laws imposed
whatever tributes exacted, she should preserve he
lineaments uneffaced." *Dis aliter visum*, to use ;
phrase which Landor, in a note to the second editior
of " Gebir," insists has generally been misunderstood
The elevation of Otho of Bavaria to the throne o
Greece in 1832 had turned out ill.   Writing ten year:
later, De Quincey said :—" The prospects at presen
are not brilliant.   A Government and a Court, drawi
from a needy aristocracy like the Bavarian, are no
suited to a needy people, struggling with the diffi
culties of a new colony."   In the autumn of 184:
there was a crisis at Athens.   A new Ministry wa:
established by the revolutionary party, who called oi
the National Assembly to prepare a fresh Constitution
Reports reached London that King Otho had beei
driven from his throne and had taken refuge on boarc
a ship off the Piræus ; but though this proved untrue
the King only saved himself by timely compliance
with the demands of Demetri Calergi and his asso
ciates.   The *Examiner* of September 16, 1843, con
tained the following letter from Landor :—

Greece and King Otho.

Sir,
        A desire has been expressed to me, from more than on
quarter, that I would recall the attention of your readers to the actua
state of Greece.   Certainly the time is unfavourable, for after th
courtesies, and (let us hope) the cordialities of Kings and Queens,
the excited mind is not easily fixed down on the commonplac
interests of a distant nation ; but, in the opinion of many, ou

---

[1] An allusion to the visit of the Queen and Prince Albert to the King (Loui
Philippe) and Queen of the French.

honour is concerned in the administration of a government we assisted in imposing. It has been demonstrated to Parliament by the principal men of both parties that King Otho has failed in his engagements, both to his people and his protectors. Having thus failed, my question is, whether he has not forfeited all right to assistance from the one, and to allegiance from the other.

In their insurrection against the Turks greatly more than half the male population, between the ages of twenty and forty, had been slain. No nation since the light of Christianity has beamed on the world had suffered so severely, at least in Europe. The Turkish authorities, we are informed by Lord Palmerston, had determined on carrying off the whole of the people, and on transporting to Africa and selling into slavery all who escaped the sword. What his Lordship calls a civil war had been raging from 1820 to 1826, and he tells us "it was devastating *the whole face* of the Morea." Ay! indeed, it was devastating a little more than the beauty-spots of the face; it was exhausting the heart itself of the last blood within it. And so we suffered six whole years to elapse, tame lookers-on!

And when the six years had elapsed, what did we? Doubtless we repaid the scattered and homeless children of Greece an instalment of the debt so long due to their ancestors for instruction in our best literature; doubtless we ensured to them protection in their cottages or their caves, for all our refinements in the arts, for the statues in our halls, and even for the lamps that light them. We promised them this, indeed, and more; we promised them exemption from the sword and slavery, we promised them free institutions. And what was done? A young prince, who probably had never heard of Greece until he was called up by his tutor to govern her, a creature of a character even more imbecile and fantastical than his father, is erected into the tutelary deity of Greece! Even under the Turks municipal rights, the best part of all Governments, Royal or Republican, were respected; but under this doll, which the people were commanded to kiss and cuddle, no vestige of them is remaining. As for taxation, King Otho squanders in one year a greater sum than entered the Treasury at Constantinople in two; and all this is extorted from a population diminished by half since the incursion of the Mahomedans.

Sir, to me, and to many in Greece, it appears far more desirable that England should insist on the performance of *all* the engagements on the part of King Otho, than that the people, now under the curse of his Government, should be indebted to the French Chambers for justice, or that another insurrection should place them, like the Servians, under the sceptre of their co-religionists.

Here permit me to lay before the public the words I have just received from a citizen of Athens :—

"When Otho came, the National Assembly of Argos was dismissed; the six thousand veterans of the army were disbanded; an absolute monarchy was imposed, and a national debt contracted. A *good tyranny* might possibly have been useful; but ours has been despicably mean, flagrantly dishonest, and injurious to every interest. The national force and the national legislature were taken from us; and, that the minds of our youth may lapse into barbarism under the feet of a barbarian, twenty-five professors are now dismissed from the University."

Will any civilized Power, will even Russia herself, see and uphold, or even tolerate, this? Would it not be more advantageous, and less disgraceful, if the Greeks again threw themselves prostrate before their ancient masters, imploring their milder sway? The Turks, always more honourable, always more observant of treaties, than any Christian Power whatsoever, would repay the money we *forced* the Greeks to borrow. It was not borrowed for their good; it was not borrowed at their request; it was not borrowed even with their consent; and the whole of it has been applied, not to the consolidation of their liberties, but of their bondage. Our political and commercial interests go along with Greek advancement: and much of our stagnant money might find a current through the fertile lands of Greece. Nothing of this is thought about. But "is it not a piteous sight," I am asked, "to see Greeks, eighteen years after the glorious conflict of Missolonghi, emigrating into Turkey?" What answer can I or any Englishman give to this question. We can only meet it with another, which we hope may be consolatory to the unfortunate who depend on the Government of England. "Is it not piteous that brave officers should be disowned by it, and thrown upon the mercy of an Asiatic despot, as ignorant, as irreclaimable, as irresponsible as Otho?" I have only one piece of advice to give the Citizen of Athens.

I will give it in the words of his countryman, entreating him to wait patiently for the signal. There will be many rockets up in the air at once: the first is not for Greece.

Σοὶ μὲν μάχεσθαι, μοῖδε βουλεύειν καλῶς.

Sept. 8.

WALTER SAVAGE LANDOR.

A second letter, entitled "Greece and King Otho," appeared in the *Examiner* of September 23, 1843 :—

Greece and King Otho.

SIR,

In my last letter I laid before the people of England the public conduct of Otho, King of Greece. I proved conclusively that he had violated his engagements with the Powers which placed him on the throne, and with the nation they appointed him to govern. I asked, and I repeat the question, whether allegiance is longer due to him. I now ask whether the English Government, or any other, will compel it. The Greeks have unquestionably the same right to resist and to expel him as the English had to resist and to expel James the Second. After this Revolution, which, for want of a better, was called the *Glorious*, both parties were unanimous that the foreign forces of William should be disbanded.

Yet by means of those forces the great work of our deliverance was accomplished. Do we then expect, or can we desire, that the Bavarians, who came only to devour the harvest which the constancy of the Greeks had reaped, should be constituted the masters of the land, holding for ever the natives in thraldom? Whatever may be the designs of the imbecile men who govern England, or of the powerful and energetic one who preponderates on the continent, or of that sagacious King[1] who has broken the back of the Pyrenees and rules at present on both sides of them, the people of France and its representatives are not become indifferent to the destinies of Greece.

In my last address to you, I stated the public crimes of the

[1] Louis Philippe of France.

puny wretch who is permitted to trample on her. I shall now lay before you certain facts in which the interests of others, and among them of Englishmen, are concerned. But, first, I must revert to my statement that, on the expulsion of the *twenty-five* professors, King Otho, who hesitates at no fraud and blushes at no falsehood, told one of them who remonstrated, that "he must complain of the Allied Powers, not of *him*: that *they* had obliged him to reduce them," an answer well worthy, as is remarked to me, of his Jesuit education and descent. Before he set off for Greece perhaps he may have seen, at no great distance from home, a monarch who robbed the national treasury, and obliged the keepers of it to make false entries. He himself is so deficient in common honesty that he never has paid for the ground on which his palace stands. Part of this appertained to the American mission, which educated five hundred children, members of the Greek Church, among which children were sixty girls of the upper classes, boarded and instructed. Finlay, an Englishman, a man of talents and enterprise, is owner of another part of the palace site : he has been treated in the same manner. Otho even stole the town water from the aqueduct, applying it to the use of his garden. But this was restored. It was remarked that too little water was likely to have the same effect on the Greeks as too much wine on the English and, like the Abbot of Edmundsbury, King Otho was fain to yield before the distaffs. One of his captains was sent into the country to extort an information from a female. The barbarian thrust a fierce cat into her trousers. Village and city, throughout the land, exclaimed loudly against this worse than Turkish brutality Whether it was by the King's order is uncertain ; but certain it is that he knew it ; certain it is that he spoke of it ; certain it is that his expression was : "le capitaine est un peu trop zélé." This villain was neither shot nor flogged ; and the viler, under whom he acted, is, by the decision of the Great Powers, against the reclamations of a whole people, King of Greece ! I am, &c.,

WALTER SAVAGE LANDOR.

Sept. 19.

A third letter, on "The Revolution at Athens," was printed in the *Examiner* of October 7, 1843 :—

The Revolution at Athens.

SIR,

The two letters you have done me the favour to insert in the *Examiner* were not intended to arouse the animosity or the courage of the Greeks, for which indeed there was no necessity, but to prepare the public mind, in England and upon the Continent, for the great event so happily accomplished.

The deliverance of that nation from insupportable tyranny was accelerated by the very means employed by King Otho to retard it. So true is the Iambic in the Fragments of Euripides,

"Ὅτανδε Δαίμων ἀνδρί πορσυνή κακά
Τὸν νοῦν ἐβλάψε πρῶτον.

Which Erasmus has turned into a Latin verse, and the quoters have turned out again :—

"Quos Jupiter vult perdere dementat prius."

But this is no half-holiday of "play for" criticism. To Greece again, if you please, and rather the present than the ancient one.

Military commissions, with every lawless engine of arbitrary power, were about to be established in all quarters of the country. Sword, imprisonment, free-quarters, torture, were in readiness to put down opposition, to stifle inquiry : in short, to reduce the most enduring of nations to a worse slavery than Turk, or Albanian, or Egyptian ever imposed. The exciting shock given at Athens was felt simultaneously at the extremities of the land, and signals shone from Hymettus to Maléa. Retaliation for the most intolerable injuries never entered the brave open heart of the plundered villager or the disbanded soldier. The one was contented to have suffered scorn and indigence, the other to have bled profusely for his country.

I promised you that my third letter should be my last in exposing the iniquities of Otho. For I knew well enough that a period was about to be placed to them, although I knew not precisely the day. Permit me, sir, through the *Examiner*, to make an appeal to the generosity and justice both of England and of France ; submitting to the Ministers and Legislature of each country, whether it would be proper and honourable to exact from the people of Greece repayment of subsidies which Otho, a King imposed on that people by the subsidizers, diverted not only from the service of the State, but against its interests and honour. We have already enabled that improvident and disgraceful youth to oppress and impoverish his subjects ; by their own high spirit the oppression is shaken off ; by our common honesty, let the impoverishment be at least alleviated. An affluent father should be accountable for the extravagances of an uncorrected son.

In a crude and inefficient project of abolishing the slavery of the Blacks, we unsacked at once on the floor of the House of Commons the enormous sum of twenty millions. The present generation of Englishmen was no party to the iniquitous traffic ; the chains of the unhappy Blacks were forged of old ; but we ourselves, we who are now living, we who exult in freedom and boast loudly of imparting it, have put a strong hand to every rivet in which Otho held the Greeks.

If the insurgents had failed in their undertaking, if the most glorious (because the most pacific and merciful) of revolutions, had been procrastinated, we might then indeed have seized on the defaulter, and have constrained him to refund the money. And indeed this advice I should have given ; in the certainty that such a pressure would have excited the people to cast off so ignominious a yoke. Otherwise it would have been the worst inhumanity, since it was by means of this very money that he was enabled to exercise his vexations. It is less than justice, it is an inadequate and a paltry compensation for the sufferings we have been the main instruments of inflicting, if we remit to the oppressed what we would have demanded from the oppressor.

I have received an " Inquiry " from a well-intentioned, calm, and reasonable man, on " *the necessity and policy* " of my last expostula-tion. He asks me whether, in case so virtuous and temperate a Minister as Sir Robert Peel, who lets everything have its own course in our own dominions, were disposed to interfere in the affairs of Greece, he yet would countenance any "violent measures" against King Otho.

Now, what measures can he mean are violent ? I never have demanded of Sir Robert Peel to scourge this youth, or even to con-fine and seclude him. Perhaps it is a bad example to the world that princes should be punished: certainly it is, if Ministers are responsible : if not, what is to be done? Are no boundaries to be fixed to the licence of power and to the sufferings of humanity? But my language, it appears, was "rather strong." Wiser and greater men have formerly used, in behalf of the same people, much stronger language against more elevated potentates. They certainly never were censured for it; but, on the contrary, have been recommended both for their sentiments and for their expression of them ; and they continue to be exhibited in admonitory contrast with the declamation and verbosity we are accustomed to hear from the sycophants and revilers of disgusted kings, the itinerant orators of the human race, the Clootzes, continental and insular. I wish at all times to say what is requisite, and never more. It is needless to add that I would not willingly undertake what must be unsuccessful. But I venture to entertain the hope, whatever may be the defects of my language, whether too strong or too weak, that it will not be uttered in vain. For not only in former ages, and in the country whose cause I am pleading, but likewise in our own days, and in more than one other country, unworthy and unprofitable princes, although they neither were nor could be oppressors, have been thrust aside. Europe never saw, contemporaneously, two Sovereigns so well adapted to the period and the people as the Emperor Nicholas and King Louis Philippe. Their courage and firmness have established them on thrones from which it was requisite, for the honour and happiness of their nations, to remove the legitimate heirs. Is it then probable that these potentates, the most sagacious that ever governed their respective countries, who excluded the unworthy of their own houses, should hesitate, if necessary, to wave away from Greece a far more unworthy alien? Perhaps it may be humane in them to wait until he relapses into his insanity. Nothing can they discover in Otho but a thriftless scion, not only not producing the fruits that were expected from it, but exhausting and corrupting the whole branch on which in an evil hour it was engrafted.

Ulterior steps must be taken for the maintenance and security of what has been achieved. The Powers adjacent to Greece are Turkey, Austria, and England. These are most interested in preserving her from the domination of Russia. Few, who have not travelled and resided some time in Germany, and conversed with the intelligent of that country, which contains three-fourths of all the intelligence of the world, few, I repeat, are aware how paramount and preponderating is the influence of Russia on surrounding states : few know or suspect the vast resources of the Emperor ; few are aware that Russia, like ancient Rome, is undeviating in aggression. Systems do not change in that country as in England ; one Minister does not raise up his power on the broken plans and thwarted measures of another, reckless if, while his faction is upholden, his country falls. The arm of Marlborough, outstretched for the deliverance of Europe, was paralysed at Utrecht; and greatly more than Wellington did was undone at Vienna. But in Russia the fiercest barbarism is guided by the most sagacious policy. The sword of Suwarof shivered the throne of Sobieski, smote the crescent where it rose in the East, and was only checked by the glaciers of the Alps. For nearly two centuries no reverses have diminished the power, abated the influence, counteracted the policy, or shortened the strides of Russia. At present, with true and deep wisdom, she abstains from injuring and irritating us : but she will not let us do what is right unless we let her do what is wrong.

Although France, not lying on the confines of Greece, has certainly less pretension than the adjacent states to interfere in her concerns, it is a wise, because it is a conciliatory policy, to invite her to assist in holding up one side of the pall at this miraculous resuscitation from the dead. At the same time, however, Belgium and Holland and Prussia should be witnesses and trustees.

WALTER SAVAGE LANDOR.

The letter which Landor wrote to Daniel O'Connell in 1838 has already been quoted. In May 1844 O'Connell, having been tried and found guilty on a charge of conspiracy, was sentenced by the Court of Queen's Bench at Dublin to a year's imprisonment and a fine of £2000. Three months later the House of Lords reversed the judgment of the Court, and O'Connell was set at liberty ; but in the meantime the *Examiner* of June 22 had published a memorial to the Queen, written by Landor, and signed by a number of residents at Bath. "We are happy," said the *Examiner*, "to lay before our readers an argument so temperate and forcible. Men of all parties may read it with advantage.' The text of the Memorial was as follows :—

Mr O'Connell's Imprisonment.

"We, the undersigned, inhabitants of Bath, yielding to none in loyalty toward your gracious Majesty or in veneration of our established laws, crave to approach the throne with our petition.

We pray of your gracious Majesty that the Royal mercy may be extended to Daniel O'Connell, against whom a verdict of 'Guilty' was delivered in Dublin on a charge of conspiracy, and who at this time is suffering the penalty of fine and imprisonment.

We presume not to question the justice of the sentence, nor the composition of the jury; but we implore your Majesty's pardon of the offence on these considerations.

First. That the Act of Union, which we hope will be indissoluble, was brought about by such practices as would disfranchise any borough in England.

Secondly. That Ireland did not obtain by it such advantages as were obtained by Scotland; namely, that the religion of the majority should be the established religion of the land.

We reflect with shame and sorrow that Ireland at the present hour is treated less liberally in regard to religion than Greece was treated under the dominion of the Turks, which dominion she was aided in overthrowing by the arms of England. And yet the Turks do not 'profess and call themselves Christians.'

We remember by what evil counsels two millions of British subjects in America were severed from the dominion of England. They had incomparably less cause of complaint than, according to the public opinion of Europe, Ireland always had, and has : on the correctness of which opinion it is not our duty or our wish to speak. Two millions, who had no free states to sympathise with them, were able, contrary to the expectation of many wise and experienced

statesmen, to declare and enforce their independence. Seeing tha
Ireland, at the present day, contains seven millions of malcontents
seeing that the nearest and the most powerful nations are ready to
espouse her cause, and omit no opportunity of displaying thei
sentiments, of uttering their threats, and of attacking the weak wh
are under your Majesty's protection ; we cannot dissemble th
danger we apprehend, nor can we believe that it is remote.

We doubt not that your Majesty's most dutiful Parliament wil
readily grant all supplies which your Majesty's Ministers (for an
purpose) may demand. But, in the poverty, the want, the almos
famine, which three millions of your Majesty's subjects are enduring
and under the long and hopeless loss of employment which anothe
million, for the most part manufacturers and artificers, impatientl
bear and angrily lament, we doubt whether it is possible to add t
the national debt, in one year, even so moderate a sum as thirt
millions of money ; a sum which we know by experience is quit
insufficient for the first year's expenditure. We are assured by th
highest authority in military affairs, that a little war is beneath th
dignity of England : we believe that it lies not in human power t
circumscribe the extent of the calamity, or in human sagacity t
calculate its duration : and we are certain that not only one peopl
nor only one continent, is alert and eager to meet us again in arms.

Formerly, when a tempestuous tide of war set in, we considere
Ireland as the great breakwater of our country ; we grieve to se
this breakwater loosened in the whole length of its foundations, an
propelled against us. We know how much easier it is to alienat
the affections of a people than to recover them when once estranged
but we believe that the virtues of your Majesty will atone for th
errors of your predecessors ; and we are confident that a single wor
of your Majesty may silence for ever that turbulence which the mos
eloquent and potent man in the empire has for a time, and perhap
only for a time, suppressed.

We deprecate the unwise and (as it seems to us) somewhat hars
and inhumane, threat that Ireland is to be conquered again. Sh
has been conquered four times already, and by the four wisest of ou
governors : Henry II., Elizabeth, Cromwell, and William. But
part was yet unwon ; a part which your Majesty has never failed t
win elsewhere ; the heart of the people. This is a conquest fa

beyond the reach of the sword, and your Majesty, without the hand or the voice of another, can achieve it.

We reflect with shame and sorrow that every other part of your Majesty's dominions is more favoured than Ireland in that which is dearest to a virtuous man, namely, in the maintenance of his religion.

We reflect with shame and sorrow that greater indulgence was recently shown to the impurest idolatry of Asia than to the religion of a Fenelon and a More.

And we cannot but wonder that all the eloquence and all the influence of Daniel O'Connell have been sufficient to restrain the passions of his countrymen, seeing these things.

We attribute solely to his great exertions the tranquil state of Ireland, which no other man in six hundred years hath been able to establish.

We entreat of your Majesty to render it durable by that gracious act, which will of itself be the truest and surest Act of Union ; and we shall be rejoiced to see the accession of seven millions to your family.

And your petitioners shall ever pray, &c., &c."

Writing to his friend Mrs (now Lady) Graves-Sawle in July 1847, Landor said that he was "outrageous against the Ministers for their action against the Liberals in Oporto"; and a week later he mentioned that he had written a petition to Parliament on the subject. In a leading article printed in the *Examiner* of June 26, 1847, that paper had warmly advocated a union of Spain and Portugal. "The old policy of *divide et impera*," it wrote, "to divide the Peninsula, to make one portion a check upon the other, is a selfish and a narrow policy. What we must desire, is to see the Peninsula great and completely independent, the Tagus its natural river and Lisbon its sea-port." This was also a favourite project of Landor's. He, moreover, as appears from his private letters, was "outrageous" about the proceedings of the British squadron under Admiral Sir William Parker, who, on June 14, accompanied by Portuguese, French, and Spanish vessels, had entered the harbour of Setubal and summoned the insurgents under Sa da Bandiera to surrender. The *Examiner* of July 3, 1847, contained the following communication from Landor:—

Portugal and Spain.

Frequently has it occurred to me that statesmen in this country are seldom to be found at the helm, and appear to think the best office is the purser's. The guides and guardians of the public mind occupy no seat in either House of Parliament. Our leading journalists not only possess incomparably more ability, but exercise it generally with more discretion. Whenever I have happened to differ in opinion from the *Examiner*, I have doubted my own judgment. It gratifies me exceedingly to find him announcing in his paper of June 26, a sentiment which I have always entertained, and publicly upheld in writing; namely, the advantage which Portugal and Spain would equally possess by the union of the two kingdoms.

Independence has a charm in the very sound of it; the first struggles of a child and the last of a man are for independence. But there is an intermediate stage in which union is the chief blessing of existence; a state in which are sought and enjoyed mutual love, mutual succour, mutual hopes and aims. This is also the condition of nations. The true policy of Spain and Portugal is perfect union, and the true policy of England is to cement it. Europe has lost her balance long ago. England in her short-sightedness helped to overturn it, by the severance of Belgium, which in twenty years France will re-annex to her dominions; but England may recover, by the conjunction of Spain and Portugal, a fresh poising power. It is not to be wondered at that men who see indistinctly things close under their eyes, see less clearly things remote. As the greater stars are farther from sight than the less, so are greater and more momentous objects. But political power and court favour are more attractive to minute and wavering minds than any present advantage of their country, or any future glory of their own. Recent events have given us manifest proofs that the interest of families is sought rather to be upheld than the rights of nations. A German comes from a German, whispers into the ear of a German, and this last German tells the Ministers of England what he wishes to see done. To gratify him, and those near him, a personal friend of his is sent over to Portugal on pretence of mediation. He mediates; on one side only. His registered and produceable orders enjoin impartiality; what were the secret ones may reasonably be suspected by his impunity, by his utter escape from censure, even from disavowal. A minister of Foreign Affairs would never offend so exalted a person as this mediator's patron. Policy turns round suddenly; the perjured are maintained in the rights of perjury; the violators of that trust of which we are joint trustees are held sacred; the defenders of that trust of which we are joint trustees are seized, confined in the holds of pestilential ships, chained, deprived of food, of water, of air, and cast to perish on the shores of Africa. Never since the reign of Charles the Second have English ministers so truckled to the court at home in favour of any court abroad. Never have English admirals been ordered to make prisoners those who defended the constitution we had sanctioned. It is high time to put an end to guarantees. But it is a pity that the Peninsula should see England a rival to France in perfidy, and more than a rival in mutability. Co-operation with that Power is an absurd idea, as was proved in Syria, proved in Egypt, proved in Greece, and proved above all in Spain, relative to which such a prevarication was committed by the Prime Minister of France as would for ever exclude any private man from all respectable society. A prevarication is baser than a lie direct; there is more of craft, of subterfuge, and of insult in it.

We may now withdraw from a confederacy which has lent us no assistance, and conferred on us no honour. Better let nations settle their own affairs in their own way. Portugal may remember that we have expended much treasure and much blood in her defence; she *must* remember that we have done her a greater injury than all our past services can atone for, in baffling her arms and in stigmatizing her cause ; but, whether united to Spain or separate, her interest will render her, as we have always found her, our truest and best ally. If united, she will draw Spain into her policy.

WALTER SAVAGE LANDOR.

Landor's opinions on the Irish question are scattered at large through his published writings. Nowhere, perhaps, are they formulated with more preciseness than in the appendix to " Pericles and Aspasia," which his editor did not think it necessary to republish. He was no Home Ruler, but he demanded justice for Ireland. "We have no right," he said, "and no interest to withhold one atom of what belongs in equity as much to Ireland as to Scotland or to England. Give that ; and then proclaim it treason to devise a repeal of the Union."[1] The following letter, printed in the *Examiner* of November 27, 1847, was written at a time when the condition of Ireland was causing grave anxiety. The reference in the opening sentences, to the state of the currency, must be explained by the then recent financial crisis in London, which had led Lord John Russell, on October 25, to authorize the suspension of the Banking Act. With regard to Ireland, the Queen's speech at the opening of the Session, on November 23, stated that " Her Majesty views with the deepest anxiety and interest the present condition of Ireland, and she recommends to the consideration of Parliament measures which, with due regard to the rights of property, may advance the social condition of the people, and tend to the permanent improvement

[1] " Pericles and Aspasia," 1836, vol. ii. p. 307.

of that part of the United Kingdom." Four days later, the *Examiner* published the following letter from Landor :—

The Condition of Ireland.

SIR,

It is right and necessary that all Members of Parliament should be made acquainted with the opinion and resolution of the English people on a question the most imminent and important. In comparison with the state of Ireland, the state of Currency bears the same value as a man's pocket-book bears to his throat.

Away with idle recriminations. The wrongs of Ireland were anterior to her actual rulers, and have been (as far as the Irish themselves would allow it) redressed by them. It would be truly a cold comfort to show, as might be shown, that the worst enemies of Ireland were the worst of England also. Let Ireland no longer be called *Gens ratione furens et mentem pasta Chimæris ;* let Ireland no longer be called ungrateful. Reckless and worthless men continue to claim, as being strictly due to them, a still larger sum than the eleven millions already cast among her scrambling squires, beggars, &c. Now, the Members of Parliament ought to be made aware that to the inconsiderate profuseness of their predecessors must be ascribed much of the present misery and crime of Ireland. Parish priests, Catholic and Protestant, subject to the revision of Justices, would have distributed, without being paid for it, all the money in due portions, well knowing the deserts and necessities of their parishioners, and rendered equitable, if ever disposed to be otherwise, by the watchfulness of their jealousy. By this would have been saved the salaries of ten or eleven thousand agents in various grades, and more than the same number of lives.

The Crown receives from certain royalties in Ireland some £4000 a year. These royalties in the market would have brought half a million of money, and would have employed 10,000 labourers for two urgent years.

The episcopal lands in Ireland were worth lately three millions sterling. Property to the amount of £200,000 a year is held under the bishoprick of Derry. No property finds at all times such ready and such responsible purchasers as redeemable copyhold. We *have* curtailed episcopal revenues; we have spliced two bishopricks into one ; we have struck off several; and not only of late, but formerly, and in what are called the good old times. There is no reason why the whole episcopal territory in Ireland should not be resumed by the Crown for the benefit and salvation of the people, and due allowances made to the prelates. We know how willingly and from what pure motives they surrendered their privileges as Spiritual Peers in Parliament ; how greatly more willingly, and from what motives, if possible, more pure, would they yield the temporal than the spiritual ! But on simple calculation they may reckon on being the gainers. They may fairly expect to receive from the Exchequer £2000 a year regularly ; and is there any one among them—is there any man in England or Ireland—so insane as to believe that their present tenure is worth two years' purchase ? People not only in Ireland, but in England also, are beginning to inquire why the prelates in these countries should be richer than all others in the world; and why the Church of England, in both of them should, as regards temporals, be the only unreformed church in Christendom ? Temporals work upon spirituals, and often powerfully against them. Hatred is excited by inequality and injustice, more especially in seasons of distress.

This is the time to effect the most salutary of reforms. Paying to the Crown annually in future as much as the Crown has received annually in these last seven years for its property in Ireland, and to each bishop £2000 a year ; selling portions of land from seventy to three hundred acres which nobody has cultivated, and paying the proprietors in future as much as they have received annually these last seven years, with the redemption of the copyholds by the noble and gentle tenants, you would find employment and the means of paying for it during the next year and the following. You may look about for other means, and you will not find them, even if you look in earnest. By these you may give labour and wages to 60,000 men, who otherwise will be driven by famine into violence and rebellion. For every labourer you keep unoccupied you must maintain a soldier to keep him down. And how long will this do ? By refusing to alienate the Crown and episcopal lands, you must hold together in the island a military force during many years, of which the expenditure will be greater in twenty months than you are called upon to raise, and to raise from sources which the whole nation is anxious to throw open. Parliament must cease to squander English money. We have already more than enough poverty at home; and we will relieve it as we can; but Parliament shall not extort one shilling more from the English poor-house. Let Ministers clearly understand that there will very soon be meetings in every part of England, protesting against the fruits of English industry going to the support of Irish idleness. It will be resolved—

1. That a great part of the money sent over has been misapplied.

2. That a great number of the richer Irish landlords not only have withdrawn their co-operation, but have exasperated the wretchedness of their tenantry.

3. That Ireland should maintain her own paupers just as England does; that is, by *Unions*, more contracted or more extensive, as circumstances may require.

This is placing the two countries on the same footing, and, indeed, is the only way of doing it. One district may agree to unite its poor with another district adjoining it; but Ireland and England never came to any such agreement; and Ireland has no better right to call upon England to support her poor than Manchester to call upon Bath. Ireland was never governed by a more temperate, a more just, or a more sagacious man than Lord Clarendon. If he has not opened the eyes of her squires, who are " *trying to live,*" let him turn his attention toward those who surely try quite as hard, and who deserve it somewhat better. There are many of these in the country; and there would be more if they who call themselves their betters (and who really are considerably so in coats and trousers) would set them an example. Whether they will do this or not, the concern which has hitherto been ours is theirs. If they do nothing but show their eloquence in pleading for vagabonds who leave their lands uncultivated, that Englishmen may come over and plow and sow them, and get shot for wages, they may go on *trying to live* and find at last the *trying* to be quite a failure.

WALTER SAVAGE LANDOR.

CHAPTER III
1848—1849

CHAPTER III

1848—1849

The events of 1848, the year of revolutions, were closely watched by Landor, but there are not many of his public letters to the press. The first one here quoted was written in the second week of April. Louis Philippe, King of the French, had abdicated on February 24, and France was once more a Republic. Italy had begun the first War of Independence against Austria. In the middle of March the Milanese had driven out the Austrian troops under Radetzky. A few days later the Austrians were expelled from Venice. The King of Sardinia had also declared against Austria. In Poland a Republic had been proclaimed at Cracow; but to the Polish refugees in Paris, asking for the sympathy and assistance of France, M. Lamartine had replied: "You must leave to her that which she alone can appoint—the hour, the moment, the mode for giving you, without aggression, without effusion of blood, the place which is due to you in the list of nations.

The Hungarians had declared their independence at the end of March, but the crisis there, accurately foreseen by Landor, was to come later. The following letter from him was published in the *Examiner* of April 15, 1848.

Things to be Done.

While the French army and navy continued in a state of inactivity, even the pens and tongues of the Provisional Government were quiescent. If the Republican fleet, already in commission and afloat, forbore to sail up the Adriatic, and to lend its aid to the Venetian States, yet moral influence at least might have been exerted on those of Hungary. Without the co-operation of the Hungarians, the difficulty of relieving Poland is extremely great. It is reported that, after declaring their own independence, they are resolved on annihilating, if they can, the independence of Lombardy. Such a report is incredible. Have the Italians injured them? And what merit can Austria claim toward them, that they who resisted her domination should assist her in her aggression? She has absorbed into her coffers all the gold and silver coin of the country, and forced upon it her base metal: she has cooped up her industrious youth in fortresses, and her intelligent patriots in garrisons. If it was lawful and just to break asunder the ancient ties which bound a great kingdom to a Duchy, it was surely just and reasonable for Lombardy to sever ties more recent and more galling, which fastened her to a nation the most alien, in language, manners, and reminiscences.

Politicians use no means to enlighten friends or enemies. But France and Germany are now under the guidance of honest citizens, of active and thoughtful men, licking up no crumbs from under a royal table, but standing up at the side of the royal chair, and suffering no poison to enter the royal lips. Let them show to Hungary the danger of leaning on the rotten throne so recently made vacant, and the firm support she would receive from Italy in return for mere neutrality. The upright are strong, and they only. If she sides with Austria, she will sink again into subjection: if she sides with Italy and Poland, she stands on ground that will never give way under her.

Little time is left for her decision. Within three months, by the season of the hay-harvest, Russia will pour her Cossacks along the Danube, even to Vienna, unless the Diet awakens to sane policy, and marches in the right direction. Force hath been too generally and too exclusively opposed to force. There are various tribes of

Cossacks, and several of them ill-disposed toward Russia. It would be no difficult matter to conciliate the leaders of these by presents and treaties ; and very far from impossible to unite many tribes under one head, such as Platoff, and to render them the efficient allies of Poland, until they are fitted to become members of the Republic. Conciliation with them, by such measures, may shorten the last war which European nations are likely to wage against one another; a war which otherwise must continue for more years, extend over more nations, and become more sanguinary than any other in modern times. Hungary, not France, is at this hour the mistress of Europe ; but France may influence Hungary, and shorten the agonies of Italy, by sending a fleet and forty thousand men up the Adriatic.

WALTER SAVAGE LANDOR.

April 10, 1848.

Landor's next letter to the *Examiner* was written on November 13, 1848. The issue of the paper in which it appeared, had accounts of the restoration of order in Vienna, lately in the hands of insurgents, and "reports of a most warlike character" from Hungary, where 150,000 of the imperial troops were in the field. Kossuth, in July, had told the Diet that "the Magyars stood alone in the world against the conspiracy of sovereigns and nations which surrounded them." Two months later, the Hungarians, with Kossuth as their Dictator, had begun their War of Independence.

In Italy King Charles Albert of Sardinia had been defeated by the Austrians at Custoza ; but he had not yet abdicated. Milan had capitulated to Marshal Radetzky in the beginning of August. Early in September King Ferdinand, who had deserted the popular cause, bombarded Messina. The following

letter from Landor was published in the *Examiner*
of November 18 :—

European Revolutions.

In my views on politics I have given offence to many good and
sensible men. Perhaps I may be erroneous in some of my opinions,
but is it quite certain that they themselves are exempt from fallibility
in all of theirs?   Permit me to ask whether they have given proofs
to the world of more research, more intellect, more information, more
independence.   I come forward not to offend, but to conduct ; not
to quarrel, but to teach ; and I would rather make one man wiser
than ten thousand friendly to me ; yet I profess no indifference to
the favourable opinion of those writers who influence the public
judgment.   I suspect both of moroseness and of falsehood such
as are guilty of this arrogant and contemptuous demeanour.   It
is only small dogs that run after the stones cast at them ; and
these small dogs, importunate to be petted and prompt at tricks,
are of a breed not remarkable for sagacity or fidelity.

Dependent on no party, influenced by none, abstaining from the
society and conversation of the few public men I happen to be
acquainted with, for no other reason than because they are in
power and office, I shall continue, so long as I live, to notice the
politics and politicians which may promote or impede the public
welfare.

It is undeniable that new forms of government are about to
supersede the old throughout the continent of Europe.   Some
fancy they see the origin of this antagonism in the commencement of the French Revolution ; others look a little higher up
on the North American Congress.   In fact, the destinies both of
America and Europe were immovably fixt when the spirit left the
body of *Old* England and transmigrated into the *New*.   Religion
and Patriotism fled together from before the throne of Charles ;
they sought only a narrow asylum, and they laid undesignedly the
foundation of the widest and most powerful empire the earth was
ever to contain.   Religion at the present time exerts but a feeble
influence over any portion of the globe.   The unwieldy wealth of
the priesthood has overturned it on the high road of the continent,
and shortly will break it into fragments here, leaving the ore at the

bottom of the stream, with fewer earthly particles.   Hatred of Religion is engendered in many hearts by the anti-Christian wealth and offices of its lordly functionaries.   France, Germany, and Italy herself, have trimmed and curtailed her phylacteries; in England and Ireland the old pattern has only been disfigured, and the massive bullion carefully covered over.   Thirty generals and thirty admirals, the saviours of our country, divide among them a smaller revenue than the Bishop of London has been enjoying for many years.

Abuses less intolerable have excited the insurrectionary spirit in France and Germany.   Taxes are more intelligible than principles; taxes, in one form or another, have shaken half the world for three-quarters of a century.   When we fall, it will be after a dreadful struggle against taxation.   This idea brings me to the point I would arrive at.   The weight of taxation has a second time put into movement the revolutionary wheel in France.   Happily for us, as we may think, she is too poor for war.   But is it more difficult for half a million of soldiers to find sustenance in Poland and Lithuania than in the streets of Paris?   Is it more difficult to conciliate nations by kindness than kings by treaties?   Are sympathies confined to the higher classes only?   War is begun between the few on one side and the many on the other.   Whether it shall be a war of extermination for the weaker party, a month probably will decide.   The weaker party, pray let me tell you, is not that whose blood now blackens the pavement of Messina: is not that which the hounds of a murderous prince are licking off his fingers at Vienna.   The brave are fallen, but not all the brave.   Dreadful will be the hour of retribution and atonement. Germans, Italians, French, perceive the impossibility of tolerating the fraudulence of princes.   All we can hope is exemption from retaliation, abstinence from the infliction of bodily pains and penalties.   Nothing would be more imprudent, or indeed more intemperate, than to let loose the dogs of war from the royal kennels.   Had I a voice in any country on the continent, I would say, " Confide no longer; but be clement; be generous; give your princes a chance and a choice of becoming honest men; grant them a sufficiency to educate their children well, and to maintain them handsomely, far away from the land of their birth, and from the breath of evil counselers."

We are now turning over the first page of *the* Revolution.   The occurrences in France, at the close of the last century, are only the Preface.   Day after day it was prognosticated, in courts and parliaments, that another campaign, another battle, would terminate the whole affair.

England lighted the forge and blew the bellows, and fabricated the armour of France.   Factions were tearing her in pieces : England declared war, and united them.   Her minister Pitt saw this contingency, and represented it to his sovran.   " *Go to war or go out,*" was the reply: we know the consequences.   The most prudent nation in the world became the most improvident, the richest became the poorest.   The armies of Italy and Germany learnt in France what the French armies had learnt in America.   Before long—after many defeats, however, and many victories—princes found it necessary to promise free constitutions.   It was never their intention to grant them, and they all descended to the grave amidst their violated pledges.   Every prince was suspicious not only of his subjects, but of his neighbours, for every one felt conscious of his own dishonesty.   Hence numerous standing armies pressed upon the people in every country.   Weary of war, sick of hope deferred, distrustful of their rulers, and galled by new debts upon the shoulders of old, at the first signal of insurrection in France, a simultaneous cry against fraudulence and despotism burst forth in all the languages of Europe.   Italy heaved off from her bosom the bloated incubus ; and Austria showed the world that among many crapulous, many distorted, she had healthy children, and never to be corrupted by indolence and sensuality.   But those standing armies, the weight of which brought about all the revolutions, stood apart from their fellow-citizens, murdered many, and drove more into exile.

What occurred at Vienna is about to occur at Berlin; and Russian armies are marching to the frontiers of Germany in order to subjugate the refractory.   Can the honour or the interest of France permit this aggression?   Will she lose the present opportunity of conciliating, or rather of recovering, the goodwill of those nations which an ungenerous, ungrateful, and unwise leader fatally betrayed?   Impossible.   Despotism and Republicanism are coming face to face.   The conflict will be terrible in the fields of Hungary and Poland.   Happy are we in England, whom neither duty nor passion urge to take a part in it; who can reduce our armaments while other nations are augmenting theirs; and who enjoy the soundest of republican institutions, without any fear or suspicion of military violence, or princely arrogance, or ministerial fraud.   Tranquilly, as at a theatre, we may hear the drum and trumpet, and see the expulsion or execution of evil-doers without rising from our seats.

WALTER SAVAGE LANDOR.

November 13, 1848.

A week later the *Examiner* (Nov. 25) published another long letter from Landor.

German Revolution.

When the Emperor of Austria, by the instigation of his generals, had resolved on overturning the Constitution, it was evident enough that another Prince in Germany, who thinks himself much wiser and wanting no advice whatsoever, would attempt the same.   In fact, the same impulse operated on both ; an impulse from without.   The Russian armies were advancing to the north and to the south, along the Baltic and along the Danube.   Every city and village of Poland was occupied to repletion from every nation of which the vast Muscovite empire is composed.   What power in the universe is adequate to contend with it ?   None.   Beside this consideration, it is manifest that the Sovereigns of Austria and of Prussia would rather owe the possession of their thrones to the favour of the autocrat than to the free-will of the people.

Armies are the glory of princes ; not industry, not morality, not contentment.   The field of battle is their only cultivation ; the bayonet is their plough, the sword their reaping-hook.   How much longer shall this be ?   Nations ! ye are silent ; I will tell you, then. It will be until ye cordially and energetically unite ; until every country has again its own boundary, its own government, its own laws.   Insensate are those princes who place their hands within the hands of others, and do homage for their crowns.   Whoever can put on a crown can take it off again ; the wearer has the least power over it.   Unsound is the rest and feverish are the dreams of those princes who lie down on broken promises.   Will they never

T

be taught how much better it is to have every wise man for a coun
sellor, every virtuous man for a friend, and every brave man for ;
sentinel ? If they refuse to learn so easy and so necessary a rudi
ment, they, like other dull and refractory ones, must be scourge(
into it. They have thrown aside the pen that signed their perfidies
and have taken up arms and halters against those who trusted them
If their own people have been traitorously abused by them, wha
confidence can neighbours, can rivals, can enemies place in them
after compulsory cessions and extorted treaties ?

It is equally the duty and interest of France to abstain fron
interference in Italy and Germany, until her aid is demanded. Thi
aid, indeed, she promised in the commencement of the struggle, an(
only thus conditionally. At that time, however, the Russians ha(
not entered the principalities on the Danube, threatening to inundat(
all Europe, and again to surmount the Alps. If she now refuses th
aid she then promised, she herself will want it. Let her press foi
ward while the giant is whirling the sling round his head, and no
wait until the stone descends. Russia is now on the Danube ; sh(
will presently be on the Elbe and on the Rhine, and, before th(
heats of summer are over, it may again be a pleasant exercise for th
Cossack cavalry to swim across the Seine. The Russian treasury i
the only one in Europe which abounds in the precious metals
Russia is the only power that works her steel with gold. Before he
armies march, a rail-road of this quality is laid down for them. I
she herself quite unassailable by arms of the same temper? Ar
no chiefs of Tartary to be subdued by it? no Khan? no Hei
man ? Surely the experiment is worth a trial by those whom i
most concerns. But we English, I repeat it, however much, ii
common with Europe, we may benefit by the disruption of thos(
fasces which hold so tremendous an axe, must abstain from th(
severest and most important conflict in which the nations of Europ
have ever been engaged. It began with the cannonade of Vienna
it will terminate on the Don. Who knows but, in twenty years
colonies of French and Irish may erect and garrison fortresses oi
the Nieper and the Dwina, boundaries of Poland? Californi;
touches Boston : who expected that?

Our children, as the steamer rolls them along the Rhine, wil
expatiate on the manifold events, of its early, its middle-aged, an(

its recent history. Julius and Germanicus, Varus and Arminius, will occupy a narrower space in the recollection, than the small island overlooked by the turrets on its right, whence princely heroism bent over cloistered beauty. The names of robbers and murderers, military and ecclesiastical, will be called over and dismissed, by some with negligence, by more with scorn. Execration and laughter will pursue the phantoms of fanatical kings, who talked of giving laws to the nations which had framed them, and of writing constitutions which it was permitted them to sign. And all this took place so recently as the year 1848, the year before they forfeited by their perfidy their palaces and estates. It was accomplished in the second year of the great Revolution; the year in which the united armies of Germany, France, and Italy delivered Poland, established Hungary, restored Finland to Sweden, and fixed the boundaries of Russia on the Don and Phasis. Territories now overpeopled will spread their superabundant population over the richest soils, lying now inert; and this will principally be owing to the arms of France, which hitherto had inflicted very grievous wounds on others, but more grievous on herself. If foreigners had wise statesmen to guide them, she would be permitted to march onward in this salutary progress, without hindrance and without altercation. Whether she meets with these annoyances or not, she will go strait (*sic*) on. The impulse is given already; the ball has exploded from the cannon; woe betide the gouty old fool who sits in his arm-chair and thrusts out his leg to stop it!

We who are now living may hope to see the day when kings will be elevated to the rank of gentlemen. But if they massacre and plunder, above all if they lie (as they have been doing lately), no gentlemen will be left to receive them into their order; for the lower classes in their indignation will sweep away all that is above them, and then will fight among themselves for the wine which they have spilt.

Revolutions are bad things, and those are the worst of men who make them necessary.   WALTER SAVAGE LANDOR.

On November 27, 1848, Louis Napoleon issued his address to the electors of France in which he said that, should he be nominated President of the French

Republic, he should ever remain faithful to the dutie
imposed on him by their votes and by the will of th
Assembly. "I would devote myself entirely, withou
any concealed view, to the consolidation of a Republi
wise by its laws, honest by its intention, and powerfu
by its arts." On December 20 he was proclaimed b
the National Assembly, President of the French Re
public, having been elected by a majority of fou
million odd votes against those given to Genera
Cavaignac. Landor's remarks on the election wer
published in the *Examiner* of December 23 :—

Remarks on the Election of Louis Napoleon.

It is improbable that the President of the French Republic wi
be influenced in his policy by a foreigner. But another thing
equally improbable, which is, that any Frenchman of integrity wi
direct his counsels. Among the public men of that country ther
are several who have distinguished themselves by abilities an
address. Guizot, the most honest of the late King's ministers, wa
guilty of such gross prevarication, in regard to the marriage of th
Infanta, as would exclude a private character from all respectabl
society. Of those who remain in their country few are exempt fror
the charge of versatility, and some have accumulated great wealt
by dishonourable means.

Under the Empire, military men became the possessors of pro
digious fortunes by permitted rapine. Junot, Massena, and Soul
exhausted the several countries they invaded : under the Bourbon:
of each branch, the stock-exchange was the area of the more silen
plunderers, and the domestic dog devoured as largely as the wol
Marceau, Brune, Bessières, and several others, have left behind ther
names which redeem in some degree the honour of France, an
stand forth in bold relief from among the hideous ruins of he
Revolution. Cavaignac was thought worthy of this select an
august assemblage. If Louis Napoleon should demand his services
such a step would tend to the consolidation of his authority. A

present the declared policy of both is the same: either of them within a few months would be constrained by circumstances to deviate widely from it: the pride, the dignity, the interests of France, permit no apathy, no procrastination. It is easier to march for ten hours than to stand on one leg for a quarter. The quarter has sounded; France is tired and uneasy; she will on. Again I repeat it, we have nothing to do with her movements on the Continent. We never interposed when Russia violated the treaty of Vienna; we never interposed when the most bestial of a bestial race over-lay and stifled the first-born of Sicilian Freedom. Woe betide the mischievous meddler who presumes to tell France that she is bound, and she alone, to abide by the very treaties which insolent despots and shameless perjurors have broken. If she collects her old allies around her, she will foster them to their mutual benefit. She will not indeed dare to look Messina in the face, but she will turn the eyes of all upon Oporto. Pacific as are the declarations of Louis Napoleon, mild and beneficent as his temper is, honourable and just as all his actions and projects may be, it lies not within his power to control the

Luctantes ventos tempestatesque sonoras

which writhe and roar not only throughout France, but over the whole continent of Europe.

Is there any man so silly as to believe that any ruler of France, emperor, king, or president, will forego the ancient influence of that Power over the destinies of Turkey? Is there any politician who calculates that a partition of that country with Russia would be so advantageous to France as its integrity? It appears to me that, at present, there will be only one accession of territory on her confines. She may permit the King of Sardinia to be King of Lombardy, on his ceding that island to her. The kingdom of Italy may be offered by the people to a Bonaparte, not under the direct influence, but not without the close alliance, of France. We may be unwilling that such additions should be made to her territories, but we have no right whatever to interfere, no more indeed than we had to resist the occupation of California by the Americans, which conquest will hereafter lay the foundation of a vast and powerful empire, to predominate at no distant period in the farthest east. If we thought it imprudent to oppose the will of France when she seized on Otaheite, and plundered and expelled our countrymen, its civilisers and protectors, with what assurance can we forbid her to recover that which was torn from her by violence? It is as little our policy to intermeddle in the conflicts or combinations of France with the other powers of Europe, as it is the policy of America, from which the provident and virtuous Washington with his dying breath dissuaded her. Men equally provident, equally patriotic, if any such existed, might be unable to check and coerce the pruriency of the impotent in their lust for war; but it is the duty of all who deprecate its calamities, and foresee its consequences, to exert their best energies against such woeful infatuation.

France must employ her armies; and it is better that she should employ them elsewhere than against *us*. If she restores the integrity of Poland, she fights our battle, she enforces the sanctity of our treaties. If she protects Turkey, she accomplishes a work which we in vain attempted. She must do both, whether we will it or will it not.

The balance of Europe, after many oscillations, will adjust itself, without a finger of ours under it or upon it. Sicily and Egypt will maintain their independence, partly by their own strength, and partly by the jealousy of others. Denmark, our most important ally, has nothing to fear from the blustering fanatic who assailed her lately; and it will be time enough for us to protect her, when an enemy no less insidious and far more powerful shall attempt to burst through the Belt. We have only to abstain; a difficult thing to ministers who have dependents and supporters to provide for. But the people of England, who love quiet homes and plentiful tables, will allow no restless man to throw a firebrand into his neighbour's house, having seen and paid for the damage, or to shovel shiploads of gold upon the coast of Ireland, to be scrambled for indiscriminately by poor and rich.

Historians will record the present Parliament as the most inefficient in our annals. Manifold have been the contrivances for warming the House; but the prevalent gas appears to have been the gas which excites to laughter. Let the honourable members shake with mirth, while the mirth is innocent, but let them abstain from the practical joke of turning our pockets inside-out at their Christmas festivities, and of making a blaze which will burn their fingers, and perhaps reach the roof of the House.

WALTER SAVAGE LANDOR.

December 18, 1848.

The Emperor Ferdinand, on Dec. 2, 1848, abdicated in favour of his nephew Francis Joseph, now reigning. The new Emperor, a youth of nineteen, signed a proclamation in which Kossuth and the Committee of Hungarian Defence were denounced as outlaws. Early in January 1849 the surrender of Pesth to the Imperial Troops compelled Kossuth with his Magyars to retire to Debreczin, but he carried with him the Iron Crown of Hungary. The Hungarians sought the mediation of Great Britain, and were told by Lord Palmerston that the British Government had no knowledge of Hungary save as part of the Austrian Empire. After suffering further reverses, the Hungarians were again victorious, and on April 19th, 1849, the Austrians were compelled to evacuate Pesth. Five days earlier, Hungary was declared a free State with Kossuth as supreme governor. To him Landor addressed the following letter, which was published in the *Examiner* of May 19, 1849 :—

To General Kossuth.

General ! There are few who have the privilege to address you, but I am of the number ; for before you were born I was an advocate, however feeble, of that sacred cause which you are now the foremost in defending. Imminent was the peril of fine and imprisonment, and certain the loss of friends and fortune: I disregarded and defied the worst. Do not trample on this paper for being written by an Englishman. We are not all of us jugglers and dupes, though we are most of us the legitimate children of those who crowded to see a conjuror leap into a quart-bottle. If we have had our Wilkeses and Burdetts, our Wilsons and Broughams, we have also had our Romillies and our Benthams. In one House we have still a Clarendon, in the other a Molesworth. Be amused, but never indignant, at the spectacle of our public men; at restlessness without activity, at strides without progress, pelted from below by petulance without wit. A wider and fairer scene is lying now before you, a scene of your own creation, under the guidance and influence of Almighty God. Merciful and just by nature, and enlightened, as the powerful of intellect always are, by the continuous lamps delivered in succession from past and passing ages, you will find them shine clearer by contraction of space and adaptation to circumstances

You have swept away the rotten house of Hapsburg. It would be an idle trick to pursue the vermin that nestled and prowled among its dark recesses, behind its moth-eaten tapestries and throughout its noisome sewers. But there is no idleness in following the guidance of the most strenuous and most provident conquerors. Sylla, Julius and Augustus Cæsar, distributed the forfeited estates of their enemies among the defenders of their cause. The justice of their cause was questionable, the justice of yours is not. In our country William of Normandy broke up the estates of the vanquished and rendered them powerless for revolt. Elizabeth and Cromwell and William of Nassau, our three greatest sovrans, pursued the same policy with the same success. In Hungary there are immense tracts of land imperfectly cultivated, and forfeited by the defection and treason of the rich and indolent proprietors. Surely no time should be lost in the distribution of this national property among the nation's defenders. Larger and smaller allotments should be holder forth as the incentives and the rewards of valour. This was promised in France by the revolutionists of that country; but what promise was ever kept by France, under any of her Governments, to any nation? least of all perhaps to her own. The Hungarians are morally the antipodes of the French; the Hungarians are calmly brave, consistently free, strictly veracious, immutably just unostentatiously honourable. The French, if they attempt an act of perfidy, which they often do, and fail in it, which they seldom do feel deeply *wronged*: their honour (peculiar to them) requires them to salve the *affront* with blood. Perfidiously did they enter Civita

Vecchia ; fraudulently did they seize the citadel ; insolently did they
scorn the remonstrances of a free and of a friendly people. Beaten
back by unprepared and undisciplined volunteers, they loudly swear
vengeance ; and, confederated with all the despots of Europe, they
certainly may inflict it.

Behold the promises of a nation which declared its readiness to
aid unreservedly in the deliverance of the oppressed ! Behold the
first public act, beyond the boundaries, of its President ! What then
is Europe to expect from France ? what, but another link and rivet
to the monarchal chain, another chin-band to the sacerdotal tiara.
She looks to Hungary who never has deceived her, and away from
France who always has.

Sir, in your hands are deposited the sword and the scales of
justice : hold them firmly ; and, if any prince calls to the stranger,
bid your lictors bind him, and perform the rest of their duty forthwith.
In the exercise of this righteous authority may God preserve you for
His glory, for the benefit of the present age, and for the example of
every age to come.

WALTER SAVAGE LANDOR.

On the very day the above letter was printed, ten
thousand Russian troops arrived at Czernowitz to
assist the Austrians, in the interests, Count Ne-
selrode informed the Powers, of " European peace
and tranquillity."   " Does any one doubt," the
Examiner asked, "that the Austrian Camarilla has
filled up the measure of its infamy in calling Russia
to its help."   But meanwhile events had occurred
in Italy which moved Landor to another outburst
of indignation.   Louis Napoleon, President of the
French Republic, had sent 10,000 troops to restore
the temporal power of the Pope.   A newly-elected
Legislative Assembly had met in Paris, to whom
the following questions, printed in the *Examiner* of
June 2, 1849, we must suppose were addressed :—

Twelve Questions, Involving Others.

1. Was there ever a period in the history of France, during seven hundred years, when she would have permitted (much less consented) that any neighbouring prince should over-run the states of Italy?

2. Did not the French, in proclaiming their own republick, proclaim also that they would aid and assist such nations as, having been by force deprived of their freedom, invoked the French republick for succour?

3. Have they not shamefully belied such proclamation?

4. Were not other nations, Italy more especially, incited by the example and encouraged by the promises of France?

5. So far from assisting the people of Rome against the Jesuits and the Cardinals, did not the republick of France refuse even to acknowledge the republick of Rome? Furthermore, did not the republick of France seize and occupy Civita Vecchia, and did not her general, Oudinot, march against Rome without any provocation?

6. Were not the movements of the Austrians and Neapolitans simultaneous with this aggression?

7. If France had interfered merely by remonstrances, would the Austrians have massacred the people of Bologna and reduced the city to ruins?

8. Were not the movements of Austrians, Russians, and Prussians, also simultaneous with those of General Oudinot?

9. Is there not as strong a probability as there can be in any events here below, that the Government of France is closely confederated with the despotic powers of Europe to subvert and stifle the liberties of nations?

10. If the Emperor of Russia, in his hatred of republicks, refused to acknowledge a *Bourbon* for *king*, what could be his motive to acknowledge a Bonaparte for President of the Republick?

11. Is there no probability that he thinks an Emperor of France and a levy of French marshals the proper instruments whereby to extend his power to the Adriatic, and to bandage and belt his green livery on every prince in Germany?

12. Whether the ministers of the French President, betrayers of all the rulers who have employed or trusted them, and seceders from

every principle they have upholden, may not have involved him in this tortuous and inexplicable policy in order to accelerate his downfall, by detaching all honest men and all friendly nations from him, by wounding the French in their sympathies for the Italians, who are fighting *their* battle for *their* order of things, and their pride by pandering to the ambition of Russia, at whose feet they are a second time laid prostrate?

WALTER SAVAGE LANDOR.

After taking possession of Civita Vecchia, the French General Oudinot met with unexpected opposition at Rome, where the citizens had summoned Garibaldi to their assistance.   M. de Lesseps was sent to treat with them; but being unable to come to terms, he left the city, having first indited the Note to which Landor takes exception in the following letter.   In this Note the French Envoy had written: "Misfortune, misfortune to the eternal city, if a hair of the head of a single Frenchman is touched!"   This was on May 24, 1849.   The *Examiner* of June 9 contained the following letter:—

France and Rome.

SIR,

Among the indignities which the Romans have endured from the French Government, none is more flagrant than the note of M. Lesseps on leaving the city.   Such arrogance, such menaces, are not only unusual, but unexampled in diplomacy.   If, instead of every courtesy and every kindness, the French aggressors had been treated with indignity and inhumanity, no worse insolence could have been directed against the illustrious rulers of that regenerate nation.   Is it because that nation *is* regenerate, and because the French require no prophet to tell them *they* can not 'be born again'?   Otherwise, surely it must be that M. Lesseps' personal vanity has somehow been sadly wounded.   Possibly it may have been askt, near the statue of Pasquin, *who*, in the name of the

Santissima, is this prodigious strutter, who wears his cock's feathe
so high. *Lesseps* has certainly a German sound, but the individua
seems to have been naturalized in Russia. Perhaps he has beer
taught his letters and his creed in some paternal school of Siberia
When people are indignant, nothing but good manners, early incul
cated and habitually seen practised, can withhold them from con
tumelious expressions. But even the violent leaders of the Frencl
Convention, exasperated as they justly were at the conduct of th
English Government, never carried their expressions to such a pitcl
of insolence. Most of these were aimed at Pitt and Coburg, taken
to be partners in the same firm of the *nation boutiquière*,[1] as Barrièr
(not Bonaparte) called us. Bonaparte, as is customary on the as
sumption of power, had a splendid civil list of witticisms voted t
him, although he never had a pennyworth of his own.

The French are generous and chivalrous toward the strong, bu
overbearing and unmerciful toward the weak. Sympathy with thos
who contend in the same cause finds no place in their bosoms. Th
most honourable and heroic man in their dominions, Toussair
l'Ouverture, would have perisht by order of Bonaparte in th
solitude and damps of a dungeon, if thirst and famine had no
by the same command, come forward to accelerate his fall. Th
menaces and notes and despatches of M. Lesseps are among th
ephemerides : but persons as low in manners as M. Lesseps have bee
exhibited and recorded in works far different. Long after the feather
of moths and butterflies have dropt away and disappeared, th
traces of their figures and the pins that held them have bee
sticking to the paper. It is evident that the French are descendin
fast toward despotism : in one form or other they have alway
lived under it. Arrogance and insolence in officials are the firs
running-footmen on the road, bedizened in the dress of envoy:
At first they only kick up the dust about them, but presently the
kick the shins of all they meet, provided they find or fancy ther
weaker than themselves. Dogs in condition worry dogs in decrep

[1] This is also pointed out in Landor's Imaginary Conversation between him
self and Archdeacon Hare. Works, 1876, v. 107. Others have traced the phras
to Adam Smith's "Wealth of Nations," — Book iv. chap. vii. ; and Dea
Tucker's "Four Tracts on Political and Commercial Subjects," 1774, p. 13;
have also been cited. But the Dean of Gloucester merely wrote :—"What :
true of a shopkeeper is true of a shopkeeping nation."

tude, and the tooth is nowhere so ferocious as on the toothless. But the hunters have discovered that the breed of the old wolf inherit the old wolf's fangs.

A few more words for the French people, since no French Government will ever heed them.   Beyond the west lies the east ; beyond freedom lies despotism.   WALTER SAVAGE LANDOR.

The *Examiner* of June 23, 1849, quoted a letter from Civita Vecchia dated June 15, saying : "Garibaldi has made a sortie with 1400 men, who have been annihilated.   The French army is fighting with unparalleled vigour.   The breach is opened, and at the present moment, perhaps, the assault of Rome is going on."   In the same issue of the paper appeared Landor's second letter on " France and Rome."

France and Rome.

The blunders of the French Government in Italy were to be intercepted from the public view by military evolutions in Paris.   For this purpose it was requisite to take advantage of rising indignation, and to stifle its expression.   A violation of the constitution was to be perpetrated, in order that remonstrances against a greater might be supprest.   An appeal to justice and honour was turned into ridicule, as might be expected, by such persons as Barrot and Falloux.[1] Indignation was just as naturally raised among the friends of Republicanism, at home and abroad.   It was foreseen that such indignation would burst forth into acts of violence ; and not only was it foreseen, but desired.   The new Republicans are now sharing the fate of the old Girondins.

Such seizure and imprisonment of respectable and intelligent men, brave soldiers, enlightened journalists, and upright representatives of the people, was beyond the ferocious grasp, beyond the bloodshot vision of Robespierre and Marat.   Neither of them was base enough to employ so dark a blinker to cover his misdeeds : neither of them

---

[1] M. Odilon Barrot was President of the Council and Minister of Justice in the new French Ministry.   M. de Falloux, Minister of Public Instruction.

was hostile to a friendly state, or treacherous to any. Yet these wretches well deserved the dishonourable death that overtook them, followed by the scorn and execration of posterity. The pages of French history, mildewed all over with large spots of perfidy, exhibit none of so deep and so corrosive a stain as this recently printed in large Roman letters. Fresh falsehood from the mouths of the ministers who defend it, can only produce the same effect as pouring sweet must on rancid wine.

The flatterers of power are always the haters of misfortune. It is probable that a majority of the French, even of the most vociferous for a Republic, will be as supple to the half-Napoleon as their fathers were to the whole one; and that despotism will become in a few months hence as fashionable as democracy was a few months ago. Surely, M. de Tocqueville, a gentleman, a scholar, a man hitherto irreproachable, will be able to stem the muddy current of the Cloaca Maxima into the midst of which he has fallen. Surely he must discern the impolicy, no less than the injustice, of murdering the Roman people and of battering down the city. The falsehood, the dishonesty, the trickery, the bigotry, of those among his associates in the Ministry, who pretended to doubt the sentiments and resolution of the Roman people, are now sufficiently manifest by its unanimity in defending the ancient honour and ancient domicile of Romans. In the eyes of such people as MM. Falloux and Barrot, such a defence may be highly criminal, and French honour (how different from Roman and English!) may demand its expiation. But the hands of M. de Tocqueville are inexpert in trickery, and his tongue has never been transferable and at a discount. Such is the great advantage he possesses over his colleagues. His knowledge of history will enlighten him. He will see clearly not only that France has broken faith, but has done it thrice in rapid succession. First, in exciting to revolt; secondly, in seizing the maritime city of a friendly power and the arms prepared for its defence; thirdly, in attacking Rome before the time promised to wait for hostilities. Even her own ambassador was ashamed of the ruffian who perpetrated this last atrocity, the least atrocity of the three. Europe cried out against the injustice and rapacity of the despots who dismembered Poland; but neither the violence nor the perfidy of these potentates, in half a century, is comparable to the violence and perfidy of one ferocious French general in a single week. The people of Poland had no treachery or ingratitude to complain of: enemies came as enemies, and were received as such. No lady of Warsaw bound up the wounds of any bleeding Cossack: no Russian officer was invited to partake the hospitalities of the city, to enjoy its promenades, to survey the strength or weakness of its walls. But the people of ·Poland, even more than the people of Rome, have proved the ingratitude of France. The most signal exploits, both in Spain and in Russia, were performed by the Polish lancers in protecting the French. Poland was trafficked away by one Bonaparte, Italy is trafficked away by another; but the glories of Rome are reinstated, the glories of· France are extinct. No arms, however successful, can cover prostrate honour. Certainly it is not a *marshal's* baton that is merited by such behaviour; and this is the opinion of all men out of France, and of many among themselves.

The French are now as detested in the whole of Italy as ever they were in Portugal and Spain. They have a wonderful facility in winning hearts and in losing them again. So long as they have an object in view, '*they fawn, feign, and flatter*'; when they have obtained it, they are contemptuous and overbearing. They began with cajoling Rome, and ended with cannonading her: they began with lies, and ended with massacres. Broadcast did they sow the wind, and abundantly do they reap the tempest. It is a tempest which is not about to terminate with the political heats of the season: it is one which already has swept away the moral of the nation whence it sprang, and will sweep away the physical of many. In the great internecine war of despots and nations has been fired only the first cannon; but the sound reverberates through Europe, and awakens the most supine. Vainly do weak men stand aloof and truckle, calling it prudence and policy to permit the aggression that (for a moment) is in another quarter and afar. But the aggressor gains strength and recovers breath at every stride, and he will presently turn round again and show it. We were parties to the ruin of Rome by not opposing it even with a word of deprecation. If 'to be weak is to be miserable,' our condition is a sorry one indeed.

When the Emperor Napoleon gave to his infant son the kingdom

304 WALTER SAVAGE LANDOR

of Rome, with the Colosseum and the Capitol as trinkets to pla
with, it was recollected that an equal piece of absurdity and im
pudence had been formerly imposed on the Roman people b
another Emperor in the nomination of his horse for consul. But
indignant as the people might have been, they accepted the appoint
ment at the hands of their capricious master; and indeed it was les:
disgraceful to be under the symbol of energy and war, '*caput acri*
equi,' than of incompetence and imbecility. Whether the presen
race would have endured the domination of a creature half-Austrian
and half-French, is uncertain: certain it is that they would rathe
tolerate such a foreign hybrid than the more monstrous one of hall
priest half-prince. No power on earth can pretend to place :
sovereign over a nation, and least of all *that* power which in thirt
years expelled from its own territories three of its own dynasties.

June 15.
WALTER SAVAGE LANDOR.

The French army entered Rome on July 3, 1849
Garibaldi having withdrawn that morning. The ke
of one of the gates had been sent to the Pope a
Gaeta, who in reply congratulated General Oudino
on his "triumph over the enemies of human society.'
The following letter was published in the *Examine*
of July 7 :—

The Pope, Temporal and Spiritual.

It would have been wiser and better if the Jesuitical an
Papistical faction in France had lookt a little to the consequence
of their hostility against the city and citizens of Rome. Duplicity
falsehood, violence, are asserted by the greater part of them to b
allowable, and even laudable, if they promote the interests of th
Church. Setting the question quite aside, whether in any case the
are laudable, whether in any case they are allowable, let us submi
to the consideration of these gentlemen, civil, military, and ecclesi
astical, whether the Redeemer of mankind ever promulgated o
sanctioned such a doctrine; whether he taught his followers tha
massacre, pillage, conflagration, rape, were necessary for sowing th

seeds or maturing the fruits of Christianity; and whether it is heretical and combustionable to believe the contrary. There are many still existing who are firmly of opinion that religion is, or ought to be, somewhat different from a mere state-engine. These, it must be confest, are a minority in all nations: but perhaps it may be argued, and almost conceded, that in every nation, excepting the gentle, the generous, the veracious French, virtuous and prudent men are also in the minority.

The most intelligent, not only in the Roman States, but in every State throughout the whole of Europe, entertain and always have entertained the opinion, that the secular power of the Pope should be disunited from the ecclesiastical. But whether they thought it or not, if the Roman people thought it, that was sufficient. The Pope had broken his word with them; he had deceived and cajoled them; he had rendered nugatory the reforms he himself had introduced. Conscious that actions so flagitious must deprive him not only of all authority but of all respect, he fled in the attire of a servant from the city; the triple crown was surmounted by the cockt hat. He became in verity, "*the servant of servants*," the servant of a Frenchman, who himself proved *he* could do what Christ said nobody could do, in serving two masters. Pio Nono carried his cross with him to Gaeta, not supported on shoulder, right or left, but on a ribbon, and out of sight. No nails for Pio! At Gaeta there fell before his knees, the murderer of Messina, the allie of Austria and of France. Rome has not fallen at his feet again. Her walls are levelled to the earth by French cannon; but subjugated France will never triumph over subjugated Rome.

The Pope in temporal concerns is an extremely weak, improvident man, and vainly attempts to supply by cunning his deficiency of strength. In spiritual concerns it may be impious to doubt his infallibility, not merely in the dogmas but also in the ordinances and duties of Christianity. Inspired by the Holy Ghost, as every good Catholick must acknowledge him to be, surely it is wonderful that he should think himself inspired to extend, not his doctrines only, but likewise his dominions, by fire and sword. It would have puzzled Pascal, and peradventure may puzzle M. de Montalembert and other devout Catholicks, to account for this discrepancy. Had only the Gospel condemned it, had only Jesus

Christ denounced it, then perhaps it might have been explained away; but even bishops and cardinals and fathers (much higher authorities in Holy Church) have set their faces against it. Pope Julius and Pope Alexander, whom many, even of the hierarchy, accused of cruelty and immorality, and what is the worst of cruelties and immoralities, an indifference to bloodshed and an indulgence in it, never instigated to them so extensively as Pio Nono. The worse of the two, whichever it may be, would have discountenanced, forbidden, and anathematised such atrocities, such meanness and ingratitude, such fraudulence and ferocity, as the French are now committing in his name. The human race cries out against them: it is only the race undescribed by Buffon, but described by Voltaire, which dips its whiskers into them and ingurgitates them greedily and gaily. If this irreclaimable race had belonged to the *genus homo*, a physiologist might designate it as *the nation that never blushes.*

WALTER SAVAGE LANDOR.

July 2, 1849.

Events in Italy had not wholly distracted Landor's attention from the struggle in Hungary. Writing to Lord Dudley Stuart early in the year, he had "suggested the propriety and practicability of raising a subsidy, however small, in aid of the Hungarians." In July he sent to the *Examiner* the following letter (published July 21) with £5 for the Hungarian Hussars. A couple of days later, it may be noted, a public meeting was held in London "for the purpose of expressing sympathy with that noble, maligned, and betrayed people, the Hungarian nation."

Subscription for the Hungarians.

SIR,

The claims of the Hungarians on our sympathy are acknowledged by Englishmen of all ranks, and by journalists of all parties. The extremely few who oppose them are little in accord with their readers on this single point. If their articles about it are perused with avidity, it is from wonder what can possibly be urged against men fighting against insidious encroachments and lawless innovations. Nearly all who follow with breathless curiosity the powerful antagonist heading the columns of the *Times*, call to mind with strong disapprobation, being religious men and strictly Protestants, that the family against whose arms and artifices the Hungarians are now contending, is that same family which, by the same arms and artifices, cut down and trod into the dust the Protestantism they found flourishing in that country. By no other hands was consumed its cradle in Bohemia.

I am no zealot "for modes of faith." What the Protestant has lost, the Papist has not gained; I wish he had. But an imposing and intolerant confraternity hems him round, telling him what quantity and of what quality he may eat, when his master has eaten first and the servants of the house after. Early in the day the Popes were at the *diggings*, and accumulated a prodigious mass of ore, which their slaves and body-guards brought into the city, forcing the poor citizens to throw in all they possessed, and turning their old habitations into smelting-houses. Ultimately there was rebuilt another Ephesus, another temple; and instead of the ancient image that was believed to have come from heaven, there was substituted one fused with human blood, gorgeous, vast, irremovable, under whose shadow sit, vociferating and bargaining, the sellers of tame doves, the scriveners and craftsmen, the artificers and solderers of States. Men, it appears, were born to support the edifice and them. The Hungarians think otherwise. They resolve to enjoy and to impart the blessings of free religion; they believe that a running stream is clearer and purer than a factitious pond, and that not only is it better to slake their thirst, but also is adapted to irrigate the field more equally and more widely.

Were I a Tory I should be, if possible, more strenuous in the cause than I have ever been. Altho' no Tory, I am truly a Conservative, and I desire no other changes, in my own country, than from profusion to economy, with the safe and certain means of maintaining it; no other in Hungary than from violence to order, from military and arbitrary government to municipal and representative. I wish every man to enjoy as much as I myself do; and, if there are inequalities and impediments in the way, to remove as many as by foresight and zeal and labour are removable. At all events I think it hard to grudge the Hungarians their ancient birthright; a birthright more ancient, more regular, more continuous than ours, more frequently assailed and more valiantly defended. Harder still is it to reproach and malign them for employing those methods of recovering it to which we ourselves in like circumstances should recur: seeing, as we do, broken promises thrown back in their faces the very hour they were made, after the dust of ancient oaths had been blown with derision into their eyes, and they had borne it.

Improperly are so many words of mine a preface to so trivial a donation as I offer. It is only intended as an aid to a few brave Hungarians now in England, who want the means of returning to their country. The truest, the most generous, the most energetick of philanthropists, Lord Dudley Stuart, thinks, with many other judicious men, that subscriptions for aiding the nation in its righteous cause should follow great publick meetings.

WALTER SAVAGE LANDOR.

July 16.

A week later, July 28, the following letter was published in the *Examiner*; a list of subscriptions for the relief of the Hungarian Hussars being appended, including that of a guinea from G. Meredith, Esq. :—

France, Italy, and the Czar.

If the Hungarians should be able to resist, for three months longer, the numerous and formidable hordes surrounding them; and if the French Government should abstain from two declarations —the first, that it will assist them; the second, that its interests and honour require their suppression—we may confidently hope for their ultimate success. That the French will secretly encourage them in hostilities, for the purpose of exhausting their resources, is probable enough, and that they will afford but a negative aid to the Austrians and Russians. Such aid, morally, they have given already; and two such declarations they have made in regard to

Rome. No weightier pledge could be offered to the Autocrat for their good behaviour. Since the time of Napoleon, there is among them no dishonour in a lie of any magnitude or any tendency; dishonour rests simply and solely in a want of courage to maintain and defend it. Liberal as are all their codes, the Code of Honour is the most so; unhappily, there is no likelihood of seeing an abridgement or a manual. Among the body of French Ministers, not a single one was ignorant that the Romans were greatly more unanimous in favour of a republick than the French were: and yet they all asserted the contrary. Doubtless they will continue with the same pertinacity of impudence to assert the contrary even now; when scarcely a Roman of any description, from the highest to the lowest, will remain in the coffee-house which a Frenchman enters. The most indigent men, women, children, brought up to live on alms, drop famished in the streets rather than ask them from the invader. Such is the aid the French bring, such is the honour they assert, such is the magnanimity they display, such the confidence they inspire. If the Polanders, the main instruments of all their victories, were surrendered and deserted by them, what can the Hungarians expect who routed them on every field where they encountered in equal numbers? They alone shared this glory with the English, and shared it amply. Never can be forgiven them their many Waterloos. Rivalry, in ancient days, was often the spring of noble sentiment, of generous emotion; and France was almost as fruitful of them as Spain herself, who inherited them equally from Goth and Moor. France, the quickest of imitators, caught them readily, but was the earliest to drop them. England placed his trophies over the slain Montcalm; and Germany over Marceau. France tramples down the monuments of the ancient Romans, and reduces their brave descendants to the vilest servitude. But which of the two nations, the Roman or the French, is the fallen?

Justice is immutable and divine; but laws are human and mutable; they are violated everyday, changed and superseded perpetually, and sometimes ejected from the judgment-seat by military power. In such a case, what remains for nations? History tells us. There springs up a virtue from the very bosom of Crime, venerably austere, Tyrannicide. The heart of Antiquity bounded before this Virtue. Religion followed Religion; new idols were worshipt; they rotted down one after another; Tyrannicide has appeared in every age, in every country, the refuge and avenger of the opprest. Can Russia have forgotten that awful vision, which hath reared its head so often over her imperial crown, and broken up, like the burst of spring, her palaces of ice? Perhaps the novel and insane idea of drawing a blockade round a vast kingdom originated at hearing the near footfall of this inevitable chastiser.

WALTER SAVAGE LANDOR.

July 22.

Late in July 1849 the English papers published a proclamation addressed by the Austrian general, Haynau, to the people of Buda-Pesth, in which he said:—" Doomed to death is every person, no matter of what rank or sex—doomed to instant death on the spot of the crime, is every one who dares to assist the cause of the rebels, by words or by deeds, or by revolutionary dress; doomed to death is every one who dares to insult any of my soldiers or of those of our allies; doomed to instant death is every one who enters into traitorous communication with the enemies of the Crown, or who maliciously presumes by rumours to assist the rebellion or to conceal weapons." In the House of Commons, on August 1, Lord Palmerston, replying to Lord Nugent, said that her Majesty's Government in common with everybody else had read the proclamation, as printed in the newspapers, with the deepest pain, but as the Government were not in possession of any information on the subject, it was impossible to say whether it were genuine or not. The *Examiner* of August 11 published the following letter from Landor, who at the same time had sent £30 for the Hungarian Committee :—

Austrian Cruelties.

Ruggiero, an Italian ecclesiastick, relates to the Bishop of Pesth a tale of devastation by the Tartars in Hungary, which Gibbon calls the "*best picture* of a barbarian invasion." If the historian were now living, he would see an imitation of this *picture* far surpassing the original in force of colouring. Tranquilly as he discourses on human crimes and sufferings, he would surely now exhibit to the indignation of mankind the cruelties which again are perpetrated in that country. They are enough to excite it even in France herself, fallen as she is from step to step in servitude. A general at the head of a German army denounces death, both on soldiers and civilians, without trial and without delay. This insolent and ferocious bastard, whom even the vilest family would disown, threatens thus the bravest men of the most illustrious. Lord Nugent, when he called upon our Parliament to interfere, would not trust his tongue (he said) with this man's name. When it was whispered in the House, there was a universal shudder. Such an effect had not been produced before, even by the murder of men made prisoners while fighting for their established and acknowledged laws. Often had soldiers and citizens been slaughtered for defending their native land, but never before were ladies scourged for lamenting it. Let us hope the hour is near when female hands will inflict this milder chastisement on the unmanly culprit, before he is committed for the remainder of his days to the grating that encloses less ferocious animals.   WALTER SAVAGE LANDOR.

August 4.

About this time Admiral Sir Charles Napier was publishing in the *Times* a series of letters on the shortcomings of the British navy. The subject attracted attention on both sides of the Channel; and the Paris *Constitutionnel* had an article on it. The French paper attributed the alarm raised by Napier to the facility with which General Oudinot's troops had been transplanted to Civita Vecchia, and went on to say :—

> "England need not entertain the slightest apprehensions. To admit the possibility of a surprise on the part of our army, we must suppose it sent against British territory without a previous declaration of war. It is true the English did not give such previous declaration when they bombarded Copenhagen, and confiscated the Danish Fleet. But the practice of the French is quite different."

This will explain the following letter of Landor's, which was published in the *Examiner* of August 18, 1849 :—

Astonishing Statements.

In the *Times* of this day, August 8, I find what is there called an "*Astonishing Statement*" in the *Constitutionnel*. Ought anything to astonish us, even in the most respectable of French journals, when we discover just as palpable falsehoods asserted by French historians, who not only were journalists, but Ministers of State? The writer, English or Continental, who should take the trouble to collect the series of falsehoods in the *Moniteur* alone, during the government of Napoleon, would render an important service both to history and to morality. At first sight the number must appear incredible, especially in the announcement of those stupendous exploits by which the English fleets were so frequently crippled, and the armies driven into the sea. France, apprehensive in her modesty that too much glory would redound to her and oppress her, proclaims to the world what contemptible cowards were her adversaries. At Acre, Sir Sidney Smith was called a madman by Napoleon. He repulsed the French army from the walls, and protected the sick and wounded. Here the expression of the *Constitutionnel* would be well placed. "*The practice of France is quite different.*" Many of them were abandoned by Napoleon ; others, with greater humanity, he poisoned. The French prisoners were protected by the English against the just indignation of the Turks ; the prisoners taken by the French were massacred in a body ; none escaped.

And now, when she seizes on Civita Vecchia, promising to Rome the blessings of peace, freedom, and fraternity, France is loud about our knavery and violence in the attack on Copenhagen, and cries, *" The practice of France is quite different."* And so indeed it is. The rulers of France and Russia had agreed on seizing the fleets of Denmark, although the Danes at that very time were their allies, and had joined in an armed neutrality against England. Remonstrances were made, and an envoy was sent to warn them of the consequences. *" The practice of France is quite different."* Tell us what provocation was given by the Romans? tell us what motive was given by the French? Again, tell us what provocation was given by Pio Settimo, and what notice was given by the French to *him.* And tell us further, what provocation was given by Ferdinand of Spain; and what notice was given to *him?* King and Pope, equally friendly, equally confiding, were circumvented and captured.

If we look up a little higher in the historical column, we find two paragraphs headed by the words *Algiers* and *Tahiti.* The French ventured not to assail Algiers until our fleet had destroyed its defences. We liberated many thousands of slaves and restored them to their several countries. *" The practice of France is quite different."* The French reduced to slavery all the nations round, and took *their* country from them, imprisoning a brave leader for defending it.

We had civilized and protected Tahiti : the French invaded the island in the time of profound peace, insulted the queen, and pillaged and expelled her protectors. They declared that the country could not justly and lawfully be considered as under English protection, since England had never seized nor conquered, but had only civilized and instructed it. According to the French code, bloodshed and rapine are the only titles to power and possession : according to the French theory and practice, violence is high-mindedness, arrogance is authority.

How extremely weak grows the moral sentiment when overshadowed by vanity ! It is probable that in twenty of the poorest French officers there are scarcely half-a-dozen who would cheat at a game of cards ; yet in the very highest it would be difficult to find a single one disinclined to act the meanest and most subordinate part in cheating where men's lives and liberties are at stake. It was done at Rome ; it was done against their promises and their conscience. Are these distinct from honour? or has honour lost its essence and changed its nature ? There are victories more calami-

tous to the conqueror than to the conquered. To be lowered i
morality is also to be lowered in prosperity. One falsehood o
fraud injurious to a thousand people is as criminal as ten thousan
frauds each injurious to one only. But the falsehoods and fraud
committed recently against the Romans are injurious to million
born and unborn, undermining the prosperity, blockading th
progress, of many nations, and exploding to atoms what little wa
left of probity in France. Aggression accompanied by treacher
not only breaks asunder all the bonds which have united, or migh
in future, the nation committing it from the nation wronged, bt
loosens all whereby every other near to her has been attached. Th
wounds inflicted by a just, a necessary, an honourable war, soo
heal again ; but Spain holds up hers in the face of France, sti
fresh and rankling; too faithful Poland scorns her worse ingratitude
and the heart of Italy by manifold perjuries is lost to her for ever.

Occasionally there is something very ludicrous in the overshot c
lying: for example, where a royalist and a papist, a priest and
publicist, tug and strain. The bow of Ulysses was fatal to th
suitors who drew it. Dexterity is only to be acquired by quic
sight and firm footing. Napoleon blundered incessantly; but a
every blunder (one excepted) there was a stroke and a leap tha
cleared it. Cunning as are the present French Ministers, for whic
quality the heterogeneous body seems to have been packed togethei
force is requisite to support their fallacies. Republics are raised b
the people, and fall by the soldiery. The cork figures now on th
table have no weight at bottom to keep them up in their places. Han
after hand will offer to steady them, but the end is a rap on th
knuckles and an outcry. Violence, which acolyte and neophyte ar
now employing, will never keep either things or men in their place
Arrogance with strong muscles, which they want, sometimes look
very like authority: but sometimes also people have found out tha
the highest in stature are not invariably the most upright or th
strongest. Few believe that the gentlemen who are actually in th
President's service are disposed to serve him faithfully under th
present form of government. Most of them are known to b
desirous of another form and another head. Whatever they ma
aim at, the French Republic will be extinct before the terminatior
of its third year. It has cried and screamed and kickt, but i

never yet has spoken, and never will at any time speak plainly. In vain does it repose in the arms of two emperors. They will treat it as our Richard is said to have treated the two children in the Tower. *Legions of Honour* must begin to march in a contrary direction, and demolish cities without *Pax Vobiscum*.

First of these exhibitions of lying was the declared *fact*, that the French Revolution was brought about by a few hundred miscreants from Marseilles : second is the declared *fact* that a few foreigners (not even so many as hundreds) domineered over Rome. If the first of these declared *facts* was well founded, to what a state of degradation and turpitude must not only the French nobility, but the French of all classes have fallen ! If the second, as M. Montalembert and M. Tocqueville have asserted, how will they venture to look in the face of any Frenchman who fought against Rome ? What ! a few foreigners kill a thousand or two of their *braves des braves*, and drive ten thousand from before the walls ! A few foreigners lead five thousand republicans out of the city to fight another day ! A few foreigners (and after they had disappeared) strike such terror into the citizens of Rome, that, knowing not what they were about, and losing all sense of salutary fear, they protested against the occupation of their city by their saviours ! I have seen no programme of hymn or anthem to be sung at the Pope's return ; but if MM. Tocqueville and Montalembert wish to sing one perfectly in accord with the service, let them, after these two facts, intone with Voltaire, like them a great Zealot,

" Descends du haut des cieux, auguste Vérité ! "

The Pope has lost her, and sadly wants her back again. France saw her last with Saint Louis on the shore of Damietta, and seems to care little about her. Paris could find a prostitute to personate the *Goddess of Reason* ; if she looks narrowly into her hospitals, she may perhaps find another, almost as fearless of ridicule, to represent the *Goddess of Liberty*. The likeness will at once be recognised, and all will cry "*patuit dea*."

WALTER SAVAGE LANDOR.

Rome had now been restored to the temporal dominion of the Papacy ; three of the Cardinals, as

Papal Commissioners, having entered the city at the end of July. A proclamation was published by them on August 1, 1849, announcing that Ministers would be appointed to control internal affairs ; foreign affairs being directed by Cardinal Antonelli. The following letter from Landor appeared in the *Examiner* of August 25 :—

The Pope.

Saint Peter, we are credibly informed, smote off the ear of the High-Priest's servant ; he seems now to have smitten off the ear of the High-Priest himself. Soldiers, who had landed from Africa, tried to catch it, and scrambled on the ground for it ; meanwhile a gang of cunning old thieves crept among their legs and carried it away in triumph. Jesuits and Cardinals now possess the relick, and blow into it shrilly from morning to night, playing a thousand odd tricks with it. Ashamed of being seen in publick with no ear belonging to him, the High-Priest claps both hands against his head-gear, and cries *Make room for the robbers*; and they turn a pretty penny by showing they have the High-Priest's ear in their possession.

Joseph Wolff, the self-sacrificer, who affronted death and the despot of Bokhara, in the shadowy and uncertain hope of saving two men he never saw, brings Peter and Pius face to face. Certainly Peter hath somewhat the advantage over Pius, who, in the words of Wolff, " exhorted his children in France to unsheath the sword against his children in Rome." Why was this ? It was not because they resisted his paternal authority in teaching them the duties of religion, but because, having now grown up to maturity, they preferred in the management of their estates the laws of jurisconsults to the decretals of theologians, and believed that the business of priests was very distinct, very different and alien, from the business of council-board and camp.

The children of France are too much in the habit of carrying crackers and serpents about them, which sometimes have blown their pockets to pieces, and singed their faces miserably. Indeed they have always been addicted to every kind of mischief. As among the children of Sparta there was a merit in thieving, if dexterously performed, so among these children there is an honour in lying if they can cleverly conceal or valiantly defend it. Whenever one of them cuts a finger, he cuts another to cure it. The children of Rome remonstrated against this practice when it was brought to bear against them; in consequence the children of France cut and slashed them in all directions, so that only their mother could recognise them. The mother did recognise them; and instead of wailing and tearing her hair, she lifted up her hands in the sight of all round about, and said only, "See ye this? see ye this? without reproof, without sympathy, without aid? Be it so. The same will befall *you* another day."

The certainty of this predictious accomplishment draws little attention, by reason of its apparent remoteness. Other events of some moment, if not more certain, are much nearer. Is it credible, is it possible, that Rome, that Italy, that Europe, are to be long without an avenger? If the laws are subverted, is there no danger to the subverter? In a moral view is it criminal to strike him down? If an offender is condemned to the gallows, and has strength enough to stifle the hangman on the scaffold and to leap off it, is it not the right and duty of any citizen to apprehend him, and to slay him should he resist? To break the laws is less criminal· than to abolish them; to rob an individual than to rob a community. It is well to cut off a thief; it is better to cut off a gang of thieves. Surely the Pope exposes the cardinals, whom he now imposes on the Roman people, to the punishments due to the stiflers of freedom and the subverters of law. If he had any courage, any honesty, any sense of religion in him, he would, instead of prevaricating and absconding, have spoken thus :—

"I tell you plainly, that being head of the Church, I will firmly maintain it ; but to every state and city now under my government I will restore its laws, and leave their regulation and improvement to the people."

He knows that the oldest of his title deeds is a forgery, and that of Peter's Patrimony not a plank or a fin is remaining. He knows that Bologna called him in as a protector, not as a prince ; as the arbiter of her disputes, not as the executioner of her citizens. Impartial History will represent not Attila nor Totila as the most devastating scourge, the most deadly plague of Italy, but Napoleon Bonaparte and his nephew Louis. The one threw her down, the

other (when she had risen) strangled her.   The two noblest cities in
the universe, the two cities longest free, were by them delivered over to
despotism.   Thus a rat and a rabbit can undermine the architecture
that has resisted ages.

WALTER SAVAGE LANDOR.

August 19.

The month of August 1849 saw the surrender o
Görgey, the Hungarian Dictator, to the Russians a
Arad, Kossuth's flight to Turkey, and the despatch
of a letter in the Czar's own hand, glorying in the
" success of our arms in the war I undertook for the
legal right of my august ally the Emperor of Austria
and for the suppression of the Hungarian insurrection.'
No more is needed to illustrate the first paragraph
of Landor's next letter (*Examiner*, Sept. 8).   In
the second paragraph he had in mind the Congress
of Universal Peace which had met in Paris, and the
opening speech of Victor Hugo, the President.

The Comfortable State of Europe.

Europe is now in that comfortable state in which all men in
power, whatever their politicks or their countries, wish to see her
Everything is settled ; no commotion, no demonstration.   The mos
speculative and the most ardent must alike acknowledge that it i
too late for interference or for intercession.   The master and arbite
of Europe sees Austria, Prussia, Sweden, Denmark, Turkey, crouch
ing at his feet, and France become his sword-bearer.   Forty year
ago the nations had little comparatively to fear from Bonaparte
His rashness and cupidity were the harbingers of his overthrow
But Russia is guided systematically by watchful and thoughtful
prompt and energetick, Ministers.   Every step of hers is considerate
and firm, is short and sure : she is exhausted by no hasty strides
she is enfeebled by no idle aspirations.   France believes it to be he
interest, and fancies it to be in her power, to divide the world with

her; and if two such nations, with ambition in accord, are resolved on it, what power upon earth can effectually interpose. It was the project of Napoleon to form a western and permit an eastern empire. He imagined the will could do everything; but no two natures are so distinct as the wilful and the wise. Never had man a quicker sight than Napoleon on the field of battle, or a shorter in the cabinet. His folly, and not our wisdom, saved us. What are we now to do? Russia has already crushed and subjugated the bravest, the most free, the most high minded people on the Continent; France has thrown Italy back into the grasp of Austria; the Germans hammer out and lay down laws, for troops of royal horse to ride over; England is laden with insolvable debts and unserviceable steam-boats. Perhaps there may, however, be time enough left her to counteract that power which she alone has been able to contend with, and lately might have coerced. France is neither able nor willing to stand up against that Colossus which strides from Archangel to Ormuz, over the snows of the Balkan and over the sandbanks of the Persian Gulph. England, by timely assistance to the Hungarians, would have saved Turkey and secured Egypt. Neither the Turks nor the Hungarians can look forward with confidence to another such opportunity. An English fleet in the Black Sea, at the invocation of the Turks, would have resuscitated the Circassians and the Polanders. Engaged with every disposable regiment against Hungary and Transylvania, the formidable monster of the north could have made *vestigia nulla retrorsum*; it must have perished in the pit-fall. A long series of future wars might thus have been prevented. Before two years are over, we must inevitably be engaged in one most formidable; one entered into not for the interests of our commerce, not for the defence of our allies, not for the maintenance of our treaties, not for sympathy with that brave nation now trampled on, the nation which bears the nearest affinity to us, in fortitude, constancy, and integrity, not for our prerogative and preeminence, but (what has never been the case these many ages) for our homes and lives. Vainly is it asserted that Russia can never hurt us, although it may indeed be conceded that she alone could never. But if Napoleon, in the blindness of his fury, had not attacked her where alone she was invulnerable, we should not at the present hour be arguing on moral duty and political expediency.

Regiments of French cavalry would have been sounding the bugle in every town and every hamlet of our land.

Virtuous men, American and English, sigh after peace in the streets of Paris! Now they are so far on the road, let them proceed to Gaeta and convert the Pope to Protestantism. There never can be universal peace, nor even general peace long together, while threescore families stand forth on the high grounds of Europe, and command a hundred millions to pour out their blood and earnings, whereon to float enormous bulks of empty dignities. Nor is it probable nor is it reasonable that young men, educated for the army and navy, should be reduced to poverty and inactivity. No breast in which there is a spark of honour would suffer this rank injustice, nor would any prudent man, however mercantile and mercenary, venture to propose it. The navy and army are the cotton-mills and spinning-jennies of Aristocracy, which she will shut up and abandon the very day Mr Cobden and Company shut up and abandon theirs. Enough was there of folly to choose France for the schoolroom of order, equity, and peace. A Frenchman is patient under the ferule if the stroke falls hard, but is always ready to filch and fib again and play with fire, and to kick his master the moment he turns his back and suspends the chastisement. Blood is as necessary to him as to a weazel. He may dip his whiskers in milk; but with a rapid and impatient motion he shakes his head and throws it off again. Away he goes, under the impulse of his nature, and washes out his disgrace in his own element. Scarves and speeches may fly about the dinner-table, but drums and fifes are the first things listened to in the morning. The people of France will presently have enough of this enjoyment. Two thunder-clouds so heavy and vast as are now impending in opposite directions on the horizon, cannot turn back; the world will be shaken to its foundations whether they collide or coalesce. Could nothing have obviated and dissipated these portents? Loudly did I denounce to the *Examiner* long ago, when the King of Prussia said he would march at the head of his army to resist the Russians, the perfidy of this man, and the certainty that he was conspiring with the two Emperors against the freedom of Germany. It was easy at that time to seize and banish him; and, since he had broken his own compact between King and people, it

was just. Nations will soon learn parables. Somebody will show them a vegetable by which they were long supported ; will show them that the distemper, which is consuming it, begins at the top ; and that, by cutting off this top in time, the sustenance of millions is secured.   WALTER SAVAGE LANDOR.
August 31, 1849.

In October of this year a dispute arose between France and the United States of America. Claims and counter-claims were made in regard to a seizure and detention of tobacco purchased by a French subject, and there was also a difference of opinion about the salvage of a French vessel. The tension between the two Governments became acute. The Washington correspondent of the *New York Herald* wrote :— " M. de Tocqueville, the Minister of Foreign Affairs, must resign; M. Poussin (French Minister at Washington), must be kicked aside; and the French Government must apologise, or a rupture must ensue . . . The case admits of no diplomatic cobbling." Guisseppe Mazzini's letter, to which Landor refers, was addressed to MM. de Tocqueville and de Falloox. In it he said :—" Rome and Italy will never forgive the Pope for having, as in the Middle Ages, called in foreign bayonets to transfix Italian hearts." The following letter from Landor was published in the *Examiner* of October 13, 1849 :—

The Presidents of France and America.

To be pacifick is as good a reason for French hostility as to be weak. Italy was so inviting that no wonder was excited at French invasion or French perfidy : but there is hardly an example in the history of policy so blind and erroneous. Detested as the French always were by every other people, the Italians, always deceived by

x

them, always plundered, always trampled on and cast off, continued to look toward them as protectors. Napoleon bartered Italy for a worthless wife; his nephew gives her up for an imperial crown under a papal consecration. He conciliated both Austria and Russia by abstaining from the consolidation of freedom throughout all the states of Europe, which might have been effected by the pressure of his foot, by only one step onward. And what has he gained by this alliance with despotism? The hatred of all free nations, the contempt even of the enslaved, not only of those who were reduced to this condition under his eye and his connivance, but also of the wretches born to servitude, the very nails and rivets of the chain that now encompasses the globe.

To what a height of glory might the President of France have attained if he had sprung up with her in her ascent toward freedom, if he had seconded and directed her energies, if he had abstained but from falsehood and fraud. History neither will nor can dissemble them : the eternal city bears the eternal testimony. The words of Mazzini are not the words of an angry zealot, but are registered in the archives of every honest heart. He accuses no man without the proof of all he utters : and there was a time when such an accusation, so confirmed, would have driven the delinquent beyond the pale of honourable men's society. A bold front and swaggering gait may reduce the cowardly to silence in presence of the ferocious ; not an inch further. It has been tried of late against the Americans, and with what success? A receiver of stolen goods is defended in his roguery by a French envoy. The French envoy is requested by the American Government to reconsider the propriety of his protection ; the American Government is answered with the same insolence as the Roman was on its calm and just expostulation. The matter was submitted by the American Government to the French Cabinet. The French Cabinet defends at once both the insolence and the fraud. Passports are delivered to the envoy ; he returns to France.

Arrogance is broken into foam when it dashes on the Western shores of the Atlantick. America knows equally her interests and her dignity. Averse to war, averse to the politicks of Europe, she is greatly more than a match against the united Powers of that Continent. France owes her money ; and she will have it, although, like many a civil suit, the contest may cost her greatly more than her demands. She is not to be shuffled off, or brought to a compromise, by a minor piece of trickery; the amount of money is not in question. The question is, whether the Americans are to be treated as ignominiously and superciliously as the Italians. At the head of the United States is a brave, a temperate, a sagacious man; no falsehood of word or deed could ever be objected to him. Americans, I hope, will pardon me in comparing their President (the indignity is unintentional) with the President of France. In one we behold the grave, sedate, veracious Englishman of England's Commonwealth, animated not indeed by a better spirit, but a spirit moving over vast and discord populations with strength to direct their energies and assign their courses; the other without any first principles, any determinate line of conduct, swearing to republicanism before the people, abjuring it before the priesthood, undermining it at home, battering it down abroad, delighted at transient cheers on a railroad, deaf to the distant voice of history, following his uncle where the way is tortuous, deviating where it is straight, and stopping in the midst of it to bow with equal obsequiousness to the heads of two religions. Symbolical of such a character is the Tree of Liberty; a tree unsound at root, shrivelled at top, shedding its leaves on the labourers who plant it, and concealing the nakedness of its branches in the flutter of the garlands that bedizen it.

Sometimes a preference makes poor amends for a comparison: but America will pardon me thus weighing a sound President against a hollow one. Temperate and strong as she is, she will treat arrogant petulance with calm derision. The resources of France, she well knows, are inadequate to set afloat, with soldiers and stores, any fleet that could make an impression. Her soldiers would find no field of operations, until by the humanity and munificence of their captors they should be employed in levelling the road to California. Beside, the Americans would rather see them perform an easier and more voluntary duty. Not only in common with the nations of Europe, but infinitely beyond them, those on the Atlantick see with abhorrence the wrongs and cruelties committed against the bravest and longest free of any on our Continent. Europe and Asia rise up simultaneously from a deathlike lethargy, which long held both, against more outrageous insolence, more unprovoked ferocity. The

God of Mahomet is called the *Merciful*; and his worship is not tl
worship of lip or knee.   Because the disciple of Mahomet is merʿ
ful to the follower of Christ, a Christian Potentate threatens him wi
a war !   America will not strike down the arm of France if she defenʿ
for once the cause of humanity and honour.   From no sympathy w
she ever do it, but from jealousy lest England should become mo
popular and more powerful in the East.

WALTER SAVAGE LANDOR.

Oct. 5.

CHAPTER IV

1850—1852

LANDOR'S first letter in the *Examiner* of 1850 was reprinted in " Last Fruit," p. 350, under the title, " What we have and what we owe." In this he wrote :—" Even in our own country many millions have been idly squandered in ships unfit for sailing and unnecessary for fighting. . . . We may soon want the ships that are no more; for ere six months are over, we shall have to support the Turkish Empire. But there are masses now inert which our machinery may raise, combine, and make combustible." His next letter, which follows, was printed in the *Examiner* of February 16 :—

The Warfare of Economy.

We never had so glorious an opportunity of engaging in a successful war as we have at present. What war? Against whom? A war of economy ; against the world. The rashness and insolence of the French have several times attempted to provoke us into one. Conscious of our strength, we looked down with calm contempt on the *bis victos Phryges.* The only war it becomes us to wage against her is the truly *Social* war ; the war of principles, the war of integrity, the war of economy. Instead of exceeding our revenue, as the French have done and will continue to do, we may without difficulty save eight or nine millions yearly. There is no necessity for much more than a colonial force in the West Indies or in Canada. They are able and willing to defray all the expenses of a just Government. If the *Crown* lands, as they are improperly called, were sold, thousands of labourers might be employed in the cultivation of them, and millions of money turned into the Exchequer. *Woods and Forests* would no longer swamp it. The Church lands should also be sold, and the proceeds be devoted to the education of the people, as was first intended. Whether the bishops should be paid better than the judges, the generals, or the admirals, will presently be decided by the publick voice. The Crown should continue to receive as much as it now receives from its lands; so should the Church: but the better part of the Church is the school-room, and next to it (as was formerly the case, until the Reformation) the hospital and poor-house. I should be sorry to see our army or our navy much diminished. Ten or twelve regiments may advantageously be disbanded, if proper steps are taken in Ireland, and if a man as wise and temperate as Lord Clarendon rules that country. When I consider what unworthy men have been entrusted with Governments abroad by those at home, I must consider it an especial dispensation of Divine Providence that the people here in power committed such an oversight as his appointment. Let Ireland be placed, in all respects, on the same footing as England and Scotland; let her have her own church as well as her own bar, and let Irishmen be alone on the bench in each. Let the taxes and duties be identical: and then let it be declared an act of treason to attempt a dismemberment of the empire. The French Government acts prudently and discreetly in coaxing the priesthood. By its suppression of liberty in Rome, she exasperated a few honest men. How few are there anywhere to be exasperated by wrongs to others! And it is questionable if the most ardent repealer in Ireland saw with any disapprobation the abolition of Roman independence and Italian freedom, in his veneration of a spiritual head, equally able to pardon and prompt to commit a perjury. The invasion of Rome under the mask of amity conciliated the whole papistical priesthood on the Continent, excepting in Rome itself, where the iniquities of its higher orders were seen and suffered daily. Even in free Belgium it was a subject of rejoicing; and it is only a reluctance to share in the national debt of France which withholds the Rhenish provinces from returning to her. Happily for Europe, her restless ambition will increase the weight of her debt, and render it every year more galling. Another revolution of the wheel will only sink it deeper in the slough.

Liberty held up a light which Popery was glad to extinguish. She has one of her own, she tells us, quite sufficient to guide us as far as we ought to go; she hates a double one, or much of any; it shows too plainly her pearl-powder and patches, her false teeth, and innumerable wrinkles. Bolstered up on her new pillow from Paris, she may be cajoled into bequeathing her patrimony to the eldest born of Perfidy, whose name announces his parentage : this will cost France very dear. Her honour is gone irretrievably with her plighted faith; her allies distrust and disown her; and her armies will presently so exhaust her treasury, that, with a little of timely economy, we shall disable her, without an effort, without a move-ment, from inflicting the injuries she meditates against us.

WALTER SAVAGE LANDOR.

January.

In the *Examiner* of June 15, 1850, there was a long reply by Landor to an article in the *Quarterly Review*, but this was reprinted in " Last Fruit," p. 339, and need not be given here. His letter on " The Monument to Sir Robert Peel" (*Examiner*, July 27), was also reprinted in " Last Fruit." The following letter, not reprinted, was published in the *Examiner* of August 24, 1850. Parliament had adjourned on the 15th of the same month.

Activity of Parliament.

Parliament is now broken up, and scattered with pointers and setters "over the hills and far away." Recollecting its last deeds in its new house, I heartily wish it sport, and not only for this autumnal season, but for the whole of the remaining and the coming year. History will take heed of these matters; we take none. Even in the reign of Charles the Second, there were conscientious and righteous men, who remonstrated against wasteful expenditure and undue claims. Shaftesbury still retained the exterior of a gentleman and man of spirit; Hyde, in the midst of an enormous expenditure from the last drainage of an impoverisht land, had somewhat of the nobleman tagged upon the lawyer. He had not forgotten that he was born among the virtuous, and that once he was one. Not within the circle but within the crescent of a century, our country had contained a greater number of great men than ever appeared anywhere in an equal period. We wonder that we can find no traces or resemblances of them now. Tergiversation and trickery are paramount. Little do we seem aware that honesty is part of intellect. It is always the best part; too often the only one. Bacon had no room for it in the vast palace of his mind; Coke threw it up into a corner, where nothing of it was seen thro' his narrow and grated window of five-inch panes. Dustmen sweep it, early in the morning, out of great houses. Poor writers pick it up, and throw it aside for anything more tempting. Improvident poets have often an allotment of it for their patrimony; but they scratch it into sore places when they suffer the flea-bites of jealousy, which induce a distemper not preventible by vaccination nor curable by sulphur. Politicians are equally subject to it; but they resolutely urge the knife and cautery, until they have extirpated the hard tubercle of honesty and salved over the cicatrice. We have seen reformers, who have somewhat of a name to rest upon, abjuring their principles and promises, protecting scourgers and murderers, and driving to desperation the most industrious and the most peaceable of colonists. Proofs of these facts are collected, examined, found undeniable, found manifold; Parliament knows of their existence, knows that many have been garbled, many withheld; and what does Parliament? goes *grousing*! Long may it remain upon the moors; may it remain there until the people of England have recovered their senses and their spirit, and have decided that inflictors of torture, and inciters to rebellion, may be and ought to be impeacht of high crimes and misdemeanours.

WALTER SAVAGE LANDOR.

During the war in Hungary, the Austrian General Haynau was accused of having ordered women to be flogged by his troops. A letter from an Englishman, published in the *Daily News* of September 29, 1849, said :—

" A few days after our departure, General Haynau arrived at Ruseberg, and, enraged apparently at the escape of Bem and Guyon, vented his fury on those who had treated them with kindness and courtesy. He ordered the lady of the house to be flogged, and she was afterwards dragged barefoot by his soldiers as far as Hatseg. Her unfortunate husband, maddened by this outrage, blew out his brains with a pistol."

A different version may be found in the reminiscences of the late Sir William Frazer, who held that General Haynau was not personally to blame for the affair. However this may be, when General Haynau came to this country on a visit in 1850 he found himself an object of public execration. On September 4 of that year the "Austrian butcher," as he was styled, was assaulted by a mob, at Barclay's brewery, and was only rescued with great difficulty by the police. This unfortunate incident naturally evoked a serious protest from the Austrian Government, as well as an excited correspondence in the English press, in which Landor joined. Beside verses on the subject in "Last Fruit," p. 367, he wrote the following letter to the *Examiner*, published by that paper on September 14, 1850 :—

Reception of Haynau.

SIR,

    Accounts have reached every part of England announcing the reception of Haynau. Whatever is new is generally more acceptable in this country than in any other ; and murderers have lately been the principal objects of solicitude and compassion. Personal wrongs, urgent necessity, and neglected education, the fault of parents or of Government, have impelled the greater part of these wretches to the commission of their crime. Yet the feeling is false and morbid which induces those of a better nature to visit them in their prisons, and to comfort them under the sentence of the laws. What excuse then is there for patronizing the deliberate murderer of brave soldiers, not met in the field of battle, not taken with arms

about them, who, if they had fought against Haynau, fought agains
the invader of their country, fought for the laws of the land, fough
for their wives and children?   What excuse is there for scourging ii
the publick market-place the most delicate of girls and mothers
Ages have past over our heads since such atrocities were committee
in Europe, and only one man has been found capable of committin;
them.   Deservedly has this wretch been designated in all language
as the *hangman Haynau*.   Is it credible that he has the audacit:
and impudence to venture into this country; to walk openly in ou
streets?   If Marat and Robespierre and Couthon had been displacee
and exiled, is ours the land in which they would have claimed the
rights of hospitality?   Yet they were only the engines of the laws
which, many as were the innocent struck down by them, many the
noble, many the aged, many the young, spared torture, sparec
degredation.

I think it probable that the gentleman in the *Times*, who defend:
on every occasion the exercise of arbitrary power, may receive i
reprimand from Petersburg.   For, the *disgrace* of Haynau (this i:
the term in Courts, where turpitude has no such meaning) came
like all other Continental movements, from that quarter.   Of existing
rulers, certainly the Emperor of Russia is the most able; and, when
ever he permits a cruelty under his subject crowns, he ensures tc
himself popularity by compassing in due time the humiliation of the
subordinate actor.   He was resolved that the youth he protected at
Vienna should lose for ever his hold on the Hungarians, while he
took himself off a little and stood aloof, breathing a tepid air o:
clemency.

There is much to be admired in the character of this potentate,
but there is, greatly more to be feared.   He is guided by one sole
star, and never turns his eyes away from it.   Variable as the winds
are the counsels of every nation round, while his are conducted by
calm sagacious men along the same line of polity from age to age.
Whatever he meditates he effects.   He knows that the hour of action
is not to be accelerated by putting on the hands of his watch.
Omnipotent not only at Athens, but through Athens at Munich;
omnipotent at Vienna, at Berlin, at Stockholm, at Copenhagen, he
excites, or suppresses, or modulates, or varies the discordant cries
of France in every Department.   The eastern empire rises up again,

with greater vigour and surer hopes than Constantine in Byzantium could impart to it, and is now overshadowing and overawing the dislocated and chaotic West. Nicholas wills the abolition of republicks; France swears to maintain them; and instantly throws down her own that she may the more readily subvert the Roman. In the hand of Napoleon his half-dozen royalets were never more pliable manikins than the nephew is in the hand of Nicholas. It will use him for a time, as for a time it used Haynau. In England, it seems, this discarded butcher, stript by Austria of his apron and cleaver, is not to be touched, but is, on the contrary, to be respected. And why? Because he has come upon our shores!

Unquestionably the hangman will find defenders here in England: but the defenders of such a wretch, whether in print or Parliament, are even worse than himself. Criminals who have been put into the pillory for much smaller offences, and indeed for one only, have undergone thereby the sentence of the law; yet public indignation pelts them; and the press acquiesces. Mr Baron Rothschild calls the unfortunate man his friend. Jews are most peculiarly citizens of the world: Baron Rothschild among the rest: but Baron Rothschild, the friend of Haynau, has a better right to be a citizen of the world than a citizen of London; and a better to be a citizen of London than its representative. Never let us hear again of the *indignities* the scourger and hangman has undergone; nor of extenuating comparisons between his crimes and the crimes of others.

The distinguished writer in the *Times* is indignant that a person of Haynau's age should be scouted and insulted. There are crimes of which age and infirmity itself are an aggravation. Age ought to be exempt from the violence of the passions: age ought to be lenient, considerate and compassionate: age should remember its past impetuosities and rejoice in their extinction: age must often have seen around its own domestick hearth the irrepressible ebullition of generous emotions, and sometimes of ungenerous. The nearer to the grave we are, the more should we be on a level with the humanities, and the more observant of those fellow-men whom we are leaving on this side of it. There is folly in calling it an act of cowardice to drive away an assassin, whatever be his age or his condition. Grey hairs are venerable only on the virtuous. We

have seen grey-whiskered wolves ; but we never have seen a body
of the most innocent villagers backward to pursue them in consideration of this merit.

WALTER SAVAGE LANDOR.

September 7, 1850.

There were one or two other letters in the *Examiner*
this year, but they have either been reprinted in "Last
Fruit" or are of no importance. It may be worth
noting, however, that a long review of a minor poet
in the *Examiner* of December 7 was evidently written
by Landor. There are several passages in it, afterwards incorporated in his acknowledged writings.

The following letter, published in the *Examiner* of
June 28, 1851, may not have lost all its interest :—

What to do with the Crystal Palace ?

SIR,

  I beg permission to lay before you the suggestion of a
gentleman no less distinguisht for his judgment than for his
liberality.

  " The last observation I heard you make was, I believe, an expression of the
high interest you felt about Mr Paxton. The newspaper talk of the day is,
' What is to become of the Crystal Palace ?' the production of his genius. Would
not that question be well referred to the parent of the Palace ? Who more competent or more fit than he would be to direct and superintend the future of his
bantling during his life ? The large funds created by the Exhibition are mainly
due to the success of the building, and some portion could not be better applied
than in a suitable testimonial to the pre-eminent contributor to the national fête.
A grant by Parliament to Mr Paxton of the site of the building for life, with the
unfettered disposal of the building during that period, would, I venture to
suggest, be a proceeding on the part of Parliament and the Commissioners which
would meet with the applause of the nation. That Mr Paxton would devise uses
for the building which would meet with public approbation, I should have the
fullest confidence. I take the liberty of submitting this notion to your judgment."

When strangers have seen in London the worst specimens of
architecture that any country in the present age has exhibited, and

have compared them with some which at the same period have adorned the poorest countries, such as Prussia and Bavaria, they will naturally inquire what honours and rewards have been conferred upon the modest architect of the *Crystal Palace*? My first hope is, that Parliament will, among the hundred acts which it passes in one session and rescinds in the following, will be wise enough to cancel its vote in regard to this noble edifice. Light as it is, it is constructed of such materials that it may outlast the most ponderous building in the whole metropolis. And, what can be said of no other on earth, tens of thousands may enjoy it daily in the most ungenial months of the year, respiring health and prolonging life, and blessing the beneficence that raised it. The wealthy, no doubt, will contribute the rarest and most beautiful plants to its embellishment. The grant is the only one worthy of the Architect's acceptance, who has already received the highest honour in the friendship of the Duke of Devonshire.

WALTER SAVAGE LANDOR.

The following letter, printed in the *Examiner* of August 16, 1851, was no doubt prompted by the appearance of Mr Gladstone's pamphlet on the State trials at Naples and the iniquities of King Bomba :—

Naples and Rome.

There is little hope that, in any nation of Europe, is the energy or the will to deliver from bondage those Romans or those Neapolitans who at this hour are groaning under it. Africans, the most barbarous, claim our pity and intervention. To exempt them from violence we snap asunder old alliances, and unite our forces with other governments of doubtful faith. Portugal has been coerced, France has been trusted, every Power has been defied. A perfidious Pope, meanwhile, and a revengeful and remorseless gang of Jesuits, are allowed to inflict on the most virtuous and the most enlightened citizens torments more intolerable than the hardest labour, indignities more cruel than the most cruel death. The *Times*, with an angry voice, a voice audible to the extremities of Europe and

America, has denounced the iniquity of these miscreants. Mr Gladstone, calm and circumspect, has laid open to the world the island-prison in which the most sanguinary and most cowardly of despots chains down the faithfullest and bravest of his people. Their only crime is, that they are witnesses to the making and breaking of his oaths, his vapouring and his fright.

In regard to the victims which the *Holiness of our Lord* shuts up for sacrifice, it is probable that a few words of our most gracious Queen, address to the President of the French Republic, would release them. One gentle breath might remove the tarnish from his glory, and moderate in some degree the animosity that rankles in the Roman heart. On the barbarian who rules at Naples there is no other agency but force and fear. Policy might induce the Americans to liberate his captives from their pestilential dens. A single ship, with a few broadsides and a few boarders, would effect it. The island would be as fairly won by them from this inhuman monster as ever slave-ship was by the bravest of our cruisers. And surely those hosts of heroic men who have fought for the same cause in Hungary and Poland will be prompt to embark in this most holy of crusades ; in a crusade at the outset against a dastard and fugitive, and ultimately against an infidel who assumes in mockery the Crown of Christ, who calls himself God's vice-gerent, subverts His attributes, effaces His laws, and stamps upon His image.

WALTER SAVAGE LANDOR.

A letter from Landor headed "Tranquillity in Europe," and published in the *Examiner* of December 13th and 20th, was reprinted in "Last Fruit" (p. 348) ; and the next letter to be quoted here is the following, which was printed in the *Examiner* of August 14, 1852. A few weeks before, a Note had been addressed to the United States Government by the English Secretary of State for the Colonies, regarding American encroachments on our fisheries.

Letter to an American.

SIR,

You are perfectly right in your opinion that I wish heartily well to the Americans. Indeed I do: I wish them prosperity, peace, and glory, all which can spring from integrity alone. Imagine to yourself the most perfect agricultural machine, brought into a field by the most industrious and intelligent farmer; imagine him entering upon ground fertile and well-prepared; then imagine him to have forgotten one thing, only one, namely, the seed. In such a condition will you be, even under the best institutions, if you neglect to bring into your rich and highly-cultivated land the article most needful both for domestic use and for external commerce, namely, honesty. I am led to these reflections by the intelligence conveyed to me in your letter, and circulated on the same day by the public newspapers, that Mr Webster has announced the probability of hostility between America and England, because we insist on the observance of a treaty. The Romans, whom you delight to imitate, were strictly observant of their treaties; and nothing was held to be more religious by a most religious people, until, in place of Mars,

"Capitolium
Scandit cum tacitâ Virgine pontifex."

An intense desire of popularity, and a dazzling prospect of high station, are suspected in America, as in England, to be the motives of the statesman who is now exciting you to an aggressive war. He knows that we have committed no violence, no injustice, in regard to the fisheries off Newfoundland. Our only fault is negligence in omitting so long to enforce our rights; we never have ceased pacifically to assert them. With reason do you laugh at our politicians, who forbore to exclude you totally; and who, when France was driven back, broken and subjugated, by the continental monarchs under our general, accepted as "indemnity for the past and security for the future" a sum of money scarcely equivalent to the expenditure of the last quarter. Our country has often been governed, within our memory, by men even less acute and provident, but never by one so ignorant as Lord Castlereagh. He signed the treaty of peace, and ceded whatever was demanded. Above all things it was necessary to retain the whole right of fishery round about the coast

Y

of Newfoundland, to the utter exclusion of the French, who had
been excluded for twenty years.   At present they give a bounty to
their sailors engaged in it; and we give the same sailors a greater
we freely give them all that they can take away from us.   This
fishery is more important to our power than whatever else o
dominion we possess in the whole circuit of the globe.   The com
merce of China must for the most part fall soon into your hands
that of India will follow gradually.   Within a period which some
already born may live to see, your territory, your United States, how
ever lax the Union, will, with interminably vast accretions and per
petual immigrations, contain a population far exceeding the census o
Europe.   You are destined to be the most numerous people, tr
also to be the greatest (which is quite another thing) that ever existe
on the earth.   Be wiser than we have been; and prepare the neigh
bouring nations for union with you, by propagating among them
your laws and language.   Our bigger boys will have been playing a
football until the bladder shall burst under the closing kicks of th
contending parties.   Rome had only one in her aristocracy; w
have two : it is easy to foresee a coalition and its result.   I am no
among those who rejoice at it; for I think our commonwealt
might with little improvement be made better, if not more durabl
than yours.   Let us be strenuous in consolidating, not in overturning
each other's work.   A few weeks ago Englishmen and American
spoke universally, and with equal emphasis, of a strict alliance; an
now, it appears, we are quarrelling, like butchers' dogs, under th
hustings of Mr Webster.   Presidency with him stands before Probit
Remember, he insisted in like manner on our receding from ou
boundary line of Oregon, believing, as he well might, in the utto
ignorance of our officials, and having the map of the territory und
his own eyes.   Well therefore did he know our right to what he wa
at that moment claiming from us.   But there is one thing which l
did not know quite so well; he did not know that an honest man
honest in all capacities, honest in private, honest in public.   H
would not appropriate to himself a bank-note left incautiously on th
table of a tavern; he would not filch a handkerchief from you
pocket; he would not defraud you of your winnings on returnir
from a race-course; he would not bring forward false witnesses
swear that a piece of land, left to you by your father, had contracte

its dimensions since your father's death. Perhaps not ; but my charity is somewhat larger than my faith. Oregon, Oregon puzzles and perplexes me. Simple as we are, we are not to be defrauded again by the same person. We recognize his features; and our policemen in blue jackets, the faithful body guard of their foster-mother Newfoundland, will arrest him and his accomplices on the coast.   I am, &c.

WALTER SAVAGE LANDOR.

The following letter, printed in the *Examiner* of October 23, 1852 was written in anticipation of Louis Napoleon's assumption of the Imperial title, the logical sequence of the *coup d'état* of December 2, 1851 :—

The Coming Empire.

To use an expression which every man uses every day, either in derision or sobriety, the coronation of Louis Napoleon is *looming in the distance*. We are unable to put it by; and I see no reason why we should desire to do so. If the terrific image comes toward us larger and nearer, when we are behind the exhibition, and discover what is in the interior, we shall find that others move it, and that the thing itself is but of moderate dimensions.

I have never shown any partiality towards Louis Napoleon since his invasion of the Roman States, which threw back the liberty of Europe far behind the lifetime of the youngest man existing ; but I rejoice in the grand exploit performed by the dexterous successor of Van Amberg. I am amused at the howlings and fawnings, the writhings and prostrations, of the mischievous animals he has scourged into subjection. If they were loose upon the earth, what interminable mischief they would do ! Even the priests he brings about him are endurable so long as he employs them in enchanting the serpents and in squeezing the venom from their fangs.

Philosophy has been making some progress in the world for nearly two centuries. Superstition was always lying in wait for her, and at last has overtaken and gagged her. Wooden images roll their eyes again and speak audibly : crucifixes are driven into the earth, show-ing the places where human victims are to be offered up as burnt

offerings to the God of peace.   Another two centuries may elapse
before such ceremonials are at an end.   All this revolution might
have been obviated by one step forward of Louis Napoleon.   But
surely it is unwise in us Englishmen to divert from him the attention
of the continent, or to take part in the vindication of the wrongs
we had the weakness to permit.   After we had abandoned Oporto
to the imaginary interests of one family, we ceded all hereditary
right of interference in the cause of freedom.   No nation can repose
any confidence in us for the future.   Why then exasperate one so
powerful by strictures on its internal concerns?   It is well for us
that the most successful of rulers sees clearly his interests on the
side of peace.   His people demand it; his treasury is empty; and
the treasuries of his neighbours are exhausted by the same expenditure, by vast armies and futile preparations.   Meanwhile we ourselves have neglected the most needful.   Long ago Sir William
Napier urged on Government the necessity of a fortification on the
Isle of Wight.   Other men saw it later and less distinctly; at last it
is about to be commenced.   We are raising a body of militia, enormous and inefficient; five thousand artillerymen would do more
service than this eighty thousand; the one taken from idleness, the
other from industry.   It was the opinion of Lord St Vincent (and
no authority can be higher) that we should always have forty sail of
the line in the English Channel.   How many have we? and what
are the crews, and where?   We are safe from conquest, but are we
quite safe from invasion?   If between the middle of November and
the middle of February the French land fifteen thousand men upon
Pevensey beach, and as many near the mouth of the Thames, direct-
ing their main force against Ireland; or indeed if only one of these
armaments reach the coast, what will be our condition!   Experienced
officers, military and naval, are more apprehensive of evil consequences than the gentlemen of the press.   These look through their
green spectacles on the sunny street below; those through their tele-
scopes on arsenal and dockyard, sail and steamer, equipage and
battalion.

Let us be ready for any enemy who may come against us, but let
us abstain from provocation.   The hour is past when we could have
defended others; the hour is come when we are called upon to
defend ourselves.   To throw a pebble at a man who is standing on

the other side of the Channel may indeed show our enmity, but neither our wisdom nor our strength. Outcries against perjury are natural and rational; but when they are raised against Louis Napoleon, they are quite as likely to wound the other princes. His perjuries, far from excluding him, place him among the legitimate sovrans of the highest order, of whom not a single one, excepting the Emperor of Russia, is guiltless of this crime against his people, God's vicar taking the precedency. Louis Napoleon is not only the hereditary successor of his uncle, but the grand referendary and representative of the French nation. I forget how many above a dozen oaths Talleyrand vaunted that he had broken; his survivors broke all these, and many since. Absolution was necessary, and Catholicism was necessary for absolution. Behold then on what a broad basis *the religion of our fathers* is set up again!

It is our duty, no less than our interest, to abstain from interference in the domestic affairs of France. I regret, as there are many who do, the vehement attacks made by the powerful engine of the *Times* on the chief magistrate of that country, whose offences lie elsewhere, and not against us, at present. I admire the magnificent instrument sounding throughout Europe from our highest organ-loft, and only wish the trumpet stop was heard less often.

W. S. LANDOR.

October 15.

In a letter to Landor published in the *Examiner* of November 6, 1852, Lord Dudley Stuart protested against the exception, in the Czar's favour, to the charge that *every* sovereign in Europe was a perjurer. His lordship's letter concluded with the remark :—
"the only real exception among the 'legitimate (Christian) sovereigns of the highest order' is not the Emperor Nicholas, but our own venerated and beloved Queen Victoria." Landor's reply, which appeared in the *Examiner* of November 13, was as follows :—

Lord Dudley Stuart and Mr Landor.

Lord D. Stuart, with his usual courtesy and frendliness, encloses in a letter to me this evening the copy of another which is to appear in the *Examiner* to-morrow.   Next week perhaps, Sir, you will insert my answer, containing the reason, however insufficient, why, having mapped and registered the Satellites of Russia, I left a blank space in the center.

The Emperor is courageous and consistent : his subordinate kings and princes are more cowardly and contemptible than the most abject of their supporters.   The scourge of Haynau, unless the backs of ladies have too much softened it, would be the proper instrument to employ against them : another fate, more accordant to usage in the palace of the Tzars, may attend its present occupant. So long as he lives, every high movement of the human heart throughout the Continent, every patriotic expression, every hopeful aspiration, and almost the hopeless sigh, will be supprest.

WALTER SAVAGE LANDOR.

To Lord Dudley C. Stuart.

MY DEAR LORD,
                    Your remark is perfectly just, that my language is too lenient towards the Emperor of Russia.   If I have represented him as guiltless of perjury, and have placed him apart from his fellows, it was only in relation to the subjects born within his proper dominions.   He swore nothing to them : he had no need for it. And indeed in regard to Poland he has done nothing worse than our administrators have done towards the Ionian Islands, Australia, Ceylon, and the Cape, by constitutions undermined, engagements broken, remonstrances derided, and the most fertile countries inundated and devastated by periodical shoals of outcast criminals.

If these administrators had only sown tares among the wheat, they had simply adhered to their traditional system of husbandry, but they have sown thistle and thorn, aconite and deadly night-shade.   Not only no worse, but better, greatly better, the harrow of Nicholas.

The close of your letter, my lord, presents an object upon which it is infinitely more gratifying to dwell. Yes, our gracious Queen deserves our affection and veneration. Men of your lordship's rank and proximity, whose benefactions have been followed by acclamation to the extremities of the world, may expatiate on her virtues, public and private, with equal decorousness and delight. But when the obscure and insignificant, like myself, attempt to praise a personage so elevated, there is generally a suspicion, and not always a groundless one, of an unworthy motive. Modesty on the right hand, pride on the left, admonish and coerce me to abstain.

With many and hearty thanks for your kindness in correcting me,
I remain, my dear Lord,
Yours most sincerely,
WALTER SAVAGE LANDOR.

CHAPTER V

1853—1855

CHAPTER V

1853—1855

On June 26, 1853, the Czar issued the famous manifesto which announced that, all means of persuasion having been exhausted, Russian troops had been ordered to enter the Danubian principalities, "and thus show the Porte how far its obstinacy may lead it." Landor rightly interpreted the signs of a coming war, but it is hardly surprising if his political information was not absolutely correct in matters of detail. The attempt made by Russia to secure the Shah's co-operation in a war against Turkey was not successful. His Minister, Mirza Agha Khan, persuaded him that the combined forces of England, France and Turkey were stronger than those of Russia. Prince Dolgorouki, the Russian Envoy at Teheran, was so enraged at finding that the project of a Russo-Persian Alliance was defeated, that in an interview with the Mirza he angrily flourished his cane and struck him on the leg. The Mirza seized the cane and throwing it to the other end of the room, requested Prince Dolgorouki to withdraw. After that, the Shah was eager to join the Allies; but, perhaps unwisely, his overtures were rejected, and he was advised to remain neutral. The following letter from Landor was published in the *Examiner* of July 9, 1853 :—

347

England, France, and Russia.

SIR,

It appears that the Emperor of Russia has at last executed his threat to invade the Turkish dominions. That such an aggression is contrary to his treaties, not only with Turkey, but with all the high powers of Europe, is acknowledged universally. The press in France and England condemns it no less as unjust and insolent, than dangerous to the freedom of other states. A general confederacy of them all would have been politic and justifiable long ago, on ground equally tenable. England has been perfidiously supplanted by the Tzar in the Court of Persia, and his influence has been active and sinister in Cabul and Afghanistan. The city and fortress of Herat felt it recently. We shall never be secure in the Punjab or Scinde until what is called Independent Tartary is really and effectually what at present it is only in the map. Persia is aware of this, and her jealousy of Turkey is turned against a Power more encroaching and more formidable. Omar and Ali join hands against it, and the King is supporter of the Khalif. No other question but this momentous one could unite France and England. On this their honour and their interests are at stake. Happily, since war is unavoidable and peace disgraceful, the expenditure of money and force can safely be moderate. France can well employ a few hundreds of her officers in disciplining the Turkish levies ; and England has need only to supply as much of arms and ammunition as will cost her less than her disbursements amounted to in a single month of her last hostilities against France. Russia is the most vulnerable of European Empires. Surely the two greatest and the least vulnerable will not omit the opportunity of lessening at once her dominions and her injustice. We are more aggrieved than France is: Austria is more aggrieved than we. Shiploads of stones, beside ballast, have been cast year after year into that mouth of the Danube which Russia was bound by treaty to keep open. This is injurious to the agriculture and commerce of all the provinces on the borders of that river, and especially of Hungary. It forces us into Odessa for grain, and largely increases the rate of tonnage and the delay of supplies. With small aid from the united fleets of France and England, would Turkey be enabled to repossess her territory as far as to the borders of the Phasis. The Circassians, the

Normans of Asia, would have beaten the Russians in a hundred battles, would drive them utterly and for ever from their country, and the Russian empire would be bounded in that direction by the Volga. Russia employs arms everywhere which England employs only in cities and boroughs. A million sterling would detach her Cossacks from her, and make independent princes of their Hetmans. But first there must be war.   WALTER SAVAGE LANDOR.

On November 1, 1853, the Czar declared war against Turkey, and the first encounter between the Russian and Turkish troops took place three days later. On December 3, the *Examiner* published the following address to the Czar, written by Landor :—

To The Emperor Nicholas.

It will be thought by some an act of indecorum, by others of somewhat like insanity, to address a king or emperor as if he were a man ; as if verily and indeed he were a rational creature, accountable here or hereafter for the government of his fellow creatures. Fellow creatures ! By what potentate, by what minister, were they ever admitted to be ? Nevertheless I have always thought that they were. And, having taken no lessons in walking backward, nor been engaged for the *minuet de la cour*, I shall do a man's duty in coming at once toward the proudest of these potentates, telling him that whoso places himself next to God is thereby the most ungodly.

Nicholas ! Tzar of Muscovy ! disturber of Europe and Asia, violator of treaties the most sacred, invader of every neighbour's lands, scoffer at his laws and allegiance, how long are thy perfidy and violence to endure? What pleasure canst thou derive from human sufferings? What benefit from the servitude of nations ? What glory from the abasement of surrounding kings ? Is there no danger in trampling on the prostrate ? The charger in the field of battle knows there is. Is it a healthy exercise, year after year, to gallop over the festering, the dying, the dead and unburied ?

Tzar Nicholas ! thy empire was built upon blood : on blood have many been constructed, none consolidated. Thou and thy pre-

decessors have purchased and fixed golden collars on sagacious an
staunch hounds, keeping them within your own kennel, and allowin
no cross from so valuable a breed. But, Tzar Nicholas, there i
one at hand who is able to run you down. There is one holdin
the same rank and title as yourself, who is followed by men c
stouter hearts and more alacrity than yours, men panting to find a
Petersburg what they lost at Moscow. Tzar Nicholas! thou, witl
out intending or perceiving it, hast fabricated in thy furnace th
electric wire that unites inseparably France and England.

WALTER SAVAGE LANDOR.

On November 30, 1853, the Turkish fleet was de
stroyed by the Russians in the harbour of Sinope
The following letter, written just after the full report
of the affair had reached England, was published i:
the *Examiner* of December 17 :—

Abettors of Revolution.

There are many honest and sagacious men who deprecate
material change in the affairs of Europe, and whose dreams are di:
turbed by the phantasmagoria of revolutions. Others there are, an
no less intelligent nor of less integrity, who are wide-awake, an
anxious for the dawn of day, when they may be up and stirrin{
These are called revolutionists: why so? for wishing to restor
the order of things, disturbed and subverted of late by lawles
violence. "Is it revolutionary," they ask, "to fly back into th
arms of Conservatism? to seize the highway robber, the maraude:
the assassin, and force him to surrender the spoil?" Such are th
sentiments of the Hungarians; such are the sentiments of th
Polanders, compatriots of Kossuth and Czartoryski. Their spirit i
not spent and lost in a flash and a detonation : it lies embosomed i
the higher regions, never to be extinguished, never to be suppres
but bursting forth from its clashing clouds in every hot season, t
renovate and to purify. That season is now advanced. Depr\
dators and murderers already betake themselves to flight and dar\
ness : the wounded rise upon their crutches, and animate by cri\
of vengeance, by appeals to honor, by adjurations to country, th

onward march of their sons.   At the present hour it is not only the
Polander, beguiled of his inheritance, and derided in open court by
the diplomatist who held his brief; it is not only the Hungarian
scourged out of his homestead, with his old laws broken and tied
about his neck; it is not only the Mussulman who refuses to acknowledge Tzar Nicholas for God; it is not only the Circassian,
our Creator's most perfect masterpiece, that is now rising up against
the homicide.   Even the Prussian, even the Austrian, upon whose
backs the cane falls naturally, are sulky at the knout.   Another
people, the highest once in military glory, is reminded of its marvel-
lous exploits against Europe's most insidious and most formidable
enemy.

The Russians, like ants, pursue invariably one beaten track.
Crush thousands; fresh thousands follow.   What they do not con-
sume, what they do not devastate, they undermine.   There is no
royal house whose sill appears to be high enough to keep them out;
and yet let us hope there is one.   Charles and Gustavus still exist
in the memory of Scandinavia.   King Oscar will remind his people
on whose soil stands Petersburg, and upon the spot itself will point
out to his army the legitimate boundary of Finland.   There are survivors among the veterans who, under Klingspor, covered their
invaded territory with Muscovite carcases, and saw with indignation
its surrender.   The Tzars pave the road to conquest with materials
from the mines of Siberia.   Other potentates use iron only; the
Tzars fuse their iron with gold.   This is the secret of their laboratory;
here stands the insurance-office of their successes.   They never won
a battle against a civilized enemy with equal numbers and honorable
arms.   In the last thirty years they have lost two hundred thousand
troops in the defiles of the Caucasus: above half the number died
in hospitals.   No great loss! they were not serfs; they were only
Polanders; refractory, rebellious, so well educated that they ought
to have known better than to talk of country!   So well-built that
they ought to be ashamed of weeping over her!   France gained few
of her victories under Napoleon the First without the Polanders,
and she may again stand in need of their co-operation.   Is it then
no interest of hers that they should be united and strong? stronger
than they ever were, and an effective barrier against barbarism?

Germany lies more exposed: has Germany then less interest in their strength and union? There are fainter hopes in that quarter for the potentates there are bound by family ties to Russia, and are mounted on Cossac saddles, and wear gilt spurs fabricated at Peters burg. The English, who hate injustice and oppression, will show that family ties never shall hold them down at the footstool of the throne. They are loyal in the truest and highest sense of loyalty and would rush into the palace were there need, to rescue their Queen from any species of degredation. The worst of any would be a secret connivance at manifest wrong, and placing a pure hand within a wholesale murderer's.

The Tzar has rushed into wrong with his eyes open, and remains there sword in hand. His adherents tell us that he must fight his way out again or feel humiliated. When he lied and prevaricated he ought to have felt so. The Turks (to use their own phrase) will make him " eat dirt" in making him eat his own words. Nothing of what is disingenuous and dishonest could unite the English people so firmly to the French. Common interest, no doubt, would have its weight, even in lighter matters : but here the interest is not com mon between the two parties only ; each of the two is stript for the race of glory on a plain and solid ground, with smaller nations standing round, afraid to enter the lists, and with bosoms swelling but not daring to applaud. How many of them are crowded into one house of bondage ! and shall none be taken out? Shall none be left in his own home ? Shall a single hand grasp the throat o twenty nations, reduce men to the condition of beasts, palisading them in a deep forest, out of which there is no escape but the cord which drags them into the field of battle ? There indeed, they again see the faces of their countrymen, of their fathers, their brothers their sons : there the homicide makes the parricide : there he com mits in one single day ten thousand crimes, any one of which would bring to the gallows the most ignorant of his subjects.

Whatever, as a free and independent man, bound to no party swayed by no personal interests, I may have written about Napoleon the Third, never have I doubted his sagacity, his courage, his per severance. Since the Government of Richelieu, of Mazarin, and of Cromwell, never has there been a ruler over any portion of mankind more firm and temperate. I deplore the success of his enterprise against the regenerate Romans : but I confidently hope that when he has done with the instruments of their ruin, he will take up others with a different stamp on them for reconstruction. He has now few enemies in France, and may safely smile at the union of the two Bourbons; the union of foolscap and blotting paper. The man who could see with gravity those two loggerheads, cheek by jowl, complimenting and kissing, then bargaining for the free-warren of France, together with the ancient court, court-leet, court-honour, and its sundry rights, royalties and hereditaments, he, I say, who could with gravity have been present at such a conference, and could abstain from strong emotions of cachinnation, must be under an inveterate aneurism of the organ of risibility.

Deplorable would it be if the inertness of an Aberdeen should neutralize the vigour of a Napoleon : deplorable if the counsels of a Court, or of any one in it, should make the whole nation stand before Europe accused of dereliction and desertion in the hour of need. Already the Orient is distrustful of England, and leans on the shoulder of her rival. If the Ottomans should be worsted[1] by the dilatoriness or duplicity of our Ministers, who can foretell how heavy will fall the responsibility, or on what heads? The firmness of the Ottomans has rescued our Court from somewhat of its ignominy ; but not from all. It is commonly thought to have been the Emperor's wish and design to declare the passage of the Pruth the commencement of hostilities. And readily may we believe it : but reluctantly must we believe that a softer voice from an opposite shore prevailed. Far different has been the result from that which was anticipated. Russia now exhibits to Europe her scheme of annexation. She seizes the richest provinces of the Ottoman Empire, ejects the magistrates, from the highest to the lowest, and compels the military to forswear their military oath and to fight under her banner. We may bear this ; France will not. The armies of France are impatient for action, and we force her into ascendancy. We possess the means of repressing the tyranny and insolence of Russia without any addition to our armaments. We can close the Baltic as easily as the Euxine. Sweden is already called to arms. She sees clearly the necessity of demolishing that enormous Power which has swallowed up nation after nation, and which threatens all. Gustavus Adolphus fixed on the Narova as the boundary

---

[1] This has now happened on the Euxine (Landor's Note).

Z

of Muscovite dominion, and the stone which marked it should be replaced. Sweden is naturally the allie of France. Should Sweden, France, and England, or (what unhappily seems the more probable) should Sweden and France efficiently aid the Sultan, Russia may be deprived of all the spoliations drawn together in two centuries, and Europe again enjoy another thirty years of peace. On this condition, and on this only, can she hope it for three. The fertile soil of Russia, thus becoming less military and more industrious, will even then contain a population of forty millions, which Sweden, Poland and Hungary, the outworks of civilization, will find it difficult enough to keep within bounds. Let each of these have its own again ; let all of them have all that was ever theirs. Nothing short of this provision can ensure the tranquillity of Europe and arrest the career of revolutions. We can do now what if we now omit we shall never be able to do hereafter. We may crush by one war the germs of many. France is ready to offer a larger aid to Turkey than we are. There is no reason why we should be jealous of it. Sufficient we can afford by the fleet already sent out ; and we are under no necessity to man a single more vessel than were displayed last summer to amuse the Queen. The Sultan would be quite as much gratified by the same evolutions. We possess the power, and we ought to exercise it, of keeping the Tzar's navy within the Baltic, forbidding any ship of war to navigate the Euxine. By this prohibition, and by this alone, we can repress a domination formidable to two continents. Unless we strenuously insist upon it, we may be incapable of avoiding more dangerous hostilities, when Austria and Prussia will be to Nicholas what they were to Napoleon the First, and when perhaps France also may have an injury to resent.

There are persons who have lived for many years in high stations, and must have seen many changes, for better, for worse, in Court and Cabinet, yet who are ignorant all the while that subserviency is not loyalty, that hesitation is not caution, that timidity is not prudence, that secession is not security. We must scrape off the Remora from our keels now stationary at the entrance of the Euxine, and we must confine the Torpedo to our own waters. The Sultan deserves our active help ; he hands us back our protocols. He writes better than we do and speaks more wisely. His dignity and self-esteem forbid him to abandon his people. He knows what we know too, but try to dissemble in the multiplicity of our fears, that Russia, with less than a third of her existing population, withstood the most warlike of nations, led against her by the greatest captain in the world. She increased her territory year after year with forces not amounting to a fifth of what she can wield at present. Can the Sultan then, or can we, suppose that the Tzar will desist from his aggressions, until all the Powers, excepting the two subservient, who lie like lapdogs on the skirts of his overcoat, hold him fast, shake him well, and tie him down with cordage stronger than the withy bands of dry diplomacy? Sometimes it is better and safer to do too much than to do too little. A wild beast is never to be wounded and run away from. The clay and the brass are hastening to disseverance and dissolution. Priest and ruler who run under the idol, and attempt to prop it up again, are crushed.

WALTER SAVAGE LANDOR.

Dec. 10, 1853.

The day before this letter appeared, the *Times* announced that Lord Palmerston had resigned his post as Home Secretary, on account of his opposition to the Government's contemplated Reform Bill. In the end, he was induced to remain in the Cabinet; but the incident serves to illustrate the opening paragraphs of the following letter, printed in the *Examiner* of January 28, 1854 :—

The Paramount Question.

Every man in Parliament thinks himself wiser than every man out: and there is an appearance of reason on his side: for, if he were not so, why should he have been sent to the place where he sits? However, the fact is not quite so certain as it seems to be in that quarter. Firmly do I believe that more than one of our newspapers contains a daily article worth all that is spoken in both Houses in seven years. Whether what I am now writing will be generally thought of such a value I am unable to ascertain: such as it is, I owe it, and offer it freely, to my country.

Parliamentary Reform is the stalking-horse which will step forward between us and Russia. We must keep it back, and walk straigh forward. Unless we now repress the aggression of Russia, we never shall. Unless we curtail her power and territory, she will enlarge them year after year. All that at present we seem ready to attempt, is to induce her quietly to retrace her steps. Does the tiger take his spring by crouching when he sees his enemy before him? no: this is the moment when he is the most formidable. We must either make the Tzar restore all that has been added to his empire, by fraud and violence, from the accession of Catherine (now with God or we must wrestle with him in the Khyber Pass. Whatever was once Poland, I have said it, and I repeat it, must again be Poland and Hungary must not draw a lengthening chain thro' Vienna to Petersburg. Austria is utterly useless to us in alliance: Hungary would take our merchandise, and furnish our garners. Austria is fertile; but the produce of Hungary would soon quintuple that of Austria.

It is wonderful that no merchant has calculated our commercial losses since the occupation of the Danube by the Muscovite wonderful that no Parisian baker has inquired how much more his flour has cost him; whether ten, or eleven, or twelve per cent. The people feel before they reason, and then the solidity of their reasoning is shaken by the intensity of their feelings. The sagacious and energetic Sovran who now rules over them, will not hazard his popularity by any unworthy compromise with the Autocrat; neither his safety nor that of Europe can allow a man so formidable and so faithless to retain the future power of devastating the most fertile lands in Europe. If twenty millions are deducted from his population, more than forty millions will continue under it. These forty millions in five-and-twenty years (years of peace, to which he must be constrained) will again amount to sixty millions. Be it so neighbouring States will have strengthened around; and his satellites will have slunk away, both on the Danube and on the Rhine.

There is no thoughtful head in Europe, no, nor even a crowned one, which the danger of Russian power and preponderance has not struck. Our Ministers are afraid to know it; but know it they must at last. Desirous as we are of peace, and sensible as we are of the benefits it has long conferred on us, we see the continuance of it only by striking down and disabling its great adversary. One single man outrages and defies the world. He tells us aloud that honour forbids him to sheathe the sword again. Did honour command him to draw it? Did honour suggest to him pretext after pretext, falsehood after falsehood? He is indignant that anybody should doubt his word: does anybody? To doubt is to question whether a matter be true or untrue, and to weigh it in the mind. He has left no room for this operation. Providence has demented him for the benefit of mankind, for the redress of long suffering, for the reparation of intolerable wrongs.

England, weary and exhausted, saw Venice and Genoa, and even Holland, deprived of their ancient laws and institutions. Nothing was to bear the semblance of republican, or even municipal: every nation was to be cast into the same charnel-house as Poland. But there is a trumpet now in the field which calls the dry bones into life again. When Louis Napoleon crossed the British Channel, the Emperor of France crossed it. I announced the fact at the time, and was called an enthusiast for announcing it. I may be called a wilder now, when I declare that a higher title is awaiting him, *Protector of Europe*. His interest will never permit him to see another Power on the Continent superior to France: from the accession of Henry the Fourth none has ever been. Conscriptions are not needed to swell his armies; they are about to rush forth, from the shores of the Mediterranean to the Euxine. Admirable has been the forbearance of Louis Napoleon. He has pardoned the Austrian and the Coburg, and smiled at the fusion of the two gutters that turned their shallow and muddy streams toward the Seine. He has tolerated the tardiness of his ally, well knowing in what quarter lay the impediments, and also well knowing that a powerful and high-minded people would remove them. Confident may we be that a sense of glory and of strength will urge him forward in the path he has taken. He will recover what he has lost in the East, and he will acquire much more than his predecessors ever hoped for. Hungary and Poland are about to be his granaries and his arsenals; Sinope and Sevastopol will succumb.

But shall Napoleon alone enjoy this glory? Shall not England share it? Safely may we leave to him the regeneration of Italy, of Hungary, and of Poland. They will be his more certainly and more

safely than by domination.   How many brave men are calling upon
him at this hour.   Italy has great names which it is dangerous to
pronounce; Hungary has her Kossuth, Transylvania her Guyon,
and Poland her Czartoryski.

Brave, generous Prince! may Heaven, who has prolonged thy
days beyond the term usually assigned to man, grant thee to rest thy
bones among thy ancestors, and may thy royal cenotaph be erected
many years hence.   WALTER SAVAGE LANDOR.
Jan. 25, 1854.

The day after this letter appeared, the Emperor of
the French wrote to the Czar inviting him to terminate
hostilities with Turkey, and adding—"if your Majesty
should refuse this proposal, then France, as well as
England, will be compelled to leave to the fate of arms
and the chances of war, that which might now be decided by reason and justice."   On February, 22, 1854
the Guards left London for the seat of war.   The
ultimatum to Russia followed five days later. Admiral
Sir Charles Napier, in command of the Baltic fleet,
left Spithead on March 11.   On the same day the
Examiner published the following :—

In the Field.

At last we are fairly in the field of battle; no more flirting with
Bellona, no more pouring out rose-water on the moustache of Mars.
Incredible as it may seem to many, and to heads of parties almost
unconstitutional, we have sent the fittest man to the fittest place;
Napier to the Baltic.   Only thrice, only upon urgent occasions, only
after grievous reverses, have we done the same by land in the course
of ninety years : the examples are Wolfe, Wellington, and that equally
great commander, who carried lately into an obscure churchyard,
among the tears of veterans, a name which is about to shake the
thousand cannon off the walls of Cronstadt.   We forget only one
thing in his appointment : we forgot to ascertain whether his flagship

was sound enough to carry him : it was not.   A delay in its restoration may allow time for the Muscovite fleets to unite from their several harbours in the Baltic, and be even more disastrous than our procrastination in the Euxine.   One benefit, unseen and unsuspected by our ministers, may arise from it ; which is, that it may induce a blind, blustering madman, at whom we have been looking so long in consternation, to make an attack on the neutrality of Sweden.   This will arouse an insulted nation, often victorious over the Giant of the Steppes : a nation which has performed on land more prodigies of valour than any other, modern or ancient.   Yes, the Swede will rise again and resume his own, altho' no Vasa can spring out of a Bernadotte.   The people is sound ; it is only the higher and slenderer branches that are withered with drought, and are liable to crack under the talons of the alighting Eagle.   We are *all* at war ; *we*, the nations.   Let us Englishmen cease the anile twaddle of *husbanding our resources*.   No husbandry is so unproductive as the parsimonious.   Give, and it shall be given unto you ; withold, and it shall be witholden.   Let us be liberal and large towards those we send forth into the world of warfare.   Let Glory take with her a befitting dower on her espousals.   WALTER SAVAGE LANDOR.

On April 20, 1854, the rulers of Austria and Prussia contracted an offensive and defensive alliance, binding themselves to guarantee each other all their respective possessions, and to hold a part of their forces in readiness for war.   The *Examiner* of April 22, printed the following from Landor :—

The Successor to the Goddess of Reason.

Since the Gallican Goddess of Reason, no other Divinity has descended among the nations until the advent of Nicholas, God of Massacres.

Chief priest to the Goddess of Reason was Maximilian Robespierre. The more exalted God Nicholas is supported and incensed by two high priests of equal dignity, the one called Francis, the other Frederick.   Francis tripped up the heels of the priest who went before him in the procession, took his place, and walked on as if nothing had happened. Frederick is too weak to trip anybody up ; but he gently shoves out of the road those who whisper in his ear to walk straiter and more erect. Nobody can be devouter than he is. Every night he prays to a God of his own, to pardon him for preferring another close at hand (meaning but not mentioning the God Nicholas), who might knock the crown off his head at the first sign of disobedience. Once in desperation he was about to start for the camp ; but he had only put on one shoe, when it occurred to him that, after all, he might sleep more comfortably under his roof at home, and with a coverlet of eyder-down about his shoulders. He has frequently been heard to practise in his inner chamber words of blustering, out of a-horn-book left there by his great-grandfather, or one before.

There have always been dissensions and quarrels about the precedency of deities and their priests. Even at the present day it is undecided whether the Goddess of Reason or the God of Massacres is the more worthy of worship. As possession is said proverbially to be nine parts in ten of the law, the God of Massacres seems to be the favourite. Men are ungrateful for past benefits ; and indeed those on whom the Goddess of Reason once conferred them are no more. Before her divinity was acknowledged by acclamation, she had, in her universal charity, led many to the hospital, and many to repentance. Her priest, Maximilian Robespierre, was greatly more abstinent of another's goods and chattels than are Frederick and Francis. Different from them, he was a man of his word, and never, like them and the hyena, whined over the blood he was spilling.

We must now raise our eyes above all three, and even above the Goddess of Liberty herself; for the God of Massacres stands before us. *Her* priest offered up human victims to her; but *he* smote them down at one blow. The God of Massacres hurls fire among aggregate thousands, sings over their cries of agony and anguish ; calls upon other Gods to rejoice with him ; imprisons and tortures tens of thousands in dark and icy caverns; tears wife from husband, brother from sister, bride from bridegroom, and breaks the ring of espousal on the finger of the espoused with the sword's hilt or the armourer's hammer.

Verily great is the God Nicholas, and worthy to be feared and praised; worthy to be held in everlasting remembrance; worthy to be worshipped in high places; yea, in the highest accessible to the feet of Britons.   WALTER SAVAGE LANDOR.

The following letter was addressed by Landor to Sir G. Hamilton Seymour, the late British Ambassador at St Petersburg, who at the Lord Mayor's banquet a few days before had explained the devious ways of Russian diplomacy. Sir Hamilton Seymour had been minister at Florence in the thirties. Landor's letter was printed in the *Examiner*, April 29, 1854:—

To Sir George Hamilton Seymour.

MY DEAR SIR HAMILTON,

The friendship you always showed towards me while you were minister at Florence, and ever since, induces me to congratulate you, not only on your safe return, but on the acclamations of your country for your manly conduct. Diplomacy, even English Diplomacy, again is held in honor: you bring her back *sans tache et sans reproche.* On reading your despatches, I was amazed at the Tzar's impudence in claiming to be on a parity with you as a gentleman. Some few are; none are more. You came too late to hear, —"*Hail, fellow! well met!*" from Jack Sheppard, and Dick Turpin, and John Thurtell, who had about the same right to accost you with easy confidence and frank familiarity as Tzar Nicholas had. The French ambassador is a partaker of your glory, in leaving at the same time as you the most perfidious of Courts, and a palace whose latest trophy is your stolen wardrobe. Happy am I in offering to his excellency this inadequate tribute of my respectful admiration. May the Emperor of France never want such upright and judicious men! M. Drouyn de Lhuys, the most intelligent and circumspect of statesmen, will take care that only such shall represent his Majesty. You know enough of me to know that I am not a flatterer. I have spoken with sufficient freedom on the Emperor's invasion of Italy and repression of liberal ideas. Before the war is over, and indeed that it may be over the sooner, he will retrace his steps, and range the nations of Europe round his throne. What could half a dozen imbecile kings do for him? What could half the number of enthusiastic nations *not* do? He has only to speak the word, and there they are. I have often seen him, often have enjoyed the wisdom of his conversation: I have no such hopes or wishes for the future; but I do wish, I do hope, I do confidently believe, that he will regenerate his own people and all those around; and that he will be more powerful because more prudent and more equitable, than any of his predecessors. I remain, dear Sir Hamilton, your faithful old friend,   WALTER SAVAGE LANDOR.

BATH, *April* 22.

In a private letter printed above (page 191), Landor has referred to a couple of articles which he had sent to the *Atlas*. These were published by that paper, as letters to the editor, on March 17, 1855, and were as follows. They may fitly conclude the present selection.

The False Politics of the War.

SIR,

The people of late have mostly occupied their time and thoughts in looking at Lord Palmerston and Lord John Russell, as they played at leap-frog over each other's shoulders. Mock inquiries have been started in the House of Commons, while this game was going on; but they excite less interest. They are merely concerning the fatal maladies of ten or twenty thousand soldiers, victorious in every field of battle. It would be thought imprudent to enquire by whose negligence or indifference such sufferings have been patiently and heroically endured. Secret committees suit better those who at the beginning were the most vociferous in threats, most urgent in denunciations. And what is likely to be the result? The fault will be scrupulously divided into infinitesimals; all will bear a little of it away, no one much. Things will go on pretty nearly as they did before, and will soon become identically the same. Meanwhile, hopes will be holden out of a fair and honourable peace. Who is to negotiate for it? The very man who declared in a public meeting, that we should demand from the Tzar no diminution of territory. A Minister of State, possessing any wisdom, any sense of duty, would reserve his sentiments, and deliver them only in the proper place, in the Council Chamber or in Parliament. A mouth eternally open is a feature of idiotcy or dotage. If we recapture no territory from the Tzar, we shall have increased not only his animosity, but also his power of showing it. When we landed in the Crimea we could have drawn his army out of it, after a battle less murderous than at the Alma. We have now to fight many more than one battle, having lost by action, or sickness, three fourths of the soldiers first landed. No fortress is impregnable; but Sebastopol is now rendered the strongest upon earth. No military man will assert that it can be captured with a smaller loss than of twenty thousand men, killed and wounded. When the Athenians lost their whole army at Syracuse, the Romans at Cannæ, and the English at Saratoga, their loss was not so great as that of one victory will be, including its past and future.

Unless we diminish the territory of Russia, her power is undiminished, and will demolish ours. Hitherto she has proved herself less vulnerable in Asia than ourselves; and in Europe all our efforts are unavailing. A few Turks have effected more against her than all our armaments by sea and land. War was procrastinated in compliance with German wishes; the same wishes as induced Lord Palmerston to sacrifice the constitutionalists at Oporto and wherever else he could. Yet he and Lord John Russell are the two men especially appointed to direct our councils. Let them suggest to those who received munificent presents from the late Tzar Nicholas, that they can now without offence, bestow the value of them on our mutilated soldiers, on helpless widows and orphan children; that such a step would be graceful, although not theatrical; and that blessings are more durable than applause.

WALTER SAVAGE LANDOR.

March 9, 1855.

SIR,

It is difficult to be quite dispassionate in the midst of politics, and most difficult when we are half-blinded by the furnace-blast of war. All parties are angry with the King of Prussia for keeping aloof from it. Little as I respect his Majesty, I think him as prudent and as honest a man as any of the other Majesties round about. Personal and private affections and disaffections ought never to warp the throne; but what throne do they not warp? Such is the material; and it is easier to cast it aside than to change its nature. The King of Prussia has gone more straightforward than his rival, the Emperor of Austria; he has not deceived us, and will not; the other has, and will. The King of Prussia owes it as a duty to his subjects to abstain from hostilities. If he is forced into them, it will not be against Russia. But let him beware of attempting to cajole the worst or the most potent ruler in the universe, him who holds the Keys of Janus in his hand, and on whose alms our famished soldiers have depended for existence. The famishers of them still direct the councils of our Sovereign, shifting from shoulder to shoulder the blame and responsibility of their misdeeds. Such men are as incapable of ensuring an honourable peace as of conducting a successful war. Let not our eyes be turned toward the Continent for objects of reproach, but toward those nearer us, on the upper seats, awaiting condign and exemplary punishment too long delayed.

WALTER SAVAGE LANDOR.

INDEX

www.ingramcontent.com/pod-product-compliance
Lightning Source LLC
Chambersburg PA
CBHW030901270326
41929CB00008B/523